Teach Yourself VISUALLY™

Word 2016

Elaine Marmel

Visual

A Wiley Brand

Teach Yourself VISUALLY™ Word 2016

Published by
John Wiley & Sons, Inc.
10475 Crosspoint Boulevard
Indianapolis, IN 46256

www.wiley.com

Published simultaneously in Canada

Wiley publishes in a variety of print and electronic formats and by print-on-demand. Some material included with standard print versions of this book may not be included in e-books or in print-on-demand. If this book refers to media such as a CD or DVD that is not included in the version you purchased, you may download this material at http://booksupport.wiley.com. For more information about Wiley products, visit www.wiley.com.

The Library of Congress Control Number: 2015952812

ISBN: 978-1-119-07466-3 (pbk); ISBN: 978-1-119-07458-8 (ebk); ISBN: 978-1-119-07499-1 (ebk)

Manufactured in the United States of America

10 9 8 7 6 5 4 3 2 1

Trademark Acknowledgments

Contact Us

For general information on our other products and services, please contact our Customer Care Department within the U.S. at 877-762-2974, outside the U.S. at 317-572-3993 or fax 317-572-4002.

For technical support please visit www.wiley.com/techsupport.

Media Credits

Sales | Contact Wiley at (877) 762-2974 or fax (317) 572-4002.

Credits

Acquisitions Editor
Aaron Black

Project Editor
Sarah Hellert

Technical Editor
Donna L. Baker

Copy Editor
Scott Tullis

Production Editor
Joel Jones

**Manager, Content Development &
Assembly**
Mary Beth Wakefield

**Vice President, Professional
Technology Strategy**
Barry Pruett

About the Author

Elaine Marmel is President of Marmel Enterprises, LLC, an organization that specializes in technical writing and software training. Elaine has an MBA from Cornell University and worked on projects to build financial management systems for New York City and Washington, D.C., and train more than 600 employees to use these systems. This experience provided the foundation for Marmel Enterprises, LLC to help small businesses manage the project of implementing a computerized accounting system.

Elaine spends most of her time writing; she has authored and co-authored more than 90 books about Microsoft Excel, Microsoft Word, Microsoft Project, QuickBooks, Peachtree, Quicken for Windows, Quicken for DOS, Microsoft Word for the Mac, Microsoft Windows, 1-2-3 for Windows, and Lotus Notes. From 1994 to 2006, she also was the contributing editor to monthly publications *Inside Peachtree* and *Inside QuickBooks*.

Elaine left her native Chicago for the warmer climes of Arizona (by way of Cincinnati, OH; Jerusalem, Israel; Ithaca, NY; Washington, D.C., and Tampa, FL), where she basks in the sun with her PC, her cross-stitch projects, and her dog Jack.

Author's Acknowledgments

Because a book is not just the work of the author, I'd like to acknowledge and thank all the folks who made this book possible. Thanks to Aaron Black for the opportunity to write this book. Thank you, Donna Baker, for doing a great job to make sure that I "told no lies." Thank you, Scott Tullis, for making sure I was understandable and grammatically correct — it's always a pleasure to work with you. And, thank you, Sarah Hellert, for managing all the players and manuscript elements involved in this book; that's a big job, and you're up to the task.

How to Use This Book

Who This Book Is For

This book is for the reader who has never used this particular technology or software application. It is also for readers who want to expand their knowledge.

The Conventions in This Book

① Steps

This book uses a step-by-step format to guide you easily through each task. Numbered steps are actions you must do; bulleted steps clarify a point, step, or optional feature; and indented steps give you the result.

② Notes

Notes give additional information — special conditions that may occur during an operation, a situation that you want to avoid, or a cross reference to a related area of the book.

③ Icons and Buttons

Icons and buttons show you exactly what you need to click to perform a step.

④ Tips

Tips offer additional information, including warnings and shortcuts.

⑤ Bold

Bold type shows command names, options, and text or numbers you must type.

⑥ Italics

Italic type introduces and defines a new term.

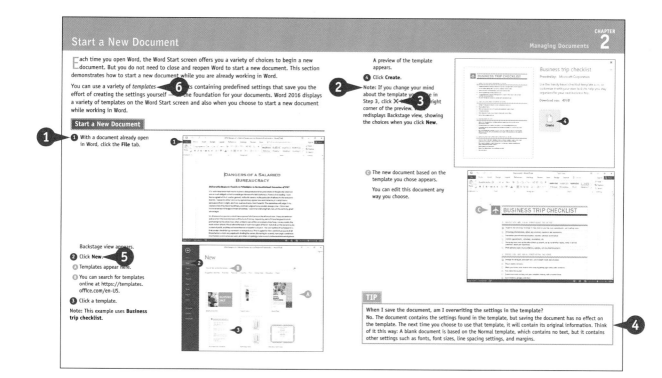

Table of Contents

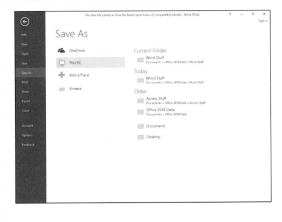

Chapter 3   Editing Text

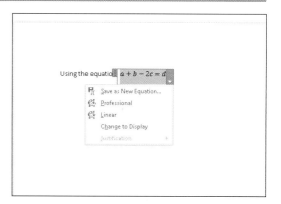

Table of Contents

Chapter 6   Formatting Paragraphs

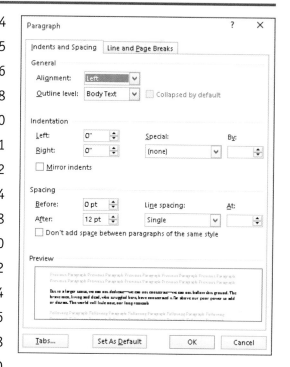

Table of Contents

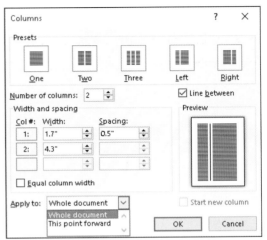

Chapter 8 — Printing Documents

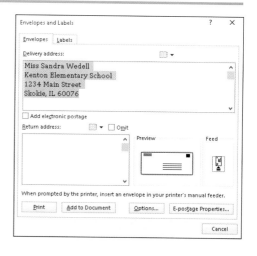

Chapter 9 — Working with Tables and Charts

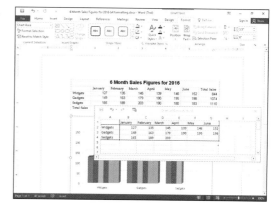

Table of Contents

Chapter 12   Working with Mass Mailing Tools

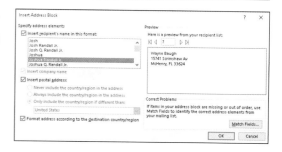

Chapter 13   Word and the World Beyond Your Desktop

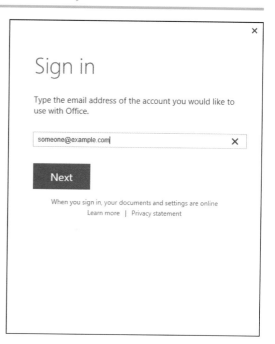

CHAPTER 1

Getting Familiar with Word

Are you ready to get started in Word? In this chapter, you become familiar with the Word working environment, including the Word Start screen and Backstage view, and you learn basic ways to navigate and to enter text using both the keyboard and the mouse. You also learn some basics for using Word on a tablet PC.

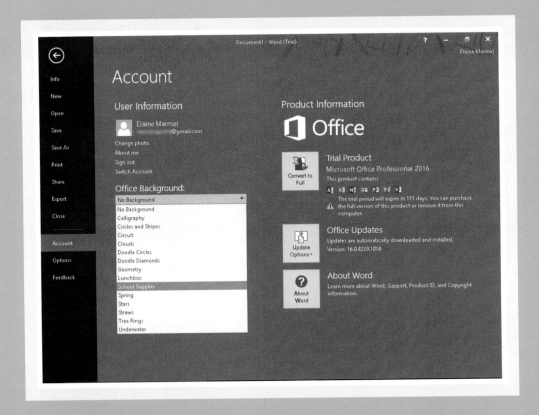

Open Word

Office 2016 runs on a 1 gigahertz (GHz) or faster x86- or x64-bit processor with 1 or 2 gigabytes (GB) of RAM, based on your processor speed, and your system must be running Windows 7, Windows 8, Windows 10, Windows Server 2008 R2, or Windows Server 2012.

This section demonstrates how to open Word from Windows 10. After Word opens, the Word Start screen appears, helping you to find a document on which you recently worked or starting a new document. For other ways to open or start a new document, see Chapter 2.

Open Word

1 Click in the search box.

A The Search menu appears.

Note: The Search menu displays popular news items from Bing, Microsoft's search engine. You can use the buttons on the left side of the Search menu to, for example, establish search settings for Cortana, the Windows Search assistant.

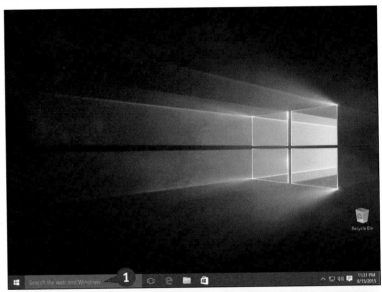

2 Start typing the name of the program; for this example, type **word**.

B A list of choices appears that match the letters you typed.

3 Click the choice matching the program you want to open.

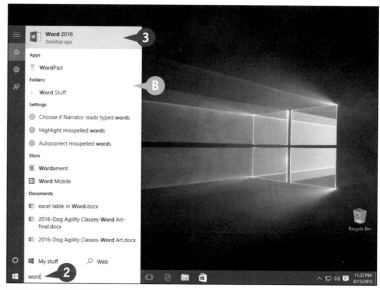

The program opens and displays its Start screen, which helps you open new or existing documents; see Chapter 2 for other ways to open documents.

C You can use this panel to open an existing document.

D You can click a thumbnail in this area to start a new document.

E This area indicates whether you have signed in to your Office 365 subscription, which enables you to work on your documents from anywhere.

Note: See Chapter 13 for details about signing in to Office 365.

F To exit from the program, you can click the **Close** button (✖).

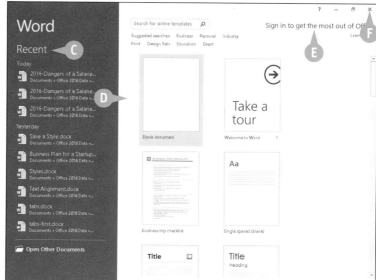

Can I create a shortcut to open an Office application?
You can, but pinning the program to the Windows taskbar or Start menu is easier. Follow Steps **1** and **2** in this section. Then, right-click the program name in the list. From the menu that appears, click **Pin to taskbar** or **Pin to Start**. Windows 10 pins the program to the Windows taskbar or the Start menu. To open the program, click the program's button on the taskbar or Start menu. Programs pinned to the Start menu appear on the right side of the menu as tiles.

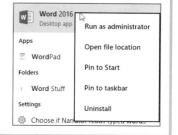

Explore the Word Window

All Office programs share a common appearance and many features, and Word is no different. These features include a Ribbon and a Quick Access Toolbar (QAT). The Ribbon contains most commands available in Word, and the QAT contains frequently used commands.

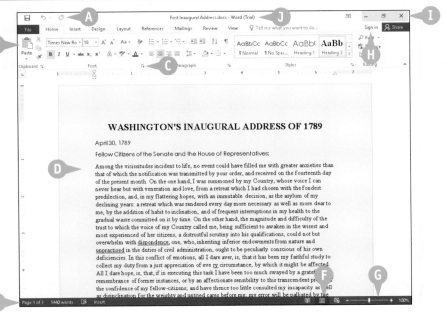

A Quick Access Toolbar (QAT)

Contains buttons that perform common actions. To customize the QAT, see Chapter 11.

B Ribbon

Contains buttons organized in tabs, groups, and commands.

C Dialog Box Launcher

Appears in the lower right corner of many groups on the Ribbon. Clicking this button (⌐) opens a dialog box or task pane that provides more options.

D Document Area

The area where you type. The flashing vertical bar, called the *insertion point*, represents the location where text will appear when you type.

E Status Bar

Displays document information and the location of the insertion point. From left to right, this bar contains the number of the page on which the insertion point currently appears, the total number of pages and words in the document, and the Proofing Errors button (⬚).

F View Shortcuts

Contains buttons to switch to a different view of your document.

G Zoom Controls

Changes the magnification of a document.

H Office 365 Indicator

If your name appears, you are signed in to your Office 365 subscription. You can click ▼ to display a menu that enables you to manage your Microsoft account settings. If you are not signed in, this area shows a Sign In link. See Chapter 13 for details about signing in to Office 365.

I Program Window Controls

These buttons enable you to control the appearance of the program window. You can minimize the Ribbon, and you can minimize, maximize, restore, or close the program window.

J Title Bar

Shows the document and program titles.

Work with Backstage View

You can click the **File** tab to display Backstage view. Backstage is the place to go when you need to manage documents or change program behavior. In Backstage view, you find a list of actions that you can use to open, save, print, remove sensitive information, and distribute documents as well as set Word program behavior options. You can also use Backstage to manage the places on your computer hard drive, in your network, or in your OneDrive space that you use to store documents.

Work with Backstage View

1 Click the **File** tab to display Backstage view.

A Commonly used file and program management commands appear here.

B Buttons representing places you commonly use to open documents appear here.

C Information related to the button you click appears here. Each time you click a button in the Open column, the information shown to the right changes.

Note: The New, Close, and Options commands behave differently; when you click any of them, Word takes the action you chose. For example, clicking **Close** closes the current document.

2 Click the **Back** button (⬅) to redisplay the open document.

Change the Color Scheme

You can use Office themes and background patterns to change the appearance of the program screen. Themes control the color scheme the program uses, and background patterns can add interest to the screen while you work. Color schemes can improve your ability to clearly see the screen, but be aware that background patterns might be distracting.

Office themes are available even if you are not signed in to Office 365, but to use background patterns, you must sign in to Office 365. For details on how to sign in and out of Office 365, see Chapter 13.

Change the Color Scheme

Note: Make sure you are signed in to Office 365. See Chapter 13 for details.

1 Click **File** to open Backstage view.

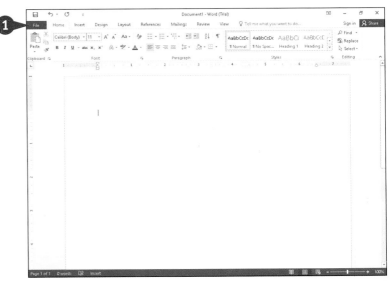

2 Click **Account**.

3 Click the **Office Theme** ▼.

4 Click an Office theme.

The colors of your program change.

Note: Some theme changes are more subtle than others.

5 Click the **Office Background** ▼.

6 Point the mouse (⍃) at a choice in the menu to highlight that choice.

Ⓐ A background pattern appears at the top of the window. The pattern remains as you work on documents.

7 Click the pattern you want to use or click **No Background**.

8 Click the **Back** button (⬅) to return to your document.

The Office theme and background you selected appear.

Ⓑ The background appears in the title bar and the tabs of the Ribbon.

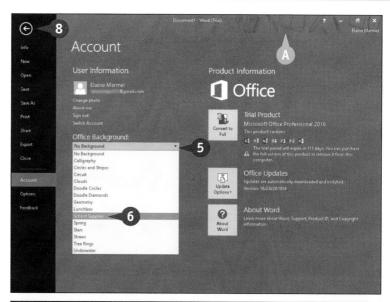

TIP

What happens if I select an Office background and then sign out of Office 365?
The background no longer appears in the program, but will reappear when you next sign in to Office 365. Similarly, theme changes you make while signed in to Office 365 might disappear when you sign out of Office 365. With themes, however, you do not need to be signed in to Office 365 to make a selection. Just complete Steps **1** to **4**.

Find a Ribbon Command

When you need to take an action that you do not take on a regular basis, you can use Word 2016's new feature, the Tell Me What You Want To Do feature. The Tell Me What You Want To Do search feature helps you find commands on the Ribbon.

You can still use the Ribbon directly, as described in the next section, "Select Commands." The Tell Me What You Want To Do search feature is most useful when you are not sure where on the Ribbon to find the command you need.

Find a Ribbon Command

1 Open a document.

Note: See Chapter 2 for details on opening documents.

2 Click here.

A A list of commonly requested actions appears.

3 Type a brief description of the action you want to take.

B The program lists possible commands you can use to complete your task.

4 Click a command to use it.

C If you click a command that displays this arrow (▶), additional options appear.

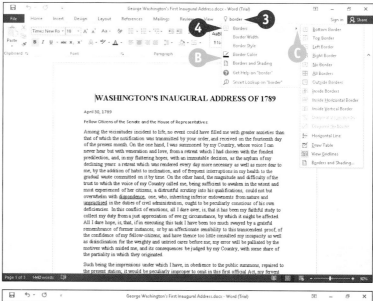

D The program performs the action you selected; in this example, Word places a border around the first paragraph of the document.

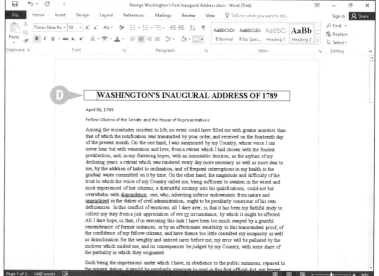

Will I need to type a description of the action I want to take if it is the same action I have previously taken?
No. The Tell Me What You Want To Do search box remembers your previous searches and displays them on the menu that appears when you perform Step **2**.

If I no longer want my previous searches to appear, can I clear them from the list?
No. The Tell Me What You Want To Do feature retains your searches in the Recently Used section of the menu that appears when you click in the search box.

Select Commands

You can keep your hands on your keyboard and select commands from the Ribbon or the Quick Access Toolbar (QAT), or you can use the mouse.

The Ribbon contains buttons organized in tabs, groups, and commands. Tabs appear across the top of the Ribbon and contain groups of related commands. Groups organize related commands; the group name appears below the group. Commands appear within each group. The QAT appears above the Ribbon and by default contains the Save, Undo, and Redo commands. To customize the Ribbon or the QAT, see Chapter 11.

Select Commands

Select Commands with the Keyboard

1 If appropriate for the command you intend to use, place the insertion point in the proper word or paragraph.

2 Press **Alt** on the keyboard.

A Shortcut letters and numbers appear on the Ribbon.

Note: The numbers control commands on the Quick Access Toolbar.

3 Press a letter to select a tab on the Ribbon.

This example uses **P**.

Word displays the appropriate tab and letters for each command on that tab.

4 Press a letter or letters to select a command.

If appropriate, Word displays options for the command you selected. Press a letter or use the arrow keys on the keyboard to select an option.

Word performs the command you selected, applying the option you chose.

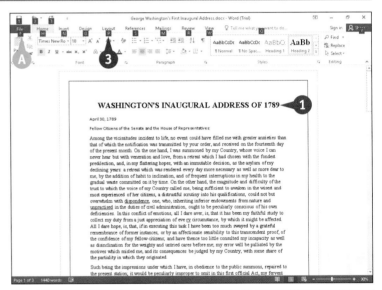

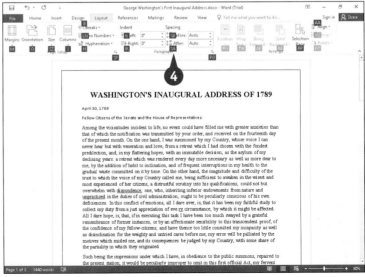

Select Commands with the Mouse

1 Click in the text or paragraph you want to modify.

Note: If appropriate, select the text; see Chapter 3 for details.

2 Click the tab containing the command you want to use.

3 Point to the command you want to use.

B Word displays a ScreenTip describing the function of the button at which the mouse () points.

4 Click the command.

C Word performs the command you selected.

Note: If you selected text, click anywhere outside the text to continue working.

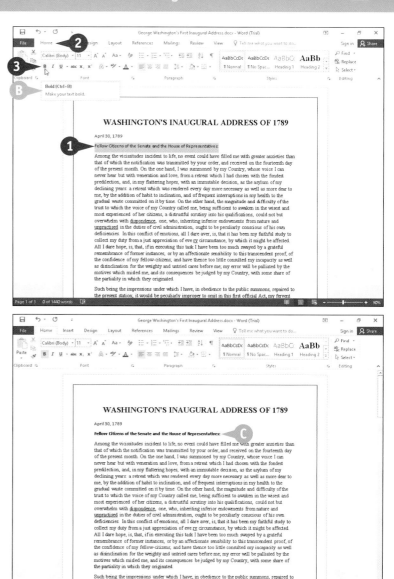

TIPS

Can I toggle between the document and the Ribbon using the keyboard?
Yes. Each time you press F6, Word changes the focus of the program, switching between the document, the status bar, and the Ribbon, in that order.

What do the small down arrows below or beside buttons mean?
The small arrow (▼) on a button means several choices are available. Click the button directly to apply a default choice. Click ▼ to view additional options. As you move the mouse () over the two parts of the button, Word highlights one or the other to alert you that you have more choices.

Using Word on a Tablet PC

Using Word 2016 on a tablet offers a different experience than using the program on a computer with a keyboard and mouse. This section shows you how to open Word on a touch device and how to switch between Touch and Mouse modes.

Enhancements for tablets are limited primarily to enlarging buttons on the status bar, the Quick Access Toolbar, and the Ribbon to make selecting commands easier. For a friendlier touch experience, consider using the universal Word app for various mobile devices, which, although not as powerful as Word 2016, were written specifically for touch devices. You can share documents across platforms.

Using Word on a Tablet PC

Start a Program

1 Tap the Windows **Start** button (⊞).

Ⓐ The Windows 10 Start menu appears.

Ⓑ Program tiles appear on the right side.

Ⓒ If the program you want to open appears in the Most Used list, you can tap it to open it. Or you can scroll through the program tiles on the right to find and tap the program you want to open.

2 Tap **All apps**.

Ⓓ An alphabetical list of programs installed on your computer appears.

3 Scroll through the list and tap **Word 2016** to open Word to the Word Start screen.

14

Using Touch/Mouse Mode

1 Tap the **Customize Quick Access Toolbar** ⬇.

2 Tap **Touch/Mouse Mode**.

Ⓔ Word adds the Touch/Mouse Mode button to the Quick Access Toolbar.

Note: By default, each Office program displays the screen in Mouse mode.

Ⓕ In Mouse mode, buttons on the Quick Access Toolbar and the Ribbon are smaller.

3 Tap **Touch/Mouse Mode**.

Ⓖ A drop-down menu appears.

4 Tap **Touch**.

Ⓗ The program enlarges the size of buttons on the Quick Access Toolbar and the Ribbon, grouping Ribbon buttons as needed.

Ⓘ The status bar, view buttons, and zoom slider also appear larger.

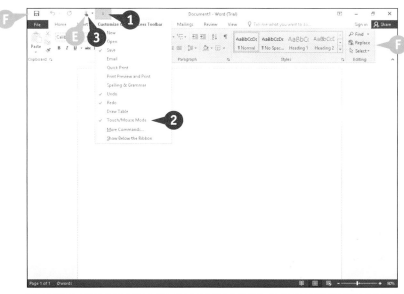

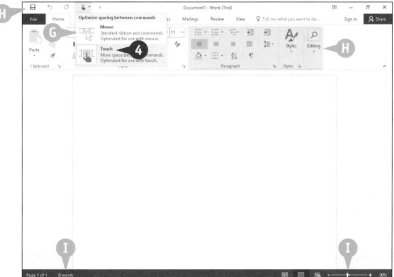

TIP

Are there any other features in Word 2016 that make the program easier to use on touch devices?

Yes, Word's Read Mode contains buttons on the left and right sides of the screen (◀ and ▶) (Ⓐ) that you can tap to change pages. See Chapter 4 for details. For a more touch-friendly experience, consider using the universal app Word, available in the Microsoft Store, on an iPad or Android device.

Work with the Mini Toolbar and Context Menus

Most of the formatting commands appear on the Home tab in Word, but you have alternatives to format text. Without switching to the Home tab, you can format text using the Mini Toolbar, which contains a combination of commands available primarily in the Font and the Paragraph groups on the Home tab.

You also can use the context menu to format text without switching to the Home tab or the Review tab. The context menu contains the Mini Toolbar and a combination of commands available primarily in the Font group and the Paragraph group on the Home tab and on the Review tab.

Work with the Mini Toolbar and Context Menus

Work with the Mini Toolbar

1 Select text.

A The Mini Toolbar appears.

Note: If you slowly slide the mouse (⬉) away from the selected text, the Mini Toolbar becomes transparent and then disappears.

2 Click any command or button to perform the actions associated with the command or button.

B Word performs the action on the selected text, leaving the Mini Toolbar visible so that you can use it again if you want.

Work with Context Menus

1 Select text.

C The Mini Toolbar appears.

2 Right-click the selected text.

D The context menu appears along with the Mini Toolbar.

Note: You can right-click anywhere, not just on selected text, to display the Mini Toolbar and the context menu.

3 Click any command or button to perform the actions associated with the command or button.

TIP

Can I turn off the Mini Toolbar?

Yes; this feature is controlled in the Word Options dialog box. To turn the feature off or on, click **File** and then click **Options**. The Word Options dialog box appears. On the General tab, deselect **Show Mini Toolbar on selection** (☑ changes to ☐). Click **OK** to close the dialog box.

Enter Text

Word makes typing easy. First, by default, when you start typing, any existing text moves over to accommodate the new text. Further, you do not need to press `Enter` to start a new line. Word uses the margins you set, the font you use, and the font's size to determine when to automatically start a new line for you. See Chapter 7 for details on setting margins and Chapter 5 to learn more about choosing a font and setting its size.

To add more than one space between words, use `Tab` rather than `Spacebar`. See Chapter 6 for details on setting tabs.

Enter Text

Type Text

1 Type the text that you want to appear in your document.

A The text appears to the left of the insertion point as you type.

B As the insertion point reaches the end of the line, Word automatically starts a new one.

Press `Enter` only to start a new paragraph.

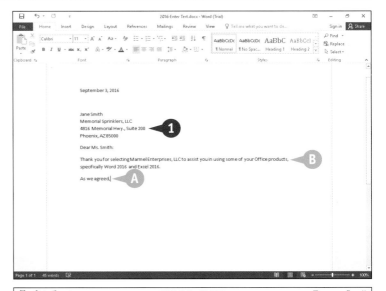

Separate Information

1 Type a word or phrase.

2 Press `Tab`.

To align text properly, you can press `Tab` to include more than one space between words.

Several spaces appear between the last letter you typed and the insertion point.

3 Type another word or phrase.

Enter Text Automatically

1 Begin typing a common word, phrase, or date.

C The AutoComplete feature suggests common words and phrases based on what you type.

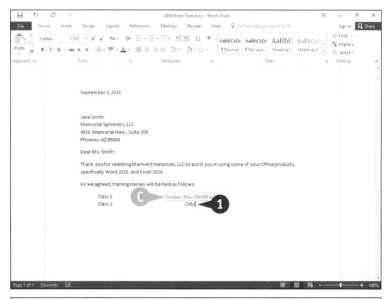

D You can press **Enter** to let Word finish typing the word, phrase, or month for you.

You can keep typing to ignore Word's suggestion.

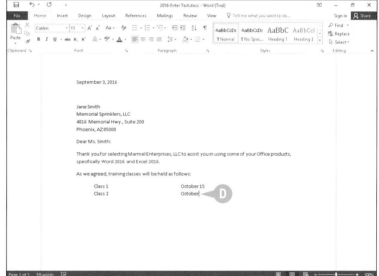

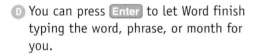

TIP

Why should I use Tab rather than Spacebar to include more than one space between words?

Typically, you include more than one space between words or phrases to align text in a columnar fashion. Most fonts are proportional, and each character takes up a different amount of space on a line. Therefore, you cannot calculate the number of spaces needed to align words beneath each other. Tabs, however, are set at specific locations on a line. When you press Tab, you know exactly where words or phrases appear on a line. For details on tab settings, see Chapter 6.

Move Around in a Document

When you edit a large document, you can move the insertion point around the document efficiently using a variety of keyboard shortcuts. Although pressing and holding an arrow key moves the insertion point rapidly in the direction of the arrow, that approach is not efficient when you are viewing Page 1 and need to edit text in the middle of the second paragraph on Page 5.

You can use many techniques to move the insertion point to a different location in a document; the technique you select depends on the current location of the insertion point and the location to which you want to move it.

Move Around in a Document

Move by One Character

1 Note the location of the insertion point.

2 Press ➡.

A Word moves the insertion point one character to the right.

You can press ⬅, ⬆, or ⬇ to move the insertion point one character left, up, or down.

Pressing and holding any arrow key moves the insertion point repeatedly in the direction of the arrow key.

You can press Ctrl+➡ or Ctrl+⬅ to move the insertion point one word at a time to the right or left.

Move One Screen

1 Note the last visible line on-screen.

2 Press ⌗Page down⌗.

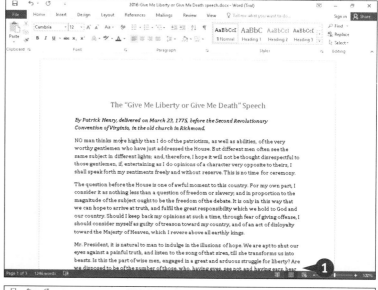

B Word moves the insertion point down one screen.

3 You can press ⌗Page up⌗ to move the insertion point up one screen.

C You can click ▲ to scroll up or ▼ to scroll down one line at a time in a document.

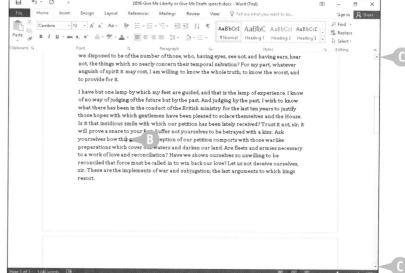

TIP

How do I quickly move the insertion point to the beginning or the end of a document or to a specific page?

Press ⌗Ctrl⌗+⌗Home⌗ or ⌗Ctrl⌗+⌗End⌗ to move the insertion point to the beginning or the end of a document. To land on a specific page, press ⌗F5⌗ to display the Go To dialog box, type the number of the page, and press ⌗Enter⌗. Press ⌗Shift⌗+⌗F5⌗ to move the insertion point to the last place you changed in your document. To move the insertion point to a specific location, use a bookmark; see the section "Mark and Find Your Place" in Chapter 3 for details.

CHAPTER 2

Managing Documents

Now that you know the basics, it is time to discover how to navigate among Word documents efficiently. In this chapter, you learn how to manage the Word documents you create, and the sections in this chapter focus on files stored on your computer; see Chapter 13 to learn about managing documents on OneDrive.

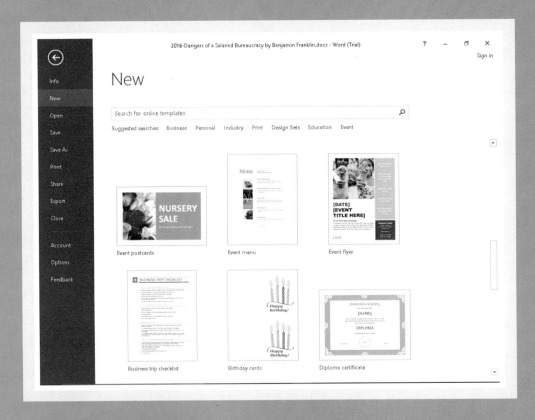

Save a Document

You save documents so that you can use them at another time in Microsoft Word. Word 2016 uses the same XML-based file format that Word 2013, 2010, and Word 2007 use, reducing the size of a Word document and improving the likelihood of recovering information from a corrupt file.

The first time you save a document, Word prompts you for a document name. Subsequent times, you can click the Save button on the Quick Access Toolbar (QAT), and Word saves the document using its original name without prompting you.

Save a Document

Ⓐ Before you save a document, Word displays a generic name in the title bar.

① Click the **File** tab.

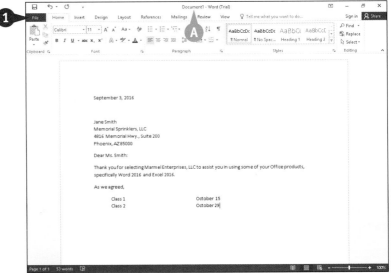

Backstage view appears.

② Click **Save As**.

Ⓑ Locations where you can save files appear here.

Note: Once you select a location, folders available at that location appear on the right side of the screen.

③ Click the location where you want to save the file; this example uses **This PC**.

Ⓒ If the folder in which you want to save the document appears here, click it and skip to Step **5**.

④ Click **Browse**.

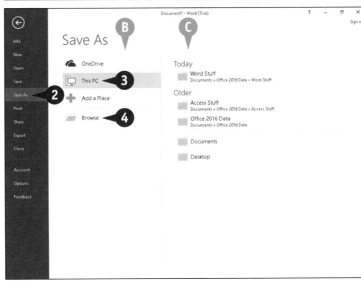

The Save As dialog box appears.

5 Type a name for the document here.

D You can click in the folder list to select a location on your computer in which to save the document.

E You can click **New folder** to create a new folder in which to store the document.

6 Click **Save**.

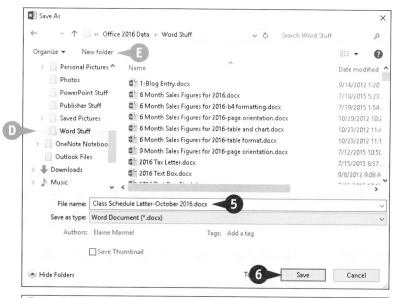

F Word saves the document and displays the name you supplied in the title bar.

G For subsequent saves, you can click the **Save** button (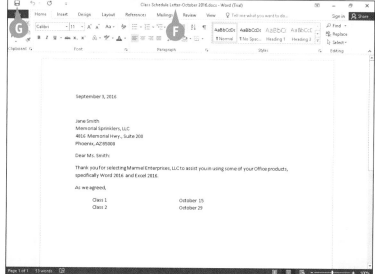) on the Quick Access Toolbar to quickly save the file.

TIPS

Will my associate who uses Word 2003 be able to open a document I save in Word 2016?

To make it easier for your associate, you can create the document in Word 2016 but save it in Word 2003 format. See the section "Save a Document in Word 97-2003 Format" for more information.

How can I tell if I am working on a document saved in Word 2016?

Check the document name in the title bar. The title of a document created in any earlier version of Word appears with "Compatibility Mode" in the title bar.

Reopen an Unsaved Document

You can open documents you created within the last seven days but did not save. It happens: You work on a document and then close it without saving because you think you will not need it again. And then, a few hours or days later, you find that you do need it.

You can reopen a document you created within the last seven days but did not save because, as you work, Word automatically saves your document even if you take no action to save it.

Reopen an Unsaved Document

1 With any document open, even a blank document, click the **File** tab.

Note: See the sections "Open a Word Document" or "Start a New Document" for details.

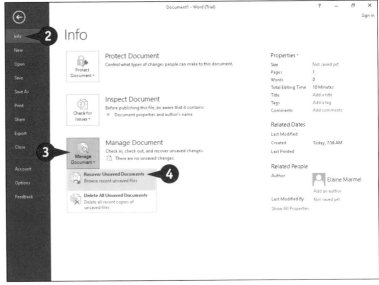

Backstage view appears.

2 Click **Info**.

3 Click **Manage Document**.

4 Click **Recover Unsaved Documents**.

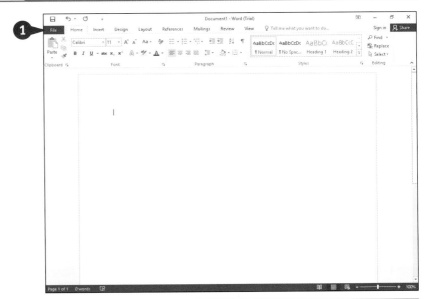

The Open dialog box appears, showing you available files that were autosaved by Word but not saved as documents by you.

5 Click the unsaved file you want to open.

6 Click **Open**.

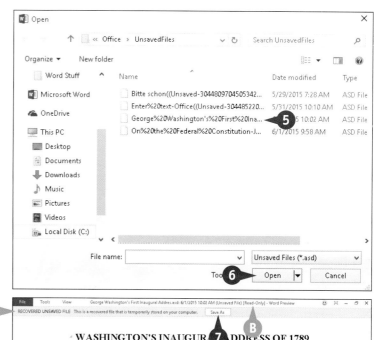

A The document appears on-screen in Reading Mode view, as indicated by this icon (📖).

B The document is a read-only file to which you cannot save changes.

C This gray bar identifies the document as a recovered file temporarily being stored on your computer.

7 Click **Save As** to save the file as a Word document.

Note: See the previous section, "Save a Document," for details.

After you save the document, the gray bar disappears.

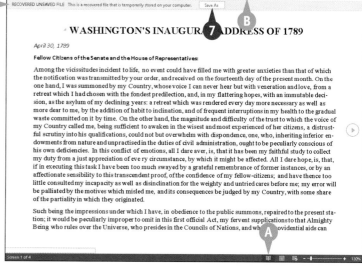

TIPS

How often does Word save a document while I work on it?
By default, Word automatically saves your work — even on documents you have not yet saved — every 10 minutes. You can control the frequency with which Word automatically saves your work by changing the options associated with saving documents; see the section "Set Options for Saving Documents" for details.

Is there another way to open the dialog box that shows unsaved documents?
Yes. Click **File**, and then click **Open**. At the bottom of the Recent Documents list in Backstage view, you will find the Recover Unsaved Documents button.

Save a Document in Word 97-2003 Format

You can save documents you create in Microsoft Word in a variety of other formats, such as Word templates, Microsoft Works files, text files, or Word 97-2003 format to share them with people who do not use Microsoft Word 2016.

Although the steps in this section focus on saving a document to Word 97-2003 format, you can use these steps to save a document to any file format Word supports. Be aware that people using Word 2013, 2010, or 2007 can open files saved as Word 2016 files; Word 2013, 2010, or 2007 users simply cannot use features available in Word 2016.

Save a Document in Word 97-2003 Format

1 Click the **File** tab.

Backstage view appears.

2 Click **Save As**.

3 Click **This PC**.

A If the folder in which you want to save the document appears in this list, click it and skip to Step **5**.

4 Click **Browse**.

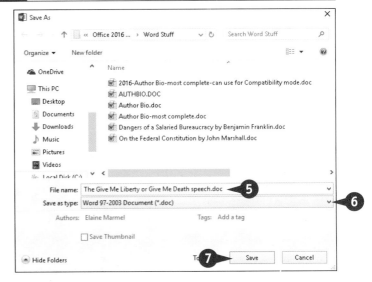

The Save As dialog box appears.

5 Type a name for the document.

6 Click ∨ to display the formats available for the document, and click **Word 97-2003 Document (*.doc)**.

7 Click **Save**.

Note: If you save a complex document, you might see the Compatibility Checker dialog box, which summarizes changes Word will make when saving your document. Click **OK**.

Word saves the document in the format that you select.

Save a Document in PDF or XPS Format

You can save Word documents in PDF or XPS formats. The PDF format is a universal format that any computer user can open using a PDF reader program. There are many free PDF reader programs; perhaps the most well-known one is Adobe System's free Acrobat Reader. Windows 8 and later come with a built-in PDF reader.

XPS is Microsoft's alternative to PDF. Windows 10, Windows 8, and Windows 7 come with an XPS viewer; users of other versions of Windows can view XPS documents using Internet Explorer 7 or higher.

Save a Document in PDF or XPS Format

1 Click the **File** tab.

Backstage view appears.

2 Click **Save As**.

3 Click **This PC**.

Ⓐ If the folder in which you want to save the document appears in this list, click it and skip to Step **5**.

4 Click **Browse**.

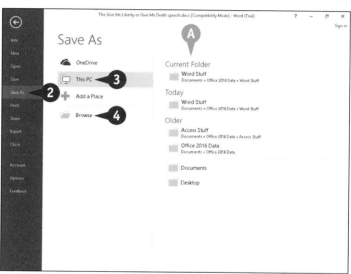

The Save As dialog box appears.

5 Click here to type a name for your document.

6 Click ⌄ to select either **PDF (*.pdf)** or **XPS Document (*.xps)**.

Note: If you choose XPS format, you can opt to save and then open the document.

Ⓑ If you plan to use your document online only, you can select **Minimum size** (○ changes to ◉).

7 Click **Save**.

Word saves the document in the selected format.

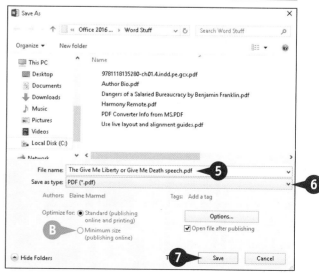

Set Options for Saving Documents

You can set a variety of options for saving documents. For example, you can choose to save documents by default in a variety of Word formats other than Word 2016, or you can save documents in any of the following formats: web page, rich text, plain text, XML, OpenDocument, or Microsoft Works. In addition, by default, Word saves documents to OneDrive and automatically saves your document every 10 minutes while you work on it, even if you have not yet saved it.

You can change any of the Save options to make Word 2016 support the way you work.

Set Options for Saving Documents

Set File-Saving Options

1 Click the **File** tab.

Backstage view appears.

2 Click **Options**.

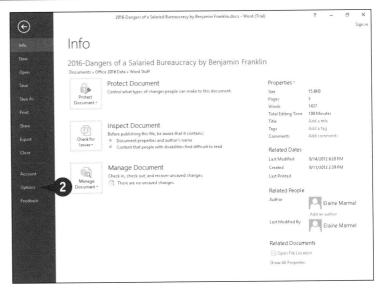

The Word Options dialog box appears.

3 Click **Save**.

Ⓐ You can select **Save AutoRecover information every** (☐ changes to ☑) and specify an interval for saving recovery information.

Ⓑ You can select **Keep the last autosaved version if I close without saving** (☐ changes to ☑) to make sure Word saves unsaved documents.

4 Click **OK** to save your changes.

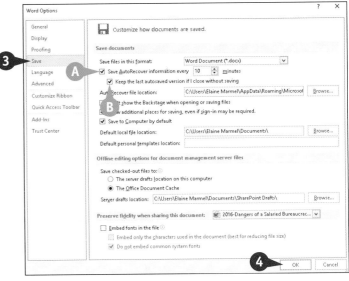

Set File-Saving Locations

1 Complete Steps **1** to **3** in the previous subsection, "Set File-Saving Options."

C To save documents to your computer rather than to OneDrive, select **Save to Computer by default** (☐ changes to ✔).

2 Click **Browse** next to Default Local File Location.

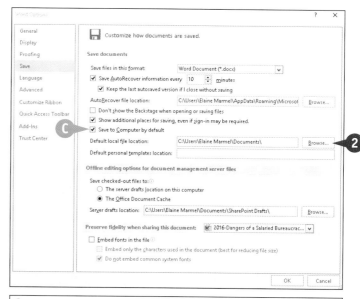

The Modify Location dialog box appears.

3 Click in the folder list to navigate to the folder where you want to save Word documents.

4 Click **OK** to close the Modify Location dialog box and redisplay the Word Options dialog box.

You can repeat Steps **2** to **4** to set the AutoRecover File and the Server Drafts locations.

5 Click **OK** in the Word Options dialog box to save your changes.

Word saves your changes.

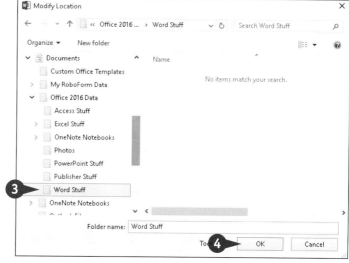

TIP

What happens if I select the Don't Show the Backstage When Opening or Saving Files option?
To take true advantage of this option, you need to add the Open and Save As buttons to the Quick Access Toolbar (QAT). When you opt not to show Backstage view, and then click the Open or Save As buttons, Word displays the Open or Save As dialog box without showing Backstage view. If you are comfortable navigating folders, enabling this option saves you time. See Chapter 11 to customize the QAT.

Open a Word Document

You can open documents that you have created and saved previously to continue adding data or to edit existing data. Regardless of whether you store a file in a folder on your computer's hard drive or on a CD, you can easily access files using the Open dialog box. If you are not sure where you saved a file, you can use the Open dialog box's Search function to locate it.

When you are finished using a file, you should close it to free up processing power on your computer. See the tip at the end of this section.

Open a Word Document

1 Click the **File** tab.

Backstage view appears.

2 Click **Open**.

A Word automatically selects Recent as the default location.

B Recently opened documents appear here. If you see the file you want to open, you can click it to open it and skip the rest of these steps.

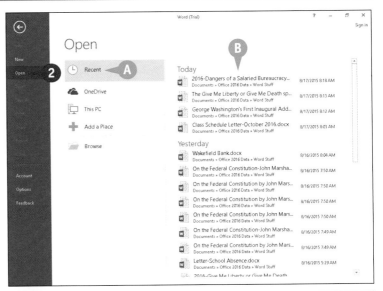

3 Click the place where you believe the document is stored. This example uses **This PC**.

C If the folder containing the document appears here, click it and skip to Step **6**.

4 Click **Browse**.

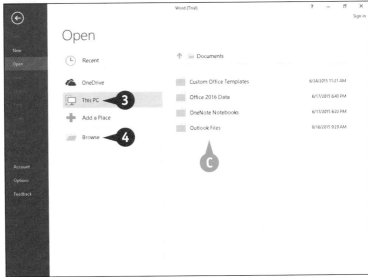

The Open dialog box appears.

D If you chose the wrong place, you can search for the file by typing part of the filename or content here.

5 Click in the folder list to navigate to the folder containing the document you want to open.

6 Click the document you want to open.

7 Click **Open**.

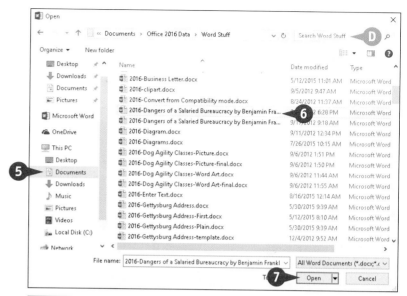

The document appears on-screen.

E To close a file, click **✕** in the upper right corner. If you have not saved the file, the program prompts you to save it.

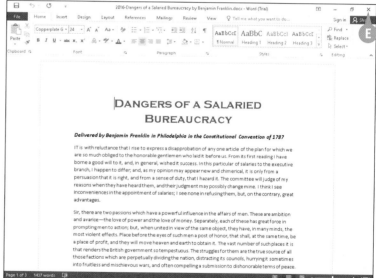

What if I cannot find my file?
You can use the search box in the upper right corner of the Open dialog box to locate files. Complete Steps **1** to **4** to display the Open dialog box. Locate and open the folder in which you believe the file was saved and type the file's name in the search box. Files containing the search term appear highlighted along with files containing a close match.

How do I close a document?
While viewing the document, click the **File** tab and then click **Close**.

Open a Document of Another Format

Y\ou can open and edit documents created by colleagues who use several other word-processing programs besides Word. For example, you can open XML, web page, rich text, plain text, OpenDocument, PDF, WordPerfect 5.x or 6.x, or Works 6-9 documents as well as documents created in earlier versions of Word.

Although you can open and edit PDF files, editing PDF files in Word works best if you used Word to originally create the PDF file. If you used a different program to create the PDF file, you will find that Word has difficulty maintaining the file's formatting.

Open a Document of Another Format

1 Click the **File** tab.

Backstage view appears.

2 Click **Open**.

A You can click **Recent** to see a list of recently opened documents. If you see the file you want to open, you can click it to open it and skip the rest of these steps.

3 Click the place where you believe the document is stored. This section uses **This PC**.

B If the folder containing the document appears here, click it and skip to Step **5**.

4 Click **Browse**.

The Open dialog box appears.

5 Click in the folder list to navigate to the folder containing the document you want to open.

6 Click ∨ to select the type of document you want to open.

7 Click the file you want to open.

8 Click **Open**.

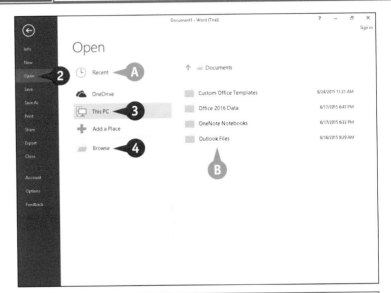

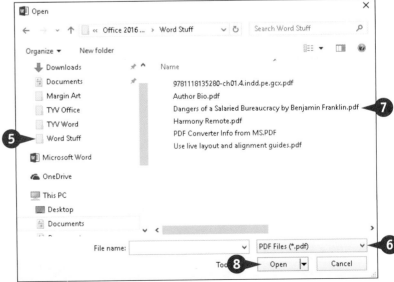

If you open a PDF file, Word displays a message indicating that it is converting your PDF file to an editable Word document; click **OK** to continue.

Note: You may be prompted to install a converter to open the file; click **Yes** or **OK** to install the converter and open the file.

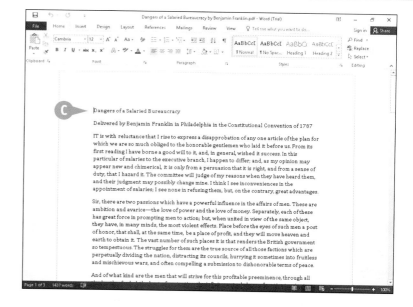

ⓒ Word opens the file.

TIP

How do I open an XPS file?

Although you can create an XPS file in Word, you cannot open the file in Word. Instead, you can use an XPS viewer as shown here, or in Windows 10, you can use the Reader app. To open an XPS file, find it using File Explorer and double-click it.

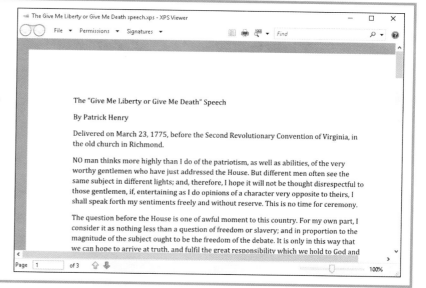

Start a New Document

Each time you open Word, the Word Start screen offers you a variety of choices to begin a new document. But you do not need to close and reopen Word to start a new document. This section demonstrates how to start a new document while you are already working in Word.

You can use a variety of *templates* — documents containing predefined settings that save you the effort of creating the settings yourself — as the foundation for your documents. Word 2016 displays a variety of templates on the Word Start screen and also when you choose to start a new document while working in Word.

Start a New Document

1 With a document already open in Word, click the **File** tab.

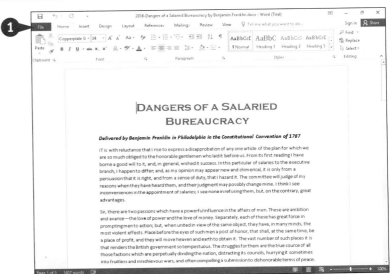

Backstage view appears.

2 Click **New**.

A Templates appear here.

B You can search for templates online at https://templates.office.com/en-US.

3 Click a template.

Note: This example uses **Business trip checklist**.

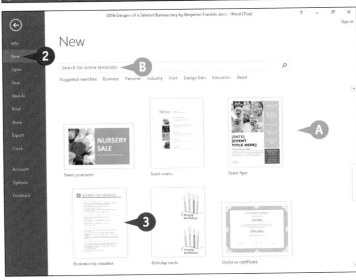

A preview of the template appears.

④ Click **Create**.

Note: If you change your mind about the template you chose in Step **3**, click ✖ in the upper right corner of the preview. Word redisplays Backstage view, showing the choices when you click **New**.

Business trip checklist

Provided by: Microsoft Corporation

Use this handy travel checklist template as is, or customize it with your own tasks to help you stay organized for your next business trip.

Download size: 49 KB

Create

ⓒ The new document based on the template you chose appears.

You can edit this document any way you choose.

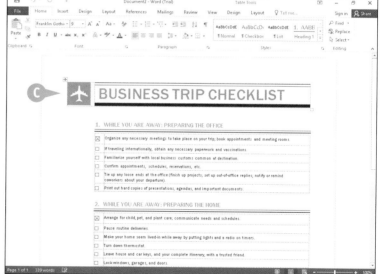

TIP

When I save the document, am I overwriting the settings in the template?
No. The document contains the settings found in the template, but saving the document has no effect on the template. The next time you choose to use that template, it will contain its original information. Think of it this way: A blank document is based on the Normal template, which contains no text, but it contains other settings such as fonts, font sizes, line spacing settings, and margins.

Switch Between Open Documents

When you have multiple documents open, you can switch between them to, for example, copy information from one document to another. You can open as many documents as you need, and you can switch between them from within Word or by using the Windows taskbar. You use the View tab in Word, or you can use the Windows taskbar to switch documents. By default, Word 2016 displays each document in its own window, and Windows identifies each open window by displaying a button on the Windows taskbar.

Switch Between Open Documents

Switch Documents Using Word

1 Click the **View** tab.

2 Click **Switch Windows**.

Ⓐ A list of all open documents appears at the bottom of the menu. A check mark (✓) appears beside the currently active document.

3 Click the document you want to view.

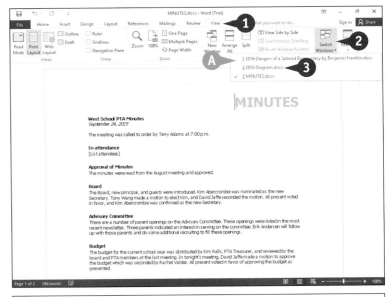

The selected document appears.

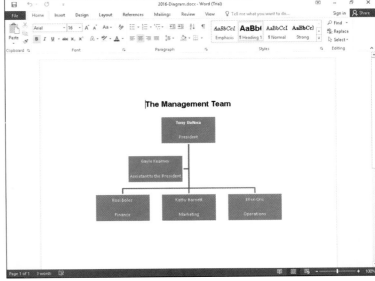

Switch Documents Using the Windows Taskbar

1 Open all the documents you need.

Note: See the sections "Open a Word Document" or "Open a Document of Another Format" for details.

2 Position the mouse (⌖) over the Word button in the Windows taskbar.

Ⓑ Preview thumbnails appear for each open document. The document over which you position the mouse (⌖) also previews in Word.

Ⓒ You can click a preview thumbnail's ✖ to close the document.

3 To view a document, click its preview.

The document appears.

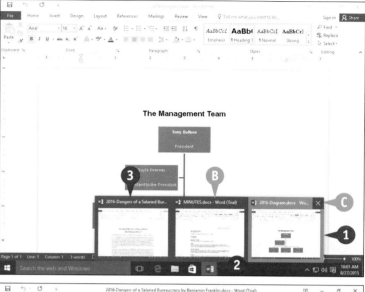

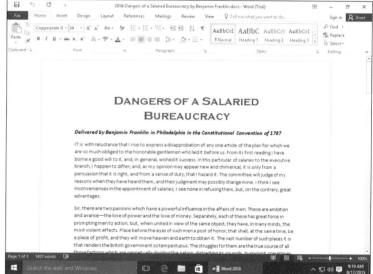

Is there a way to keep the taskbar buttons separate from each other instead of stacked on top of each other?

Yes. Right-click a blank spot on the taskbar, and click **Properties** in the menu that appears. The Taskbar and Start Menu Properties dialog box appears. Click the **Taskbar location on screen** ⌄ and choose **Combine when taskbar is full** or **Never combine** (Ⓐ). Click **OK** to save your changes.

Compare Documents Side by Side

You can view two open documents side by side to compare their similarities and differences. Although you could open both documents in their own windows and switch between them, that process can be cumbersome if you want to compare them. Switching between documents is better when you want to copy or move text from one document to another. But viewing documents side by side is the more effective tool for comparing document content.

Using the technique described in this section, you can scroll through both documents simultaneously.

Compare Documents Side by Side

Compare Documents

1. Open the two documents you want to compare.

Note: See the sections "Open a Word Document" or "Open a Document of Another Format" for details.

2. Click the **View** tab.

3. Click **View Side by Side**.

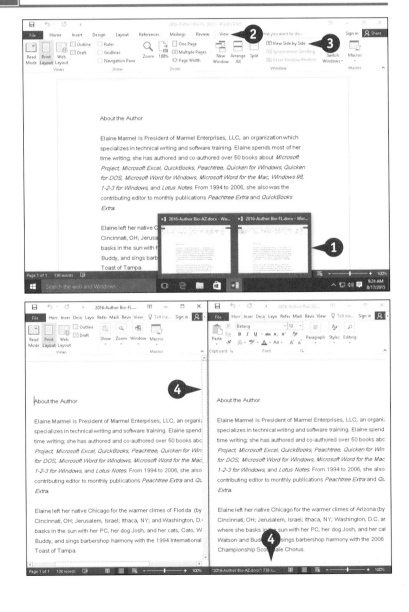

Word displays the documents in two panes beside each other.

4. Drag either document's scroll bar.

Word scrolls both documents simultaneously.

Stop Comparing Documents

1 Click **Window** in the document on the left.

A Options drop down from the Window button.

2 Click **View Side by Side**.

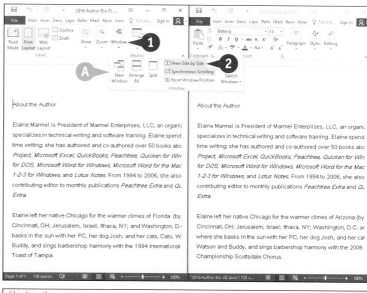

Word redisplays the document in a full screen.

B The second document is still open. You can see preview thumbnails for both documents in the Windows taskbar or click Switch windows to view open documents in a list, and you can click a preview thumbnail or an open document to switch to the other document.

Note: For details on this technique, see the previous section, "Switch Between Open Documents."

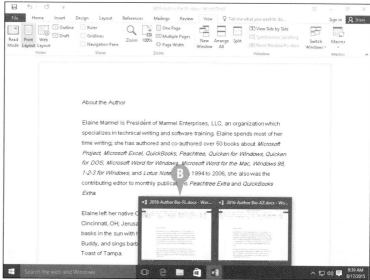

TIPS

Can I compare two documents with their differences highlighted?

Yes. When you have sent the same document to several people for review, each will return the document with his or her comments. You can compare the different document versions to see their differences. See the section "Combine Reviewers' Comments" in Chapter 4 for details.

What does the Reset Window Position button do?

With respect to comparing documents side by side, the **Reset Window Position** button has no effect. But you can use **Arrange All** to place one window above the other, each in its own separate pane. To return to side-by-side viewing, click **Reset Window Position**.

Inspect a Document Before Sharing

You can remove any personal information that Word stores in a document. For issues of privacy, you may want to remove this information before you share a document with anyone.

The Document Inspector searches your document for comments, revision marks, versions, and ink annotations. It searches document properties for hidden metadata and personal information. It inspects for task pane apps saved in the document as well as text that has been collapsed under a heading. If your document contains custom XML data, headers, footers, watermarks, or invisible content, the Document Inspector alerts you.

Inspect a Document Before Sharing

1 In the document you want to check for sensitive information, click the **File** tab.

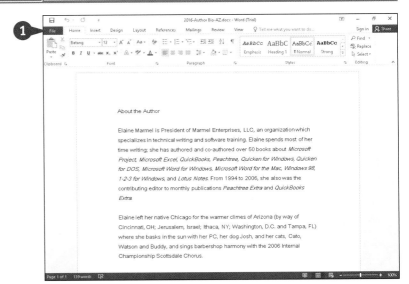

Backstage view appears.

2 Click **Info**.

3 Click **Check for Issues**.

4 Click **Inspect Document**.

Note: If you have unsaved changes, Word prompts you to save the document, which you do by clicking **Yes**.

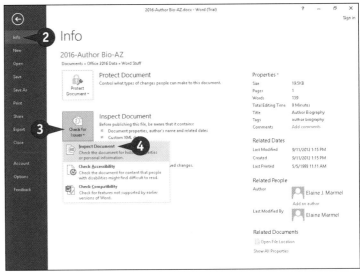

The Document Inspector window appears.

Ⓐ You can deselect check boxes (☑ changes to ☐) to avoid inspecting for these elements.

❺ Click **Inspect**.

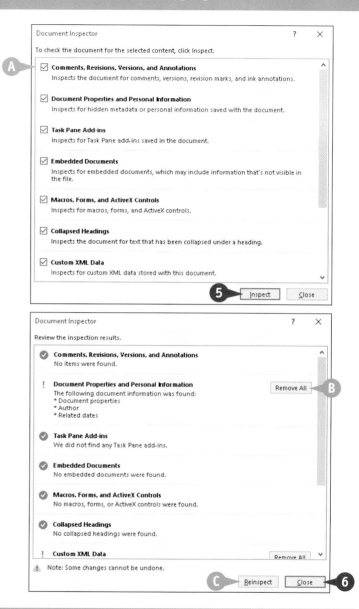

The Document Inspector looks for the information you specified and displays the results.

Ⓑ You can remove any identified information by clicking **Remove All** beside that element.

Ⓒ You can click **Reinspect** after removing identifying information.

❻ Click **Close**.

Can I review the information that the Document Inspector displays before I remove it?

No. The only way to review the information before you remove it is to close the Document Inspector *without* removing information, use the appropriate Word features to review the information, and then rerun the Document Inspector as described in this section.

What happens if I remove information and then decide that I really want that information?

You cannot undo the effects of removing the information using the Document Inspector. However, to restore removed information, you can close the document *without* saving changes and then reopen it.

Work with Protected Documents

You can limit the changes others can make to a document by protecting it with a password. Word offers two kinds of protection: Password and User Authentication. User authentication, not shown in this section, relies on Windows authentication.

You can limit the styles available to format the document, the kinds of changes users can make, and the users who can make changes.

Work with Protected Documents

1 Click the **Review** tab.

2 Click **Protect**.

3 Click **Restrict Editing**.

Note: Depending on your screen resolution, you may or may not see **Protect**.

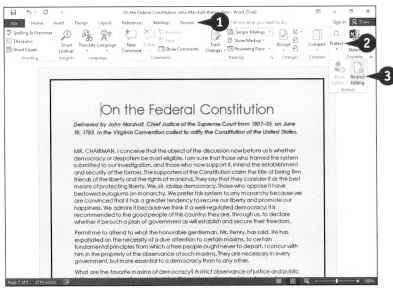

The Restrict Editing pane appears.

4 Select this option to limit document formatting to the styles you select (☐ changes to ☑).

5 Click the **Settings** link.

The Formatting Restrictions dialog box appears.

6 Deselect the styles you want unavailable (☑ changes to ☐).

7 Click **OK**.

8 Select this option to specify editing restrictions (☐ changes to ☑).

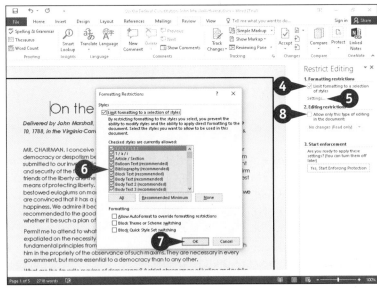

9 Click ▼, and select the type of editing to permit.

You can select parts of the document to make them available for editing.

10 Select this option to identify users who are allowed to edit the selected parts of the document (☐ changes to ☑).

11 Click **Yes, Start Enforcing Protection**.

12 In the Start Enforcing Protection dialog box, type a password, and then retype it.

Note: If your computer uses Information Rights Management (IRM), you can opt to use User Authentication, which also encrypts your document; only users you specify can remove document protection.

13 Click **OK**.

14 Click the **Save** button (🖫).

Word protects the document and saves the protection.

15 Click ✖ to close the Restrict Editing pane.

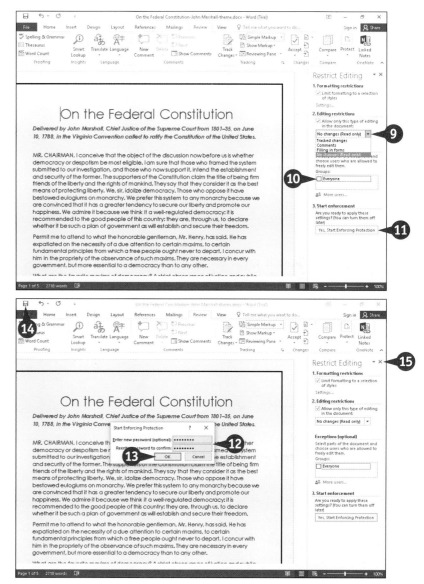

TIP

How do I open a protected document and work in it?
You open a protected document as you would open any document. Areas you can edit are highlighted. If you try to change an area that is not highlighted, a message appears in the status bar, explaining that you cannot make the modification because that area of the document is protected. Follow Steps **1** to **3** in this section to display the Restrict Editing pane, which contains only two buttons in a restricted document, and click **Show All Regions I Can Edit** to find areas you can change. To turn off protection, you need the protection password.

Mark a Document as Final

When you mark a document as final, Word makes the document read-only; you cannot make changes to it or inspect it.

Marking a document as final is not a security feature; instead, it is a feature that helps you focus on reading rather than editing because it makes editing unavailable. If you want to focus on security, consider assigning a password to the document that others must supply to open the document. Alternatively, you can assign a digital signature to indicate that a document has not changed since you signed it, or you can restrict editing as described in the previous section, "Work with Protected Documents."

Mark a Document as Final

Mark the Document

1. Click the **File** tab.

   Backstage view appears.

2. Click **Info**.

3. Click **Protect Document**.

4. Click **Mark as Final**.

   A message explains that Word will mark the document as final and then save it.

5. Click **OK**.

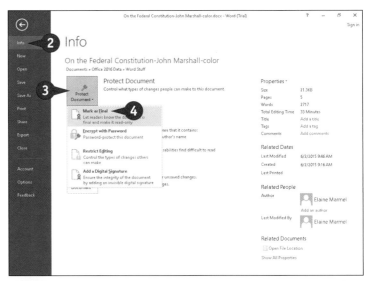

A. Word saves the document and displays another message confirming that the document has been marked as final and editing commands are unavailable. If you do not want to see this message again, select this option (☐ changes to ✔).

6. Click **OK**.

   Backstage view highlights the Protect Document button in yellow to draw your attention.

7. Click the **Back** button (⬅).

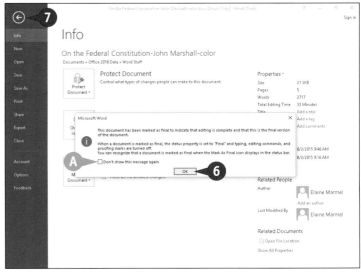

Edit a Final Document

B The document is now read-only.

C Commands on the QAT become unavailable.

D Word hides the Ribbon buttons because most editing commands are not available.

E This yellow bar appears, indicating that the document has been marked as final.

8 Click **Edit Anyway** in the yellow bar at the top of the document.

F Word no longer marks the document as read-only.

G Word redisplays and makes available all Ribbon buttons.

H QAT buttons are available.

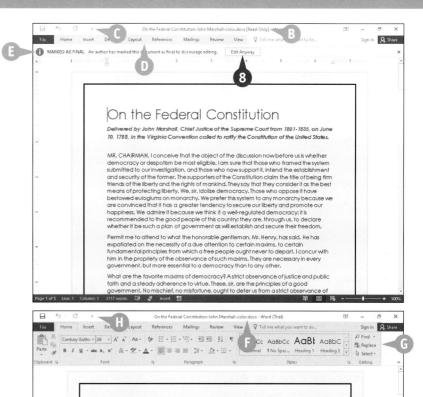

Can any user remove the "Marked as Final" status from a document?

Yes. If you absolutely do not want others to edit or change your document, consider other security options. For example, you can restrict editing with a password but, if you mark the document as final, you cannot require a password to open the document. You also can consider saving your document as a PDF or XPS document, as described in the section "Save a Document in PDF or XPS Format."

Convert Word Documents from Prior Versions to Word 2016

You can convert existing Word 97-Word 2003 documents to the new format introduced by Word 2007. You also can convert Word 2007, Word 2010, and Word 2013 documents to Word 2016 documents.

It is helpful to convert documents created in older versions of Word to Word 2016 format when you want to take advantage of tools available in Word 2016 that are not in earlier versions of Word. For example, you can open a Word 2010 document that contains an image and you can move the image, but you will not see alignment guides during the move unless you convert the Word 2010 document to Word 2016.

Convert Word Documents from Prior Versions to Word 2016

1 Open any prior version Word document; this example uses a Word 2003 document.

Note: See the sections "Open a Word Document" or "Open a Document of Another Format" for details.

A In the title bar, Word indicates that the document is open in Compatibility Mode.

2 Click the **File** tab.

Backstage view appears.

3 Click **Info**.

4 Click **Convert**.

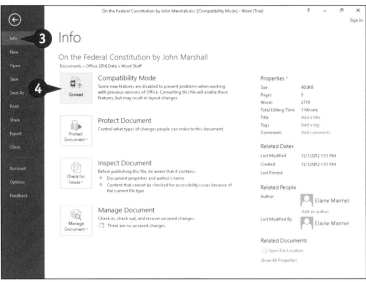

Word closes Backstage view and displays a message indicating it will convert the document to the newest file format.

Ⓑ If you do not want to view this message in the future when you convert documents, select this option (☐ changes to ☑).

❺ Click **OK**.

Ⓒ Word converts the document and removes the Compatibility Mode indicator from the title bar.

❻ Click the **Save** button (🖫).

The Save As dialog box appears.

Ⓓ Word suggests the same filename but the new file format extension (.docx).

❼ Click **Save**.

Word saves the document in Word 2016 format.

TIP

Do I need to convert my documents from earlier versions of Word before I work on them in Word 2016?
No. You can work on a document created in an older version of Word and even incorporate Word 2016 features not available in earlier versions of Word. You only need to convert documents in which you expect to include features available only in Word 2016. Also note that, if you use the Save As command while working in an older version document, Word prompts you to convert the document to the Word 2016 format using the Convert command as described in this section.

CHAPTER 3

Editing Text

After you know how to navigate around Word, it is time to work with the text that you type on a page. In this chapter, you learn editing techniques that you can use to change text in documents you create.

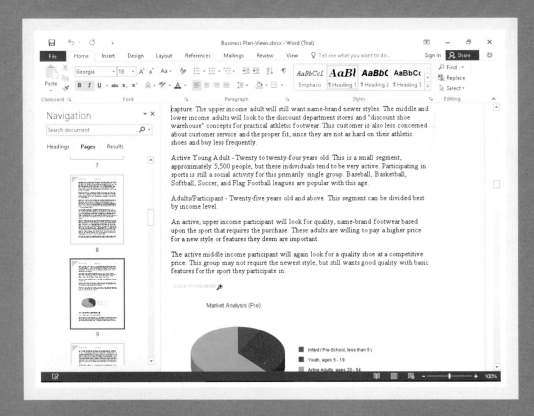

Insert Text

Word makes typing easy; you can quickly type a letter, memo, or report in Word. You can insert text into a document by adding to existing text or replacing existing text. By default, Word is set to Insert mode; when you start typing, Word moves any existing text to the right to accommodate the new text. In Overtype mode, Word replaces existing text to the right of the insertion point, character for character. If you have set up Word to toggle between Insert mode and Overtype mode, you can press `Insert` to switch between Insert and Overtype modes.

Insert Text

Insert and Add Text

1 Click the location where you want to insert text.

The insertion point flashes where you clicked.

You can press ←, →, ↑, or ↓ to move the insertion point one character or line.

You can press `Ctrl`+→ or `Ctrl`+← to move the insertion point one word at a time to the right or left.

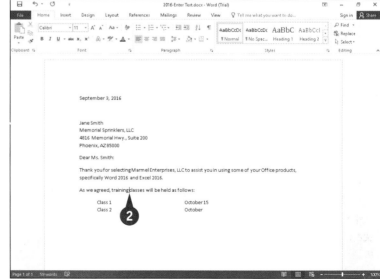

2 Type the text you want to insert.

Word inserts the text to the left of the insertion point, moving existing text to the right.

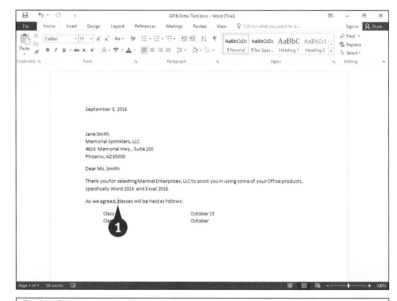

Insert and Replace Text

1 Position the insertion point where you want to replace existing text.

2 Right-click the status bar.

3 Click **Overtype** to display a check beside it.

A An indicator appears in the status bar.

4 Click the indicator to switch to Overtype mode.

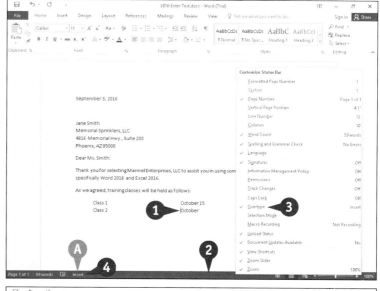

B The indicator switches to Overtype.

Note: Each time you click the indicator, you switch between Overtype and Insert mode.

5 Type the new text.

As you type, Word replaces the existing text with the new text you type.

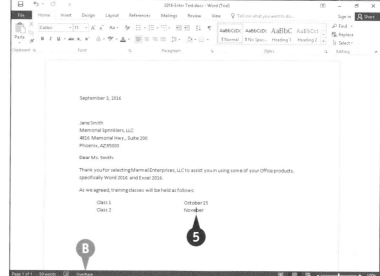

TIP

How can I use the keyboard to control switching between Insert mode and Overtype mode?
Perform the steps that follow: Click the **File** tab and click **Options** to display the Word Options dialog box. Click **Advanced** and select **Use the Insert key to control overtype mode** (☐ changes to ✔). Click **OK**, and then press ⎀Insert⎀. Word switches between Insert mode and Overtype mode.

Delete Text

When you make a mistake or simply change your mind about text you have already typed, you can easily remove the text from your document. Whether you have a large or a small amount of text to remove, you use either **Delete** or **Backspace** on your keyboard. This section demonstrates how to remove one character at a time. Note that when you need to delete a larger amount of text, you do not need to remove it one character at a time, but you use the same basic technique demonstrated here.

Delete Text

Using the Delete Key

1 Click to the left of the location where you want to delete text.

The insertion point flashes where you clicked.

You can press **←**, **→**, **↑**, or **↓** to move the insertion point one character or line.

You can press **Ctrl**+**→** or **Ctrl**+**←** to move the insertion point one word at a time to the right or left.

2 Press **Delete** on your keyboard.

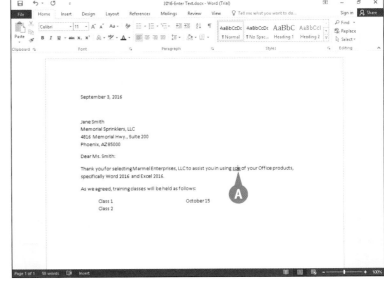

A Word deletes the character immediately to the right of the insertion point.

You can press and hold **Delete** to repeatedly delete characters to the right of the insertion point.

You can press **Ctrl**+**Delete** to delete the word to the right of the insertion point.

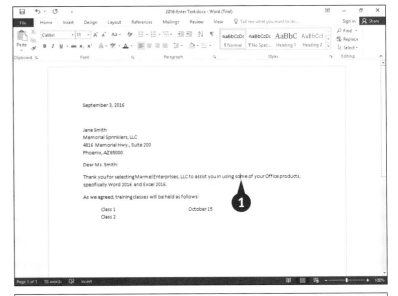

Using the Backspace Key

1 Click to the right of the location where you want to delete text.

The insertion point flashes where you clicked.

2 Press **Backspace** on your keyboard.

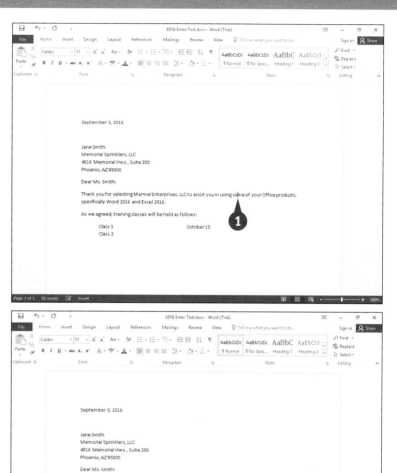

B Word deletes the character immediately to the left of the insertion point.

You can press and hold **Backspace** to repeatedly delete characters to the left of the insertion point.

You can press **Ctrl**+**Backspace** to delete the word to the left of the insertion point.

TIPS

Do I have to delete a large block of text one character or one word at a time?

No, and in fact, to work efficiently, you should not delete a large block one character or word at a time. You can select the block of text and then press either **Delete** or **Backspace**; either key deletes selected text. For details on selecting text, see the section "Select Text," later in this chapter.

What should I do if I mistakenly delete text?

You should use the Undo feature in Word to restore the text you deleted. For details on how this feature works, see the section "Undo Changes," later in this chapter.

Insert Blank Lines

Y ou can insert blank lines in your text to signify new paragraphs by inserting paragraph marks or line breaks. Word stores paragraph formatting in the paragraph mark, which you can display by clicking the **Show/Hide** button (¶) on the Home tab. When you start a new paragraph, you can change the new paragraph's formatting without affecting the preceding paragraph's formatting.

You use line breaks to start a new line without starting a new paragraph; typically, when you type the inside address of a letter, you use line breaks. For more information on styles and displaying paragraph marks, see Chapter 6.

Insert Blank Lines

Start a New Paragraph

1 Click where you want to start a new paragraph.

2 Press Enter.

A Word inserts a paragraph mark and moves any text to the right of the insertion point into the new paragraph.

3 Repeat Steps **1** and **2** for each blank line you want to insert.

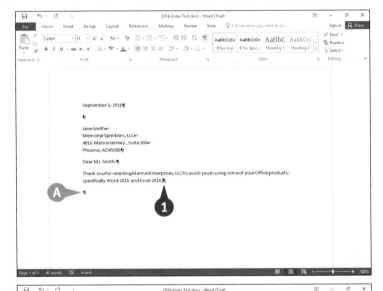

Insert a Line Break

1 Click where you want to start a new paragraph.

2 Press Shift + Enter.

B Word inserts a line break.

Note: Any text on the line to the right of where you placed the insertion point in Step **1** moves onto the new line.

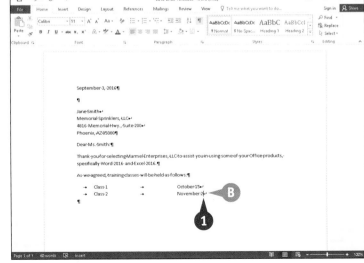

Undo Changes

You can use the Undo feature to reverse actions you take while working in a document. For example, suppose that you accidentally delete text that you meant to keep. In this case, you can use the Undo feature to recover the text you accidentally deleted.

You also can use the Undo feature to remove formatting you might have applied, particularly if you decide that you do not like the look of the formatting. Rather than take steps to remove the formatting, simply undo your actions.

Undo Changes

Note: The position of the insertion point does not affect using the Undo feature.

1 Click the **Undo** button (↶ ▾).

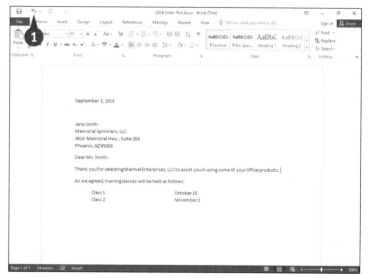

(A) Word reverses the effects of the last change you made.

You also can press Ctrl+Z to reverse an action.

Note: You can repeatedly click the **Undo** button (↶ ▾) to reverse each action you have taken, from last to first.

(B) If you decide not to reverse an action after clicking the **Undo** button (↶ ▾), click the **Redo** button (↷), which reverses the action of the Undo button (↶ ▾).

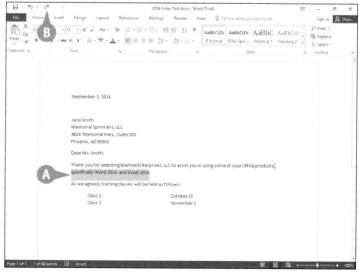

Select Text

Before performing many tasks in Word, you identify the existing text on which you want to work by selecting it. For example, you select existing text to underline it, align it, change its font size, or apply color to it.

You can take advantage of shortcuts using the keyboard and the mouse together to select a word, a sentence, or your entire document, and the text you select does not need to appear together in one location. If you like to keep your hands on the keyboard as much as possible, you can select text using only the keyboard.

Select Text

Select a Block of Text

1 Position the mouse (⬚) to the left of the first character you want to select.

2 Click and drag to the right and down over the text you want to select and release the mouse button.

A The selection appears highlighted, and the Mini Toolbar appears.

Note: This example hides the Mini Toolbar so that you can see the beginning and end of the selection.

To cancel a selection, you can click anywhere on-screen or press ⬅, ➡, ⬆, or ⬇.

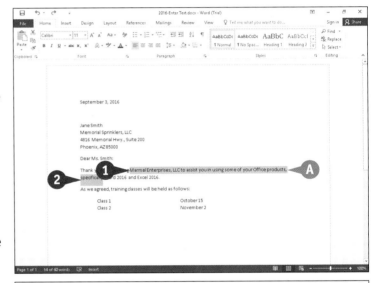

Select a Word

1 Double-click the word you want to select.

B Word selects the word, and the Mini Toolbar appears.

You can slide the mouse (⬚) away from the Mini Toolbar to make it disappear.

Note: See Chapter 1 for details on using the Mini Toolbar.

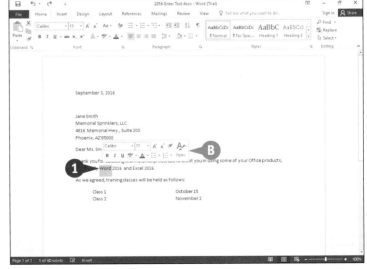

Select a Sentence

1 Press and hold [Ctrl].

2 Click anywhere in the sentence you want to select.

C Word selects the entire sentence, and the Mini Toolbar appears.

You can slide the mouse (⬉) away from the Mini Toolbar to make it disappear.

Note: See Chapter 1 for details on using the Mini Toolbar.

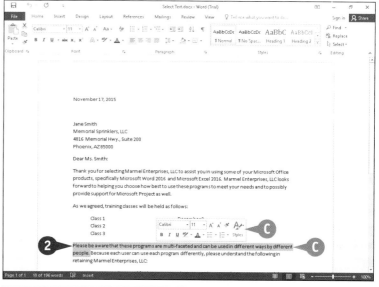

Select the Entire Document

1 Click the **Home** tab.

2 Click **Select**.

3 Click **Select All**.

D Word selects the entire document.

You also can press and hold [Ctrl] and press [A] to select the entire document.

To cancel the selection, you can click anywhere.

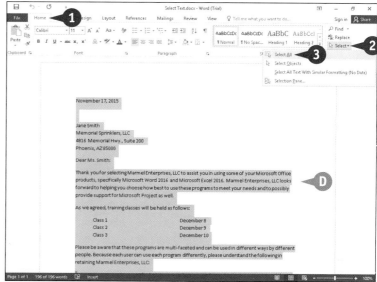

TIPS

Can I select text using the keyboard?
Yes. Press and hold [Shift] while pressing ⬅, ➡, ⬆, or ⬇. You also can press [Shift]+[Ctrl] to select, for example, several words in a row. If you press and hold [Shift]+[Ctrl] while pressing ➡ five times, you select five consecutive words to the right of the insertion point.

How can I select noncontiguous text?
You select the first area using any of the techniques described in this section. Then press and hold [Ctrl] as you select the additional areas. Word selects all areas, even if text appears between them.

Mark and Find Your Place

When you want to mark your place in a document as you edit it so that you can easily return to it later, you can use the Bookmark feature. You can also use bookmarks to identify text that, for example, you plan to change but do not have the time to do so at the present. You can place the text in a bookmark so that you can easily locate it when you do have time to change it.

Bookmark indicators do not appear by default, but you can choose to display them as shown in this section. Bookmark indicators do not print.

Mark and Find Your Place

Mark Your Place

1 Click the location you want to mark.

Note: If you select text instead of clicking at the location you want to mark, Word creates a bookmark containing text and names it using the text you select.

2 Click the **Insert** tab.

3 Click **Links**.

4 Click **Bookmark**.

The Bookmark dialog box appears.

5 Type a name for the bookmark.

Note: Do not include spaces in a bookmark name.

6 Click **Add**.

Word saves the bookmark and closes the Bookmark dialog box.

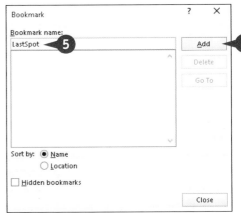

Find Your Place

① Click the **Home** tab.

② Click ▼ beside the **Find** button.

③ Click **Go To**.

The Go To tab of the Find and Replace dialog box appears.

④ Click **Bookmark**.

⑤ Click ✓, and select a bookmark.

⑥ Click **Go To**.

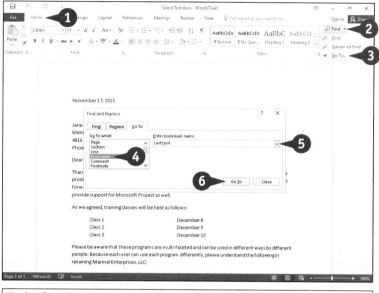

Ⓐ Word moves the insertion point to the bookmark.

Note: If the bookmark contains text, Word selects the text in the bookmark.

⑦ Click **Close**, or press Esc.

Word closes the Find and Replace dialog box.

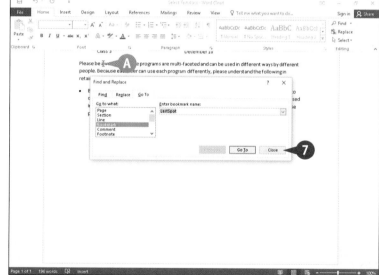

TIP

How can I display bookmarks in my document?
Perform the steps that follow: Click the **File** tab and then click **Options**. In the Options dialog box, click **Advanced**. In the Show Document Content section, select **Show bookmarks** (☐ changes to ☑). Click **OK**, and Word displays open and close brackets representing the bookmark. A bookmark that marks a location looks like an I-beam (Ⅰ).

Move or Copy Text

You can move information in your document by cutting and then pasting it. You also can repeat text by copying and then pasting it. For example, you might cut or copy information in a document and paste it elsewhere in the same document.

When you move text, the text disappears from the original location and appears in a new one. When you copy and paste text, it remains in the original location and also appears in a new one. You can move or copy information in two ways: using buttons on the Ribbon or using the drag-and-drop method.

Move or Copy Text

Using Ribbon Buttons

1 Select the text you want to move or copy.

Note: To select text, see the section "Select Text."

2 Click the **Home** tab.

3 To move text, click the **Cut** button (✂); to copy text, click the **Copy** button (📋).

Note: If you cut text, it disappears from the screen.

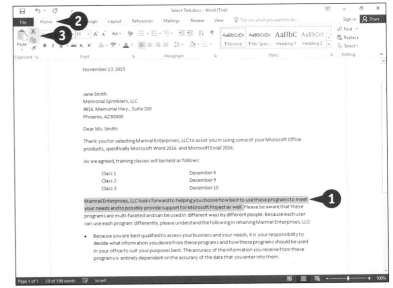

4 Click to place the insertion point at the location where you want the text to appear.

5 Click the **Paste** button.

A The text appears at the new location.

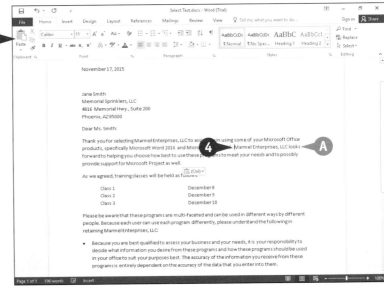

Drag and Drop

1 Select the text you want to move or copy.

2 Position the mouse over the selected text ($\mathcal{I}$ changes to h).

3 Either move or copy the text.

To move text, drag the mouse (h changes to h).

To copy text, press and hold **Ctrl** and drag the mouse (h changes to h).

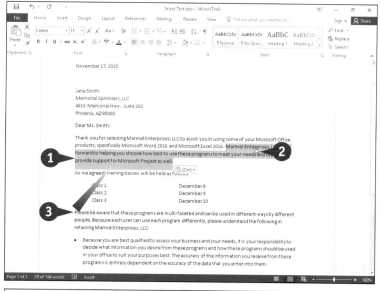

B The text appears at the new location.

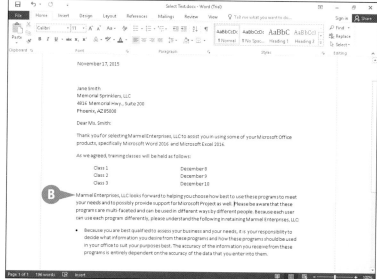

Can I can move or copy text using menus?

Yes. Select the text that you want to move or copy, and then right-click it. The context menu and the Mini Toolbar appear; click **Cut** or **Copy**. Then place the insertion point at the location where you want the text to appear, and right-click again. From the context menu, click **Paste**.

Can I copy or move information other than text?

Yes. You can copy or move any element that you can select, such as text, pictures, tables, graphics, and so on. You also can copy or move text from one Word document to another; see the next section, "Share Text Between Documents."

Share Text Between Documents

You can move or copy information both within the current document and between two or more documents. For example, suppose that you are working on a marketing report and some colleagues provide you with background information for your report. You can copy and paste the information from the colleagues' documents into your document.

Any text that you cut disappears from its original location. Text that you copy continues to appear in its original location and also appears in the new location you choose.

Share Text Between Documents

1 Open the documents you want to use to share text.

2 Select the text you want to move or copy.

Note: For details on selecting text, see the section "Select Text."

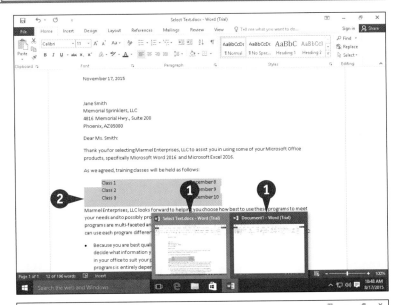

3 Click the **Home** tab.

4 Click the **Cut** button (✂) to move text, or click the **Copy** button (🗐) to copy text.

5 Switch to the other document by clicking its button in the Windows taskbar.

The other document appears.

6 Place the insertion point at the location where the text you are moving or copying should appear.

7 Click the **Paste** button.

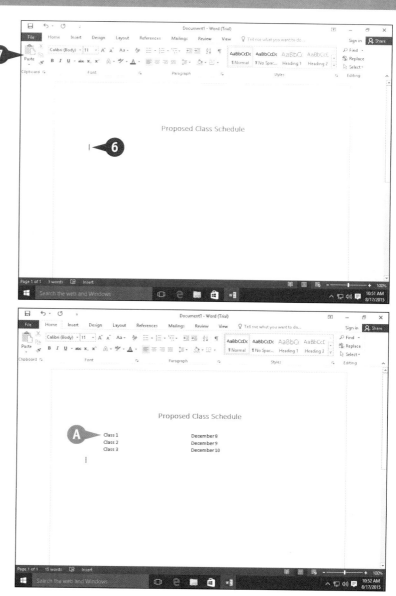

Ⓐ The text appears in the new location.

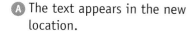

TIPS

Why do I see a button when I paste?
Word displays the Paste Options button (🗐 (Ctrl)▾) to give you the opportunity to determine how to handle the formatting of the selection you are pasting. See the section "Take Advantage of Paste Options" for details on how to use Paste options.

What format will Word use by default for text I paste?
The default appearance of pasted text depends on options set in the Word Options dialog box. To view or set the default appearance, click the **Paste Options** button (🗐 (Ctrl)▾), click **Set Default Paste** to display the Word Options dialog box, and set options in the Cut, Copy, and Paste section.

Move or Copy Several Selections

Using the Office Clipboard, you can move or copy several selections at the same time. The Office Clipboard is the location where Word stores information you cut or copy until you paste it. By default, Word stores only the last information you cut or copied, making only that information available when you paste. However, if you open the Office Clipboard, Word can save up to the last 24 selections that you cut or copied. You can paste the items from the Office Clipboard into a single document or multiple documents in any order you want.

Move or Copy Several Selections

① Click the **Home** tab.

② Click the Clipboard group dialog box launcher (⌐).

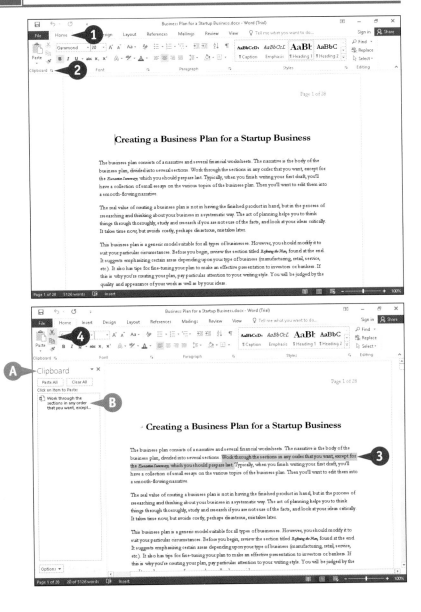

Ⓐ The Office Clipboard pane appears.

Note: If you cut or copied anything prior to this time, an entry appears in the Clipboard pane.

③ Select the text or information you want to move or copy.

④ Click the **Cut** button (✂) or the **Copy** button (📋).

Ⓑ An entry appears in the Clipboard pane.

5 Repeat Steps **3** and **4** for each selection you want to move or copy.

C Word adds each entry to the Clipboard pane; the newest entry appears at the top of the pane.

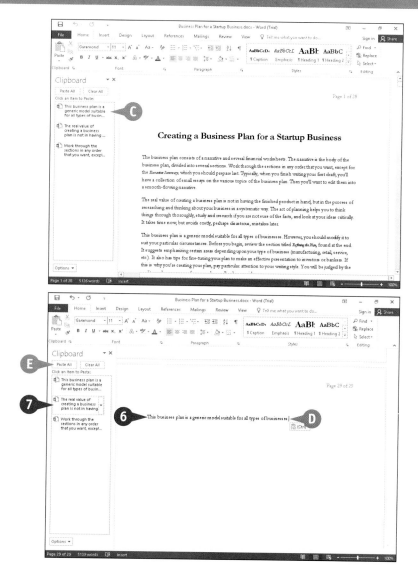

6 Click in the document or in a different document where you want to place text you cut or copied.

7 Click a selection in the Clipboard pane to place it in the document.

D The entry appears in the document.

8 Repeat Steps **6** and **7** to paste other items from the Clipboard.

E If you want to place all the items in one location and the items appear in the Clipboard pane in the order you want them in your document, you can click **Paste All**.

TIPS

Why does a down arrow appear when I point at an item in the Clipboard pane?

If you click ▼, a menu appears. From this menu, you can click **Paste** to add the item to your document, or you can click **Delete** to remove the item from the Clipboard pane.

Must I display the Office Clipboard to collect copied elements?

No. Click the **Options** button at the bottom of the Clipboard pane, and then click **Collect Without Showing Office Clipboard**. As you cut or copy, a message appears in the lower right corner of your screen, telling you how many elements are stored on the Office Clipboard. You must display the Office Clipboard to paste any item except the one you last cut or copied.

Take Advantage of Paste Options

Sometimes, when you move or copy information, the formatting at the original location is not the formatting that you want to use at the destination location. Using Paste Options, you can choose the formatting Word applies to the selection at its new location. You can preview the formatting for a particular paste option without actually applying that formatting. The formatting options available depend upon the information you copy. This section shows how to paste information from an Excel workbook into a Word document; in this scenario, you see several options that might not appear if you paste information from one Word document to another.

Take Advantage of Paste Options

1 Make a selection; this example uses an Excel spreadsheet selection, but you can select text in a Word document.

2 Click the **Copy** button (⧉) or the **Cut** button (✄).

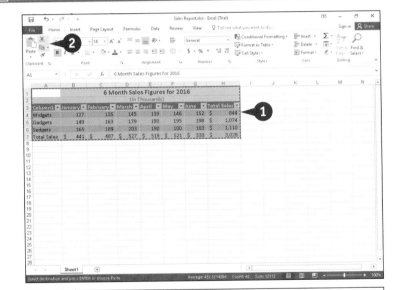

3 Position the insertion point in your Word document where you want to paste the information.

4 Click the bottom half of the **Paste** button.

A Buttons representing paste options appear.

5 To preview formatting for the selection, point at the **Keep Source Formatting** button (📋).

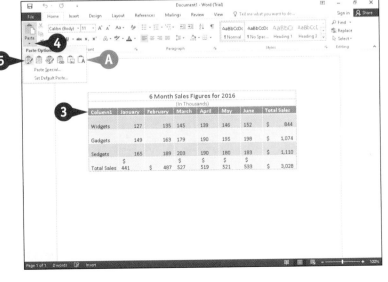

6 To preview formatting for the selection, point at the **Use Destination Styles** button (▤).

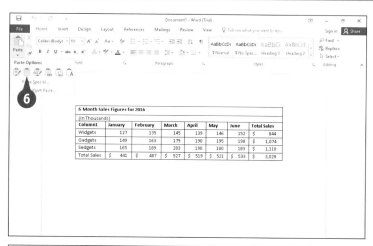

7 To preview formatting for the selection, point at the **Keep Text Only** button (▤A).

8 Click a **Paste Options** button to paste the selection and specify its format in your Word document.

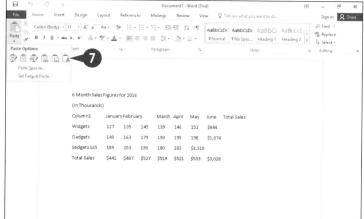

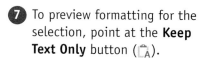

TIP

What do the various Paste Options buttons mean?

Button	Function	Button	Function
	Uses the formatting of the selection you copied or cut.		Formats the selection using the style of the location where you paste the selection and links the selection at the new location to the selection at the original location.
	Formats the selection using the style of the location where you paste the selection.		Formats the selection as a graphic that you cannot edit in Word.
	Uses the formatting of the selection you cut or copied and links the selection at the new location to the selection at the original location.		Applies no formatting to the selection; only text appears.

Switch Document Views

You can view a document five ways. The view you use depends entirely on what you are doing at the time; select the view that best meets your needs. For example, if you are working with a long document that has headings and sub-headings, and you want to work on the document's organization, Outline view might work best for you. On the other hand, if you are reviewing a document, consider Read Mode view, which has been updated to support tablet PC motions.

For more on the various views, see the next section, "Understanding Document Views."

Switch Document Views

1 Click the **View** tab.

2 Click one of the buttons in the Views group on the Ribbon: **Read Mode**, **Print Layout**, **Web Layout**, **Outline**, or **Draft**.

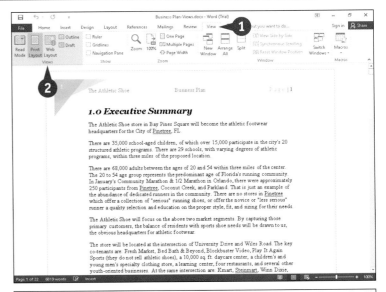

Word switches your document to the view you selected.

Note: In this example, the document switches from Print Layout view to Outline view, showing four outline levels, each representing a heading style.

A Outline view displays its own tab of outline-related tools.

B Buttons for three of the views also appear at the right edge of the status bar; position the mouse (⬚) over each button to see its function, and click a button to switch views:

▤ — Read Mode

▤ — Print Layout

▤ — Web Layout

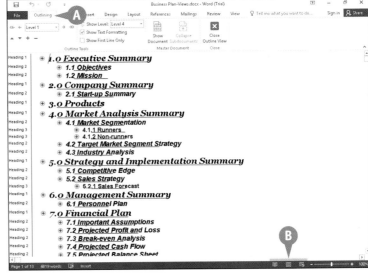

Understanding Document Views

You can control the way that you view your document by choosing from five different views: Read Mode, Print Layout, Web Layout, Outline, and Draft.

Read Mode View

Read Mode view, which supports tablet motions, optimizes your document for easier reading and helps minimize eyestrain when you read a document on-screen. This view removes most toolbars. To return to another view, click **View** and then click **Edit Document** or press **Esc**.

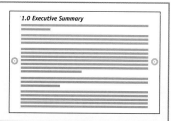

Print Layout View

Print Layout view presents a "what you see is what you get" view of your document. In Print Layout view, you see elements of your document that affect the printed page, such as margins, headers, and footers.

Web Layout View

Web Layout view is useful when you are designing a web page because it displays a web page preview of your document.

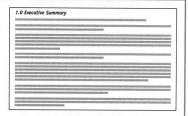

Draft View

Draft view is designed for editing and formatting; it does not display your document the way it will print. Instead, you can view elements such as the Style Area — which shows the formatting style for each paragraph — on the left side of the screen, but you cannot view certain document elements such as graphics or the document's margins, headers, and footers.

Outline View

Outline view helps you work with the organization of a document. Word indents text styled as headings based on the heading number; you can move or copy entire sections of a document by moving or copying the heading. You also can display the Style Area, as shown here.

Heading 1	⊕ **1.0 Executive Summary**
Heading 2	⊕ *1.1 Objectives*
Heading 2	⊕ *1.2 Mission*
Heading 1	⊕ **2.0 Company Summary**
Heading 2	⊕ *2.1 Start-up Summary*
Heading 1	⊕ **3.0 Products**
Heading 1	⊕ **4.0 Market Analysis Summary**
Heading 2	⊕ *4.1 Market Segmentation*

Work with the Navigation Pane

I f you are working with a very long document, using the scroll bar on the right side of the screen or the Page Up and Page Down keys on your keyboard to locate a particular page in that document can be time-consuming. To rectify this, you can use the Navigation pane to navigate through a document. This pane can display all the headings in your document or a thumbnail image of each page in your document. You can then click a heading or a thumbnail image in the Navigation pane to view the corresponding page.

Work with the Navigation Pane

Navigate Using Headings

Note: To navigate using headings, your document must contain text styled with Heading styles. See Chapter 6 for details on styles.

1 Click the **View** tab.

2 Select **Navigation Pane** (☐ changes to ☑).

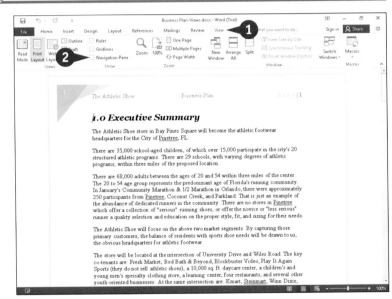

A The Navigation pane appears.

B Heading 1 styles appear at the left edge of the Navigation pane.

C Word indents Heading 2 styles slightly and each subsequent heading style a bit more.

D This icon (◢) represents a heading displaying subheadings; you can click it to hide subheadings.

E This icon (▷) represents a heading hiding subheadings; you can click it to display subheadings.

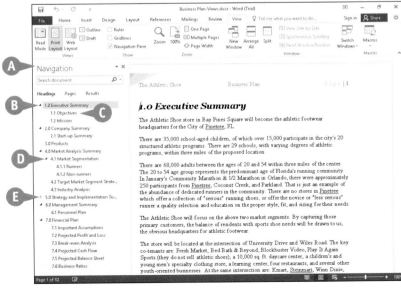

3 Click to select any heading in the Navigation pane.

F Word moves the insertion point to that heading in your document.

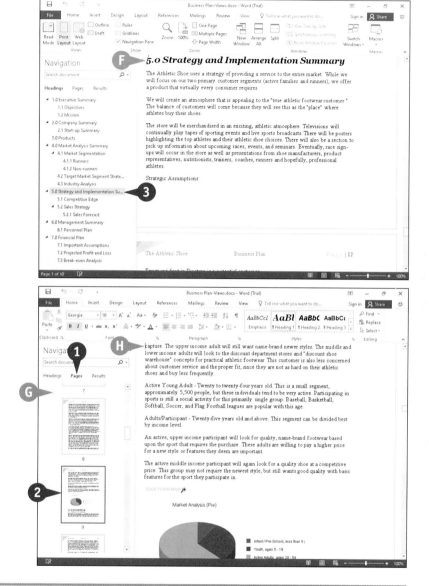

Navigate by Page

1 Click **Pages**.

G Word displays each page in your document as a thumbnail.

2 Click a thumbnail.

H Word selects that page in the Navigation pane and moves the insertion point to the top of that page. Word surrounds the current page's thumbnail with a heavy blue border.

What do I do with the Search Document box?

You can use the Search Document box, which is visible in the Navigation pane, to find text in your document; see Chapter 4 for details on using this box and on other ways you can search for text and information in your document.

Can I control the headings that appear?

Yes. While viewing headings, right-click any heading in the Navigation pane. From the menu that appears, point at **Show Heading Levels** and, from the submenu that appears, click the heading level you want to display, such as **Show Heading 1**, **Show Heading 2**, and so on through **Show Heading 9**.

Insert a Symbol

From time to time, you might need to insert a symbol such as a mathematical symbol or special character into your Word document. From the Symbol gallery, you can insert many common symbols, including mathematical and Greek symbols, architectural symbols, and more. If you do not find the symbol you need in the Symbol gallery, you can use the Symbol dialog box. The Symbol dialog box displays a list of recently used symbols as well as hundreds of symbols in a variety of fonts. You also can use the Symbol dialog box to insert special characters.

Insert a Symbol

1 Click the location in the document where you want the symbol to appear.

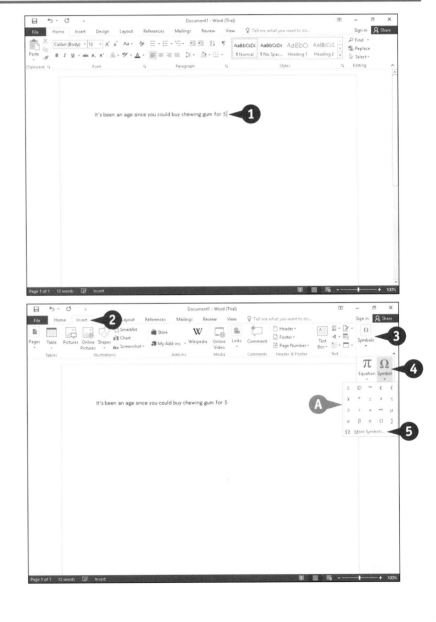

2 Click the **Insert** tab.

3 Click **Symbols**.

4 Click **Symbol**.

Note: Depending on your screen resolution, you may or may not see the Symbols button.

A A gallery of commonly used symbols appears. If the symbol you need appears in the gallery, you can click it and skip the rest of these steps.

5 Click **More Symbols**.

74

The Symbol dialog box appears.

6 Click ∨ to select the symbol's font.

The available symbols change to match the font you selected.

B You can click ∧ and ∨ to scroll through available symbols.

7 Click a symbol.

8 Click **Insert**.

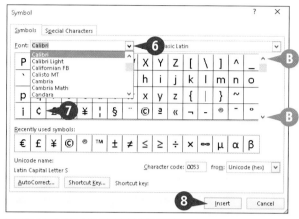

C The symbol appears at the current insertion point location in the document.

Note: You can control the size of the symbol the same way you control the size of text; see Chapter 5 for details.

The dialog box remains open so that you can add more symbols to your document.

9 When finished, click **Close**.

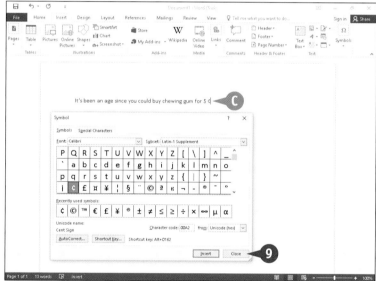

How do I add a special character?
To add a special character, open the Symbol dialog box and click the **Special Characters** tab. Locate and click the character you want to add, and then click **Insert**. Click **Close** to close the dialog box.

Character:		Shortcut key:
—	Em Dash	Alt+Ctrl+Num -
–	En Dash	Ctrl+Num -
-	Nonbreaking Hyphen	Ctrl+Shift+_
¬	Optional Hyphen	Ctrl+-
	Em Space	
	En Space	
	1/4 Em Space	
°	Nonbreaking Space	Ctrl+Shift+Space
©	Copyright	Alt+Ctrl+C
®	Registered	Alt+Ctrl+R
™	Trademark	Alt+Ctrl+T
§	Section	
¶	Paragraph	
…	Ellipsis	Alt+Ctrl+.
'	Single Opening Quote	Ctrl+`,`
'	Single Closing Quote	Ctrl+`,`
"	Double Opening Quote	Ctrl+`,`"
"	Double Closing Quote	Ctrl+`,`"

Work with Equations

You can easily create complex equations in Word 2016. The Equations gallery contains many commonly used equations, such as the area of a circle or, for you physicists out there, the Fourier Series. If you do not see the equation you want, you might find it on Office.com.

If you add a structure to an equation, Word supplies dotted box placeholders for you to click and substitute constants or variables. Using the Equation Tools Design tab on the Ribbon, you can select formatting choices for your equation. Note that the Equation feature does not function when you work in Compatibility Mode.

Work with Equations

Insert an Equation

1 Position the insertion point where you want to insert an equation.

2 Click the **Insert** tab.

3 Click **Symbols**.

4 Click ▼ beneath the **Equation** button.

Note: Depending on your screen resolution, you may or may not see the Symbols button.

A The Equation gallery, a list of commonly used equations, appears.

You can click an equation to insert it and then skip Steps **5** and **6**.

5 Click **Insert New Equation**.

B Word inserts a blank equation box.

C The Equations Tools Design tab appears on the Ribbon.

6 Type your equation.

You can click the tools on the Ribbon to help you type the equation.

7 Press ➡, or click outside the equation box.

Word hides the equation box, and you can continue typing.

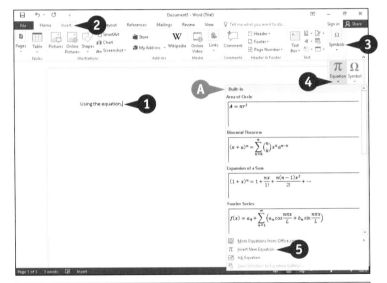

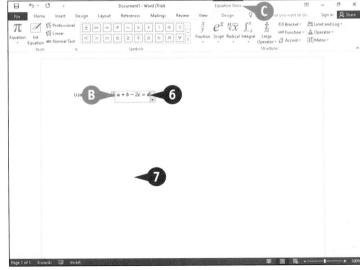

Delete an Equation

1 Click anywhere in the equation to display it in the equation box.

2 Click the small gray square on the left side of the box.

Word highlights the contents of the equation box.

3 Press Delete.

Word deletes the equation from your document.

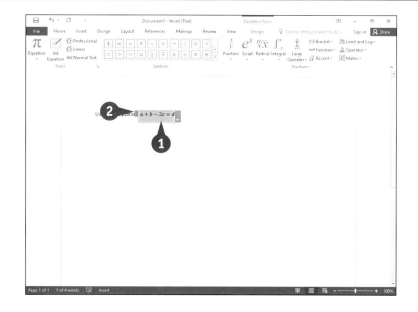

TIP

Can I save an equation that I use regularly so I do not have to create it each time I need it?

Yes. Follow these steps:

1 Click anywhere in the equation.

2 Click ▼ on the right side of the equation.

Word selects the equation and displays a drop-down menu.

3 Click **Save as New Equation**.

4 In the Create New Building Block dialog box that appears, click **OK**.

The next time you display the Equation gallery, your equation appears on the list.

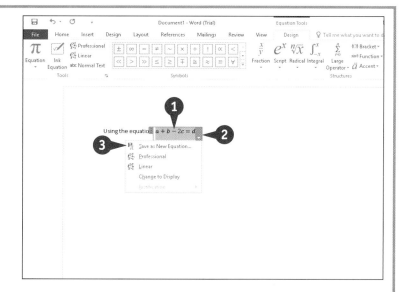

Zoom an Object

In Read Mode view, you can enlarge an image to get a better view of it. You can enlarge any type of image, including pictures, shapes, clip art, and inserted online videos, and you can zoom images in Word documents or in PDF files that you open in Word.

When you zoom an object, you can enlarge it twice from its original size; the first zoom level magnifies the image some, and the second zoom level makes the image fill the majority of your screen. Note that, although you can zoom inserted online videos, you can zoom them only to the first zoom level.

Zoom an Object

1 Open a document containing an image of any type.

2 Click 📖 to switch to Read Mode view.

3 Double-click the image.

A Word enlarges the image.

4 Click the **Zoom** button (🔍) in the upper right corner of zoomed image.

B Word enlarges the image even further and 🔍 changes to 🔍.

C You can click the **Zoom** button (🔍 or 🔍) repeatedly, and Word switches between the first and second levels of zoom.

5 Press Esc, or click anywhere outside the image

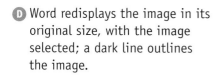

D Word redisplays the image in its original size, with the image selected; a dark line outlines the image.

Note: See Chapter 10 for details on working with images.

TIP

I tried to zoom an image in a PDF file, but more than just the image zoomed; why?
In all probability, the PDF file you opened was not created in Word. Although you can open a PDF file in Word, if the file was not created in Word, the original PDF layout will probably not translate properly. Word tends to read the PDF file content as objects rather than text and images, so in all likelihood, Word zoomed the image as well as text surrounding it that was part of the original PDF file layout.

Zoom In or Out

The Zoom feature controls the magnification of your document on-screen; you can use it to enlarge or reduce the size of the text. Zooming in enlarges text. Zooming out reduces text, providing more of an overview of your document. Zooming does not affect the printed size of your text; it simply makes text larger or smaller on-screen.

You can zoom using the Zoom dialog box, as shown in this section, or for less precise zooming, you can use the Zoom slider bar located in the lower right corner of the Word window.

Zoom In or Out

1 Click the **View** tab.

2 Click **Zoom**.

The Zoom dialog box appears.

3 Click a zoom setting.

A You can click the **Many pages** button and select to display multiple pages.

Note: The number of pages you can view depends on the resolution you set for your monitor.

B A preview of the settings you choose appears here.

4 Click **OK**.

The document appears on-screen using the new zoom setting.

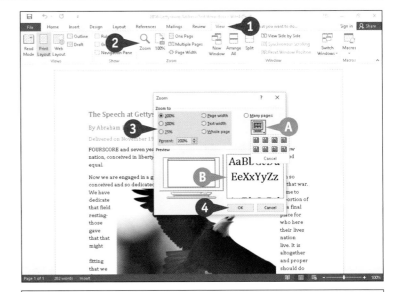

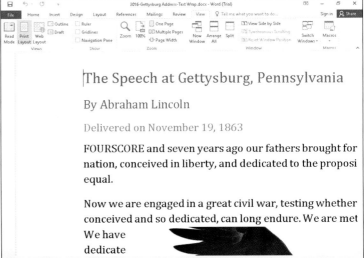

Translate Text

You can translate a word from one language to another using language dictionaries installed on your computer. If you are connected to the Internet, the Translation feature searches the dictionaries on your computer as well as online dictionaries.

You can choose Translate Document from the Translate drop-down menu to send the document over the Internet for translation, but be aware that Word sends documents as unencrypted HTML files. If security is an issue, do not choose this route; instead, consider hiring a professional translator.

Translate Text

1 Select a phrase to translate.

2 Click the **Review** tab.

3 Click **Translate**.

4 Click **Translate Selected Text**.

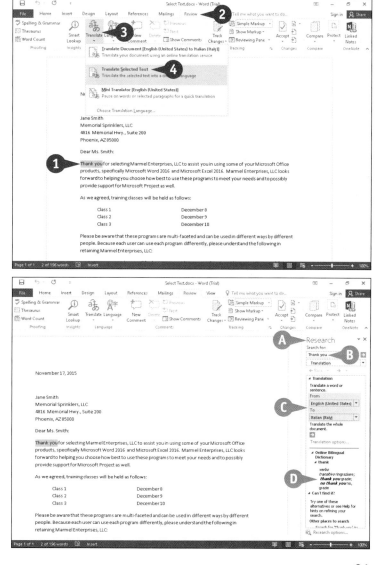

Note: A message box might appear, telling you that your text will be sent over the Internet for translation; click **Yes** to continue.

Ⓐ The Research pane appears.

Ⓑ The phrase you selected appears here.

Ⓒ The current translation languages appear here.

You can click the boxes beside each language to display available translation languages.

Ⓓ The translation appears here.

Set Options for Additional Actions

The Additional Actions feature provides you with a way to save time. When you enable this feature, Word recognizes certain types of context-sensitive information, such as an address or a date, and gives you the opportunity to use the information to take extra steps. For example, for an address, you can display a map or driving directions or add the information to Outlook contacts. For a date, you can display your Outlook Calendar.

You can control the kinds of information Word recognizes and identifies for additional actions that can save you time. You also can turn off additional action recognition entirely.

Set Options for Additional Actions

1 Click the **File** tab.

Backstage view appears.

2 Click **Options**.

The Word Options dialog box appears.

3 Click **Proofing**.

4 Click **AutoCorrect Options**.

The AutoCorrect dialog box appears.

5 Click the **Actions** tab.

6 You can select this option (☐ changes to ✔) to turn on recognition of additional actions.

7 Turn additional action recognition on (✔) or off (☐).

8 Click **OK** to close the AutoCorrect dialog box.

9 Click **OK** to close the Word Options window.

Word saves your preferences.

Using Additional Actions

You can use the Additional Actions feature to save time. Using this feature, Word recognizes certain context-sensitive information and provides extra information. With this feature, Word can convert measurements, add a person or telephone number to Outlook Contacts, schedule a meeting, display a map of a location, or get you driving directions to that location.

This feature may not be on by default; see the previous section, "Set Options for Additional Actions." This section shows you how to use the Additional Actions feature.

Using Additional Actions

1 Right-click text for which you have enabled additional actions. In this example, a date is used.

A A context menu appears.

2 Click **Additional Actions**.

B Word displays the selected action.

3 Click an action in the list of available actions.

Word performs the action, or the program that performs the action you selected appears on-screen.

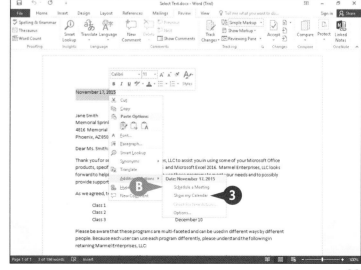

CHAPTER 4

Proofreading

This chapter shows you how to handle proofreading tasks in Word. You can search through text to find something in particular or to replace text. Word contains some features to help you define words and address spelling and grammar issues. This chapter also shows you how to track revisions and work with revisions and comments provided by reviewers.

Work in Read Mode View

ead Mode view optimizes your document for easier reading and helps minimize eyestrain when you read a document on-screen. This view removes most toolbars. Read Mode view supports mouse, keyboard, and tablet motions. To move from page to page in a document using your mouse, you can click the arrows (◁ and ▷) on the left and right sides of the pages or use the scroll wheel. To navigate using the keyboard, you can press the Page Up, Page Down, spacebar, and Backspace keys on the keyboard, or press any arrow key. If you use a tablet or other touchpad device, swipe left or right with your finger.

Work in Read Mode View

Look Up Information

1 Click 📖 to display the document in Read Mode view.

2 Select the word you want to look up and right-click.

3 From the menu that appears, click **Smart Lookup**.

Ⓐ The Insights pane appears.

4 Click **Define** to display the word's definition.

Ⓑ To close the Insights pane, you can click the **Close** button (✖).

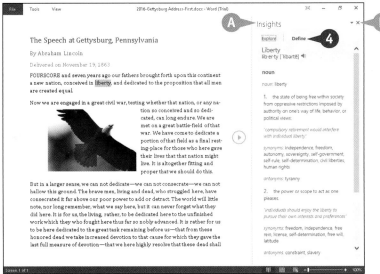

Translate a Word or Phrase

1 Click 📖 to display the document in Read Mode view.

2 Select the word or phrase you want to translate and right-click.

3 From the menu that appears, click **Translate**.

Note: A message might appear, indicating that text will be sent over the Internet for translation; click **Yes**.

C The Research pane opens, displaying a translation of the word or phrase you selected in Step **2**.

4 To close the Research pane, click ✖ in the upper right corner of the pane.

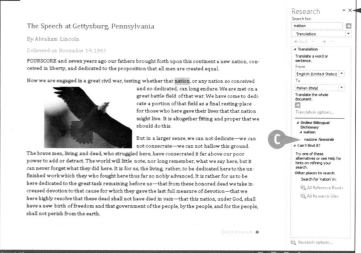

continued ▶

TIP

Can I change the color of the page?
Yes. Follow these steps:

1 Click **View**.

2 Click **Page Color**.

3 Choose a page color.

This example uses **Sepia**.

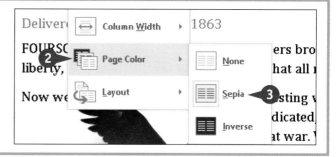

Read Mode view offers more than just minimized eyestrain; while you work in Read Mode view, you can look up words in the dictionary, translate a word or phrase, highlight important text, and insert comments in documents you are reviewing. If you are viewing a long document in Read Mode view, you can also use the Navigation pane to move around the document. You can open the Navigation pane from the Tools menu in Read Mode view; for details on using the Navigation pane, see Chapter 3.

Work in Read Mode View (continued)

Highlight Important Text

1 Click 📖 to display the document in Read Mode view.

2 Select the words you want to highlight and right-click.

3 From the menu that appears, click **Highlight**.

4 Click a highlight color.

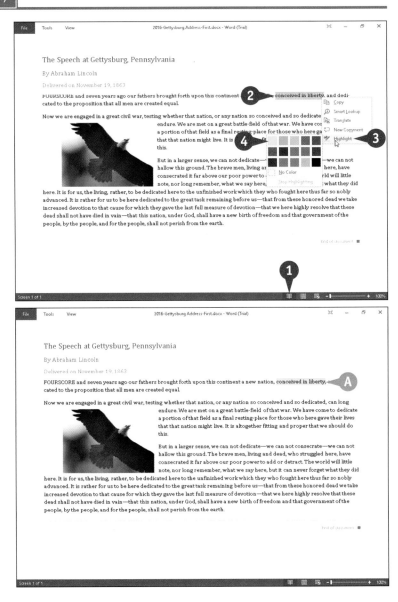

A Word highlights the selected text in the color you chose.

You can click anywhere outside the highlight to see its full effect and continue working.

Insert a Comment

1 Click 📖 to display the document in Read Mode view.

2 Select the words about which you want to comment, and right-click.

3 From the menu that appears, click **New Comment**.

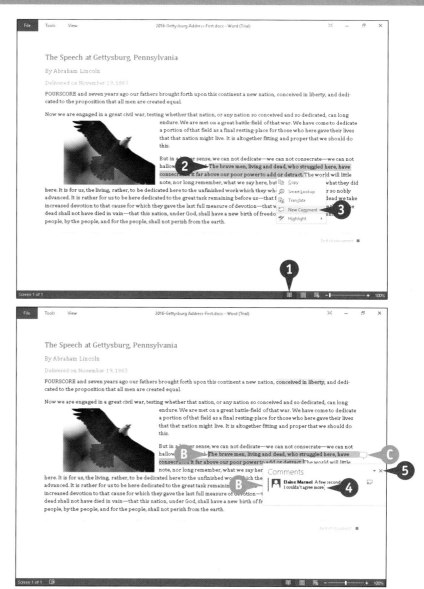

B Word changes the color used to select the text and displays a comment block containing the insertion point.

4 Type your comment.

5 Click ✖ to close the comment block.

C This symbol represents your comment; click it at any time to view the comment.

What are some of the different views available in Read Mode?

To display all comments in the document, click **View** and then click **Show Comments**. To view your document as if it were printed on paper, click **View** and then click **Layout**. From the menu that appears, click **Paper Layout**.

Can I change the column width?

Yes. Click **View** and then click **Column Width**. From the menu that appears, choose **Narrow** or **Wide**; click **Default** to return to the original column view. Note that on a standard monitor, Default and Wide look the same; Wide takes effect on widescreen monitors.

Search for Text

Occasionally, you need to search for a word or phrase in a document. For example, suppose you want to edit a paragraph in your document that contains a specific word or phrase. You can use Word's Find tool to search for the word or phrase instead of scrolling through your document to locate that paragraph. You can search for all occurrences simultaneously or for each single occurrence in the order in which it occurs from the current position of the insertion point.

This section focuses on finding text; see the next section, "Substitute Text," for information on finding and replacing text.

Search for Text

Search for All Occurrences

1. Click the **Home** tab.

2. Click **Find**.

A. The Navigation pane appears.

3. Type the word or phrase for which you want to search.

B. Word highlights all occurrences of the word or phrase in yellow.

4. Click ✕ to clear the search and results.

5. Click ✕ to close the Navigation pane.

Search for One Occurrence at a Time

1 Press **Ctrl**+**Home** to position the insertion point at the beginning of your document.

2 Click the **Home** tab.

3 Click ▼ beside the **Find** button.

4 Click **Advanced Find** to display the Find and Replace dialog box.

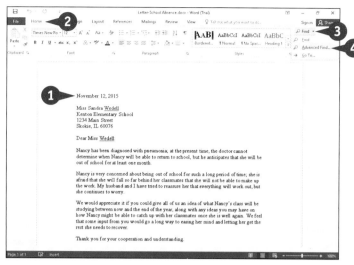

5 Type the word or phrase for which you want to search.

C You can click **More** (More changes to Less) to display additional search options.

D You can click **Reading Highlight** and then click **Highlight All** to highlight each occurrence.

E You can click **Find in** to limit the search to the main document or the headers and footers.

6 Click **Find Next** to view each occurrence.

7 When Word finds no more occurrences, a dialog box appears telling you that the search is finished; click **OK**.

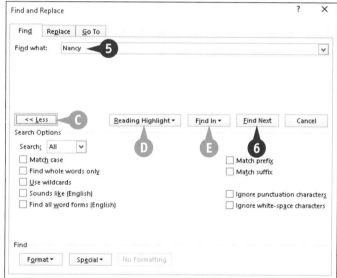

TIPS

How can I set options to limit my search in the Navigation pane?

Complete Steps **1** and **2** in the subsection "Search for All Occurrences" to open the Navigation pane. Click ▼ in the Search Documents box. Click **Options** to display the Find Options dialog box, where you can set the same options you set when following the steps in the subsection "Search for One Occurrence at a Time."

Can I search for elements other than words?

Yes. Complete Steps **1** and **2** in the subsection "Search for All Occurrences" to open the Navigation pane. Click ▼ in the Search Documents box. From the menu that appears, you can search for graphics, tables, equations, footnotes or endnotes, and comments.

Substitute Text

Often, you want to find a word or phrase because you need to substitute some other word or phrase for it. For example, suppose you complete a long report, only to discover that you have misspelled the name of a product you are reviewing. You do not need to hunt through the document to change each occurrence; you can use the Replace tool to substitute a word or phrase for all occurrences of the original word or phrase.

On the other hand, you can selectively substitute one word or phrase for another — a particularly useful tool when you have overused a word.

Substitute Text

① Press **Ctrl**+**Home** to position the insertion point at the beginning of your document.

② Click the **Home** tab.

③ Click **Replace**.

The Find and Replace dialog box appears.

④ Type the word or phrase you want to replace here.

⑤ Type the word or phrase you want Word to substitute here.

Ⓐ You can click **More** to display additional search and replace options (More changes to Less).

⑥ Click **Find Next**.

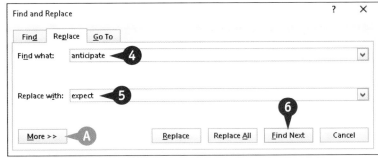

Ⓑ Word highlights the first occurrence of the word or phrase that it finds.

Ⓒ If you do not want to change the highlighted occurrence, you can click **Find Next** to ignore it.

7 Click **Replace**.

Ⓓ To change all occurrences in the document, you can click **Replace All**.

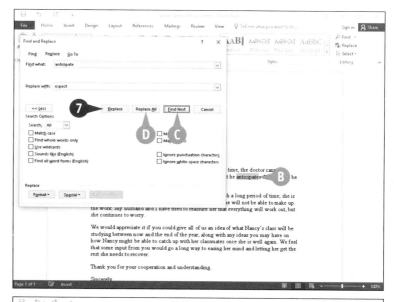

Ⓔ Word replaces the original word or phrase with the word or phrase you specify as the substitute.

8 Repeat Steps **6** and **7** as needed.

9 When Word finds no more occurrences, a dialog box appears telling you that the search is finished; click **OK**.

The Cancel button in the Find and Replace dialog box changes to Close.

10 Click **Close** to close the Find and Replace dialog box.

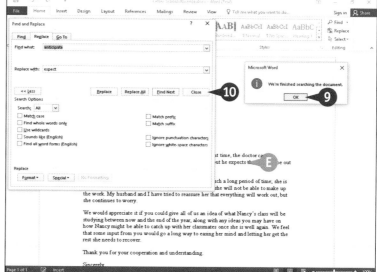

TIPS

Can I find italic text and change it to boldface text?

Yes. Follow Steps **1** to **3**, and click **More** to expand the window. Follow Steps **4** and **5**, but, instead of typing text, click **Format** and then click **Font**. In the Font Style list of the Font dialog box that appears, click **Italic** for Step **4** and **Bold** for Step **5**. Then complete Steps **6** to **10**.

Can I search for and replace special characters such as tabs or paragraph marks?

Yes. Follow Steps **1** to **3**, and click **More** to expand the window. Then follow Steps **4** and **5**, but instead of typing text, click **Special** to display a menu of special characters. For Step **4**, select the special character you want to find. For Step **5**, select the special character you want to substitute. Then complete Steps **6** to **10**.

Count Words in a Document

You can count the number of words in a selection, sentence, paragraph, or document or in any portion of a document. Suppose, for example, that your history teacher just assigned you to write a paper describing the First Continental Congress, and the paper must be at least 500 words long. You can use the Word Count feature to count the words you have written.

This feature also comes in particularly handy when you must limit the number of words in a section of a document. For example, college application essays often require that you write no more than 500 words.

Count Words in a Document

Display the Word Count

1 Right-click the status bar.

A The Customize Status Bar menu appears.

B The number of words in the document appears here.

2 If no check mark appears beside Word Count, click **Word Count**; otherwise, skip this step.

3 Click anywhere outside the menu.

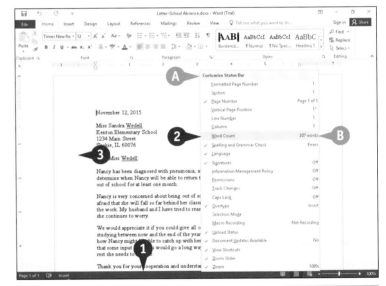

C Word closes the menu, and the number of words in the document appears on the status bar.

Display Count Statistics

1 Click the word count on the status bar.

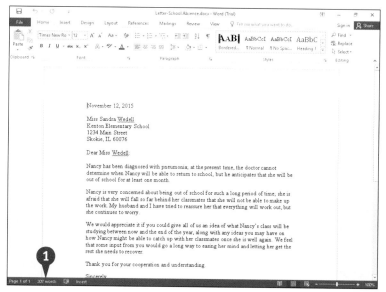

The Word Count dialog box appears.

The Word Count dialog box reports the number of pages, words, characters with and without spaces, paragraphs, and lines in your document.

2 When you finish reviewing count statistics, click **Close**.

TIP

Can I count the number of words in just one paragraph?
Yes. Do the following:

1 Select the text containing the words you want to count.

A Both the number of words in the selection and the total words in the document appear in the Word Count box on the status bar.

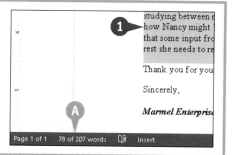

Automatically Correct Mistakes

As you may have noticed, Word automatically corrects your text as you type. It does this using its AutoCorrect feature, which works from a preset list of misspellings.

To speed up your text-entry tasks, you can add your own problem words — ones you commonly misspell — to the list. The next time you mistype the word, AutoCorrect fixes your mistake for you. If you find that AutoCorrect consistently changes a word that is correct as is, you can remove that word from the AutoCorrect list. If you would prefer that AutoCorrect not make any changes to your text as you type, you can disable the feature.

Automatically Correct Mistakes

1 Click the **File** tab.

Backstage view appears.

2 Click **Options**.

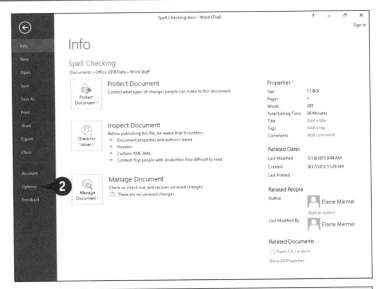

The Word Options dialog box appears.

3 Click **Proofing** to display proofing options.

4 Click **AutoCorrect Options**.

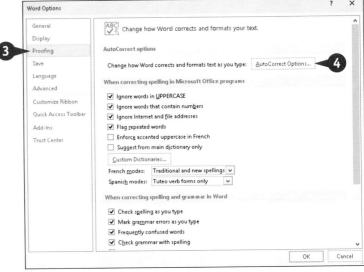

The AutoCorrect dialog box appears.

Ⓐ The corrections Word already makes automatically appear in this area.

⑤ Click here and type the word you typically mistype or misspell.

⑥ Click here and type the correct version of the word.

⑦ Click **Add**.

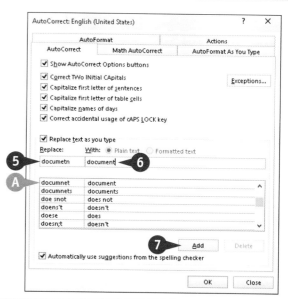

Ⓑ Word adds the entry to the list to automatically correct.

You can repeat Steps **5** to **7** for each automatic correction you want to add.

⑧ Click **OK** to close the AutoCorrect dialog box.

⑨ Click **OK** to close the Word Options dialog box.

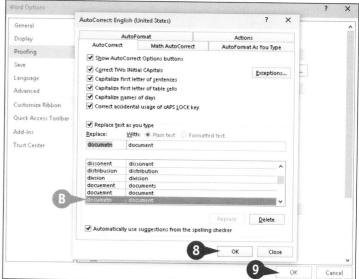

How does the automatic correction work?

As you type, if you mistype or misspell a word stored as an AutoCorrect entry, Word corrects the entry when you press Spacebar, Tab, or Enter.

What should I do if Word automatically replaces an entry that I do not want replaced?

Position the insertion point at the beginning of the AutoCorrected word and click the **AutoCorrect Options** button (≡·). From the list that appears, click **Change back to**. To make Word permanently stop correcting an entry, follow Steps **1** to **4**, click the stored AutoCorrect entry in the list, and then click **Delete**.

Automatically Insert Frequently Used Text

Suppose you repeatedly type the same text in your documents — for example, your company name. You can add this text to Word's Quick Parts gallery; then, the next time you need to add the text to a document, you can select it from the gallery instead of retyping it.

In addition to creating your own Quick Parts for use in your documents, you can use any of the wide variety of preset phrases included with Word. You access these preset Quick Parts from Word's Building Blocks Organizer window. (See the tip at the end of this section for more information.)

Automatically Insert Frequently Used Text

Create a Quick Parts Entry

1 Type the text that you want to store, including all formatting that should appear each time you insert the entry.

2 Select the text you typed.

3 Click the **Insert** tab.

4 Click the **Quick Parts** button (⊞ ▾).

5 Click **Save Selection to Quick Part Gallery**.

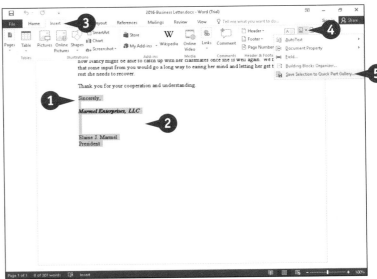

The Create New Building Block dialog box appears.

6 Type a name that you want to use as a shortcut for the entry.

Ⓐ You can also assign a gallery, a category, and a description for the entry.

7 Click **OK**.

Word stores the entry in the Quick Part gallery.

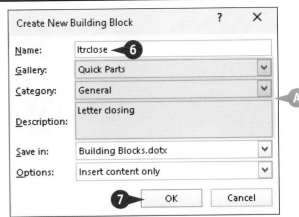

Insert a Quick Part Entry

1 Click in the text where you want to insert a Quick Part.

2 Click the **Insert** tab.

3 Click the **Quick Parts** button (▣ ▾).

All building blocks you define as Quick Parts appear in the Quick Part gallery.

4 Click the entry that you want to insert.

Ⓑ Word inserts the entry into the document.

How can I find and use an AutoText entry?

Click the **Insert** tab, and then click the **Quick Parts** button (▣ ▾). In the menu that appears, point at **AutoText**. A gallery of all the AutoText entries appears.

How do I remove a Quick Parts entry?

To remove a Quick Parts entry, use the Building Blocks Organizer window. Click the **Insert** tab, click the **Quick Parts** button (▣ ▾) and then click **Building Blocks Organizer**. In the Organizer window, locate and select the entry you want to remove, click **Delete**, and click **Yes** in the dialog box that appears.

Check Spelling and Grammar

Word automatically checks for spelling and grammar errors as you type. Misspellings appear underlined with a red wavy line, and grammar errors are underlined with a blue wavy line. If you prefer, you can turn off Word's automatic Spelling and Grammar Check features, as described in the next section.

Alternatively, you can review your entire document for spelling and grammatical errors all at one time. To use Word's Spelling and Grammar checking feature, you must install a dictionary; see Chapter 13 for details on installing apps for Word.

Check Spelling and Grammar

Correct a Mistake

1 When you encounter a spelling or grammar problem, right-click the underlined text.

2 Click a correction from the menu that appears.

Ⓐ To ignore the error, you can click **Ignore All**.

Ⓑ To make Word stop flagging a word as misspelled, click **Add to Dictionary**.

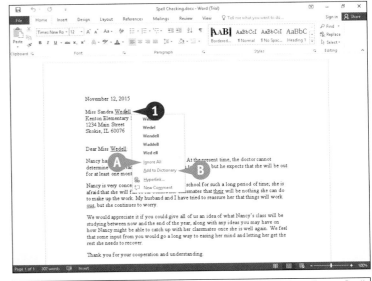

Run the Spell Checker

1 Click at the beginning of your document.

2 Click the **Review** tab.

3 Click **Spelling & Grammar**.

Ⓒ Word selects the first spelling or grammar mistake and displays the Spelling or Grammar pane.

Ⓓ The spelling or grammar mistake appears here.

Ⓔ Suggestions to correct the error appear here.

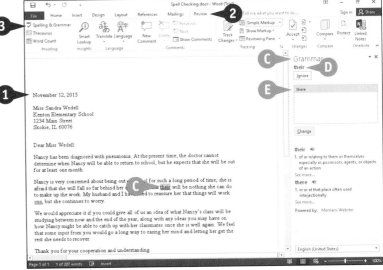

④ Click the suggestion you want to use.

⑤ Click **Change**.

Ⓕ You can click **Ignore** or **Ignore All** to leave the selected word or phrase unchanged.

⑥ Repeat Steps **4** and **5** for each spelling or grammar mistake.

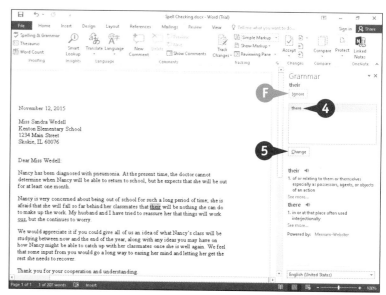

Word displays a dialog box when it finishes checking for spelling and grammar mistakes.

⑦ Click **OK**.

Note: To check only a section of your document, select that section.

TIP

When should I use the Add to Dictionary button?
Word identifies misspellings by comparing words in your document to whichever dictionary you chose to install. (See Chapter 13 for details on downloading and installing apps like the dictionary for Word.) When a word you type does not appear in the dictionary Word uses, Word flags the word as misspelled. The word might be a term that you use regularly; if so, click **Add to Dictionary** so that Word stops flagging the word as a misspelling.

Disable Grammar and Spell Checking

By default, Word automatically checks spelling and grammar by displaying red and blue squiggly lines whenever it identifies a spelling or grammar mistake. If the red and blue squiggly underlines annoy you, you can turn off automatic spelling and grammar checking, in which case Word no longer displays red and blue squiggly lines under words or phrases it does not recognize. You can always check spelling and grammar after you complete your work on your document but before you send it to the recipient or to co-workers for review.

Disable Grammar and Spell Checking

Ⓐ When automatic spelling and grammar checking is enabled, red and blue squiggly lines appear in the document.

① Click the **File** tab.

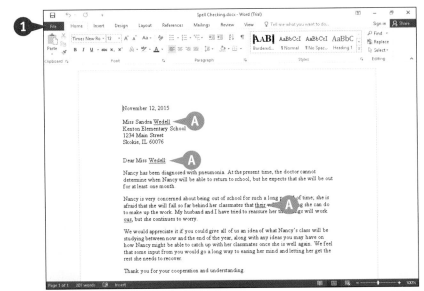

Backstage view appears.

② Click **Options**.

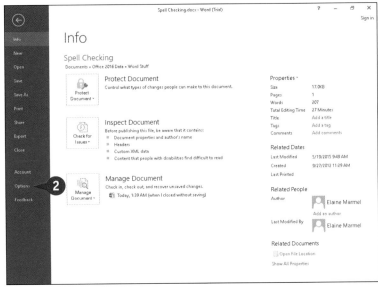

The Word Options dialog box appears.

3 Click **Proofing**.

4 Deselect **Check spelling as you type** (☑ changes to ☐) to disable automatic spell checking.

5 Deselect **Mark grammar errors as you type** (☑ changes to ☐) to disable automatic grammar checking.

6 Click **OK**.

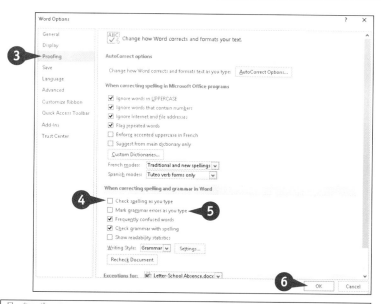

B Word no longer identifies the spelling and grammar errors in the current document.

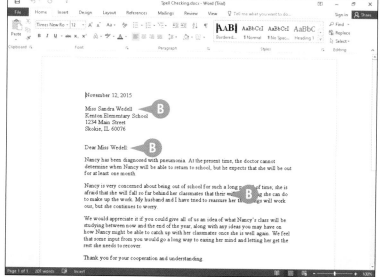

If I disable automatic spelling and grammar checking, how do I check spelling and grammar?
Use the procedure described in the section "Check Spelling and Grammar." When you follow the procedure in that section, you disable only the portion of the feature where Word automatically identifies misspellings or grammar mistakes with squiggly red or blue underlines.

What should I do if I change my mind and decide that I want to see the red and blue squiggly lines?
Repeat the steps in this section, selecting the options you deselected previously (☐ changes to ☑).

Find a Synonym or Antonym with the Thesaurus

If you are having trouble finding just the right word or phrase, you use Word's thesaurus to find a more suitable word than the one you originally chose. The thesaurus can help you find a synonym — a word with a similar meaning — for the word you originally chose, as well as an antonym, which is a word with an opposite meaning.

Word displays synonyms and antonyms as major headings in the Thesaurus pane; you can identify a major heading because a carat appears beside it. Each word under a major heading is a synonym or antonym that you can substitute in your document.

Find a Synonym or Antonym with the Thesaurus

1 Click the word for which you want to find an opposite or substitute.

2 Click the **Review** tab.

3 Click **Thesaurus**.

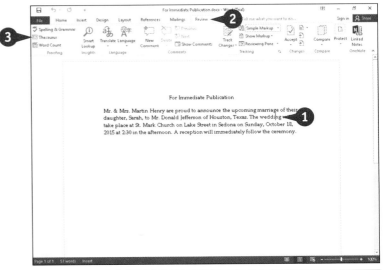

Ⓐ The Thesaurus pane appears.

Ⓑ The word you selected appears here.

Ⓒ Each word with a carat on its left and a part of speech on its right represents a major heading.

Note: You cannot substitute major headings for the word in your document.

Ⓓ Each word listed below a major heading is a synonym or antonym for the major heading.

Ⓔ Antonyms are marked.

④ Point the mouse (⩘) at the word you want to use in your document, and click the ▼ that appears.

⑤ Click **Insert**.

Ⓕ Word replaces the word in your document with the one in the Thesaurus pane.

⑥ Click ✖ to close the Thesaurus pane.

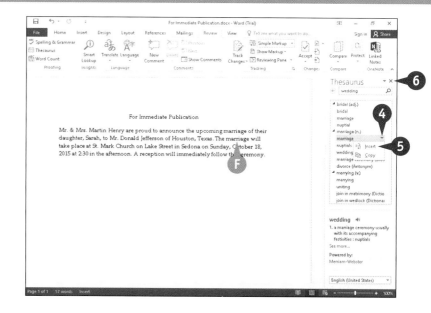

Is there a faster way I can display synonyms and antonyms?

Yes. You can use the keyboard shortcut Shift+F7 to open the Thesaurus pane, or you can perform the steps that follow: Right-click the word for which you want a synonym or antonym (Ⓐ) and click **Synonyms** (Ⓑ) from the menu that appears. Click a choice to replace the word in your document (Ⓒ).

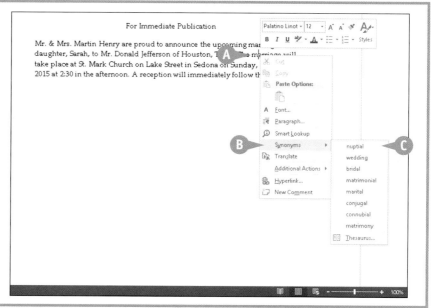

Find a Definition

Using the Smart Lookup feature, you can use Bing to explore the web using a word in your document, or you can look up the word's definition. The Smart Lookup feature replaces the Dictionary feature in earlier versions of Word.

When you explore the web, Bing returns a variety of entries found on the web that are related to a word you select in your document. Alternatively, Bing can provide you with a definition of a word you select in your document. Bing uses the Oxford University Press Dictionaries to provide definitions.

Find a Definition

1 Click anywhere in the word for which you want a definition.

2 Click the **Review** tab.

3 Click the **Smart Lookup** button.

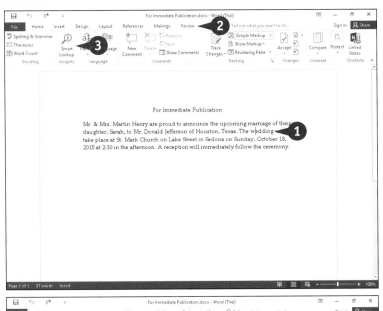

A The Insights pane appears on the right side of the screen, displaying the Explore tab.

4 Click **Define**.

B Word displays various definitions for and other information about the word you selected.

C You can click ✖ to close the Insights pane.

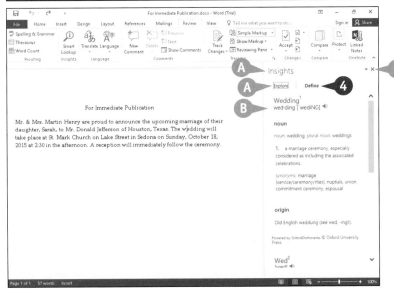

Track Document Changes During Review

Word can track the editing and formatting changes made to your document. This feature is useful when more than one person works on the same document. When Word tracks document revisions, it uses different colors to track the changes made and who made them, so that you can easily identify who did what to a document. By default, Word displays changes in Simple Markup view, which indicates, in the left margin, areas that have changes. If you prefer to see changes as you make them, switch to All Markup view.

Track Document Changes During Review

1 Click the **Review** tab.

2 Click **Track Changes** to enable change tracking.

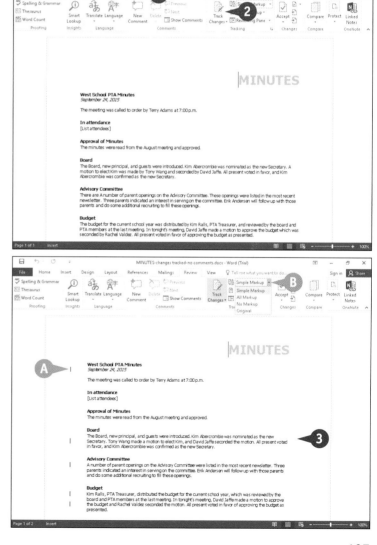

3 Make changes to the document as needed.

A Red vertical bars appear in the left margin beside lines containing changes.

B If you prefer to view changes as you work, click ▼ beside the **Simple Markup** button and choose **All Markup**.

Note: When you open a document containing tracked changes, Simple Markup is the default view.

Lock and Unlock Tracking

You can control who can turn change tracking on and off using the Lock Tracking feature, which requires a password to turn off change tracking. You no longer need to deal with the situation where you turn on change tracking and send out a document for review. Then, when you get the document back, it contains no change markings because the reviewer turned the Track Changes feature off.

In the past, you needed to use the Compare Documents feature to determine how the reviewed document differed from the original. But now, you can lock change tracking.

Lock and Unlock Tracking

Lock Tracked Changes

1 In the document for which you want to lock tracked changes, click the **Review** tab.

2 Click **Track Changes** to turn on tracking.

3 Click ▼ at the bottom of the **Track Changes** button.

4 Click **Lock Tracking**.

The Lock Tracking dialog box appears.

5 Type a password here.

6 Retype the password here.

7 Click **OK**.

Note: Make sure you remember the password or you will not be able to turn off the Track Changes feature.

Word saves the password and the Track Changes button appears gray and unavailable.

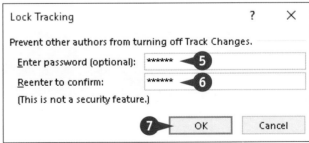

Unlock Tracked Changes

1 Open a document with tracked changes locked.

2 Click the **Review** tab.

3 Click ▼ at the bottom of the **Track Changes** button.

4 Click **Lock Tracking**.

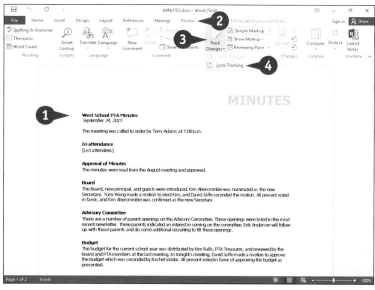

The Unlock Tracking dialog box appears.

5 Type the password.

6 Click **OK**.

The Track Changes button becomes available again so that you can click it and turn off the Track Changes feature.

TIP

What happens if I supply the wrong password?

This message box appears. You can retry as many times as you want. If you cannot remember the password, you can create a new version that contains all revisions already accepted, which you can then compare to the original to identify changes. Press Ctrl+A to select the entire document. Then press Shift+← to unselect just the last paragraph mark in the document. Then press Ctrl+C to copy the selection. Start a new blank document and press Ctrl+V to paste the selection.

Work with Comments

You can add comments to your documents. For example, when you share your documents with other users, you can use comments to leave feedback about the text without typing directly in the document, and others can do the same.

To indicate that a comment was added, Word displays a balloon in the right margin near the commented text. When you review comments, they appear in a block. Your name appears in comments you add, and you can easily review, reply to, or delete a comment, or you can indicate that you have addressed a comment.

Work with Comments

Add a Comment

1 Click or select the text about which you want to comment.

2 Click the **Review** tab.

3 Click **New Comment**.

Ⓐ A comment block appears, marking the location of the comment.

4 Type your comment.

You can click anywhere outside the comment to continue working.

Review a Comment

1 Click ▼ to switch to Simple Markup view.

2 Click a comment balloon.

Ⓑ Word highlights the text associated with the comment.

Ⓒ Word displays the Comments block and the text it contains.

Ⓓ To view all comments along the right side of the document, click **Show Comments**.

You can click anywhere outside the comment to hide the Comments block and its text.

Reply to a Comment

1 While working in Simple Markup view, click a comment balloon to display its text.

2 Click the **Reply to Comment** button (☞).

Ⓔ Word starts a new comment, indented under the first comment.

3 Type your reply.

You can click anywhere outside the comment to continue working.

Delete a Comment

1 Click the comment that you want to remove.

2 Click the **Review** tab.

3 Click **Delete**.

Note: You can also right-click a comment and click **Delete Comment**. And, you can delete all comments in the document by clicking ▼ at the bottom of the **Delete** button and then clicking **Delete All Comments in Document**.

Word deletes the comment.

TIP

Can I indicate that I have addressed a comment without deleting it?

Yes, you can mark the comment as done. Right-click the text of the comment and choose **Mark Comment Done**. Word fades the comment text to light gray.

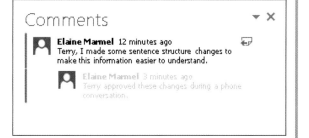

Comments ▼ ✕

Elaine Marmel 12 minutes ago
Terry, I made some sentence structure changes to make this information easier to understand.

Elaine Marmel 3 minutes ago
Terry approved these changes during a phone conversation.

Review Tracked Changes

When you review a document containing tracked changes, you decide whether to accept or reject the changes. As you accept or reject changes, Word removes the revision marks.

When Word tracks revisions, it uses different colors to track the changes made and who made them so that you can easily identify who did what to a document. By default, Word displays changes in Simple Markup view, which indicates, in the left margin, areas that have changes. You can use the Reviewing pane to identify who made each change, or you can hide the pane and work directly with the revisions.

Review Tracked Changes

Display the Reviewing Pane

1 Open a document in which changes were tracked.

2 Click the **Review** tab.

3 Click **Reviewing Pane**.

A In the Revisions pane, Word displays the reviewer's name, the date, time, and the details of each change.

B You can click ∨ to hide the summary of revisions and view only the details of each revision.

C You can click ✖ to close the pane.

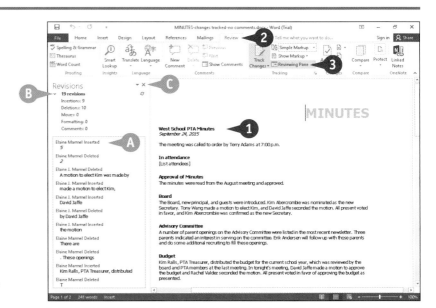

Review Changes

Note: Documents containing tracked changes open in Simple Markup view. Red vertical bars appear in the left margin to indicate locations where changes were made.

1 Click any vertical bar in the left margin.

All vertical bars turn gray, and Word changes the view to All Markup and displays all changes in the document.

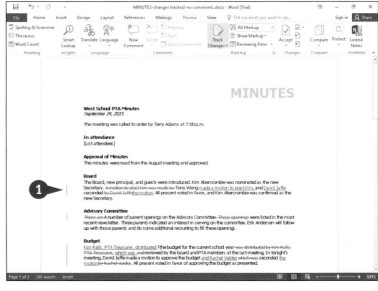

D Deleted text appears in color with strikethrough formatting.

E Added text appears underlined and in color.

Note: Each reviewer's changes appear in a different color.

2 Press `Ctrl`+`Home` to place the insertion point at the beginning of the document.

3 Click the **Next** button (🔁) to review the first change.

F Word highlights the change.

You can click the **Next** button (🔁) again to skip over the change without accepting or rejecting it.

4 Click **Accept** to incorporate the change into the document or click the **Reject** button (🗙 ▾) to revert the text to its original state.

G Word accepts or rejects the change, removes the revision marks, and highlights the next change.

5 Repeat Step **4** to review all revisions.

H If you need to move backward to a change you previously skipped, you can click the **Previous** button (🔁).

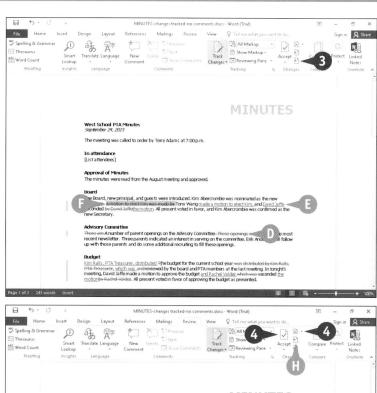

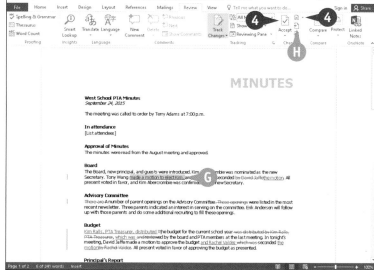

Can I print revisions?

Yes, you can print revisions in the document by simply printing the document. Or you can print a separate list of revisions by performing the steps that follow: Click the **File** tab to display Backstage view, and then click **Print**. Click the button below **Settings** (Ⓐ). From the menu that appears, click **List of Markup** (Ⓑ). Click **Print**.

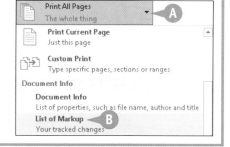

Combine Reviewers' Comments

Suppose that two different people review a document, but they review simultaneously using the original document. When they each return the reviewed document, you have two versions of the original document, each containing potentially different changes. Fortunately, you can combine the documents so that you can work from the combined changes of both reviewers.

When you combine two versions of the same document, Word creates a third file that flags any discrepancies between the versions using revision marks like you see when you enable the Track Changes feature. You can then work from the combined document and evaluate each change.

Combine Reviewers' Comments

Note: To make your screen as easy to understand as possible, close all open documents.

1. Click the **Review** tab.

2. Click **Compare**.

3. Click **Combine**.

   The Combine Documents dialog box appears.

4. Click the **Open** button (📁) for the first document you want to combine.

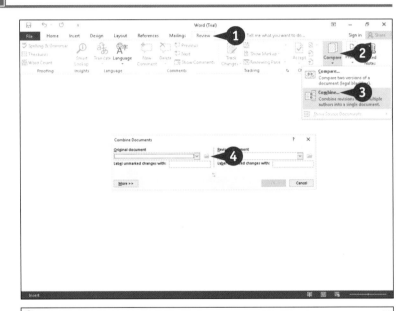

   The Open dialog box appears.

5. Navigate to the folder containing the first file you want to combine.

6. Click the file.

7. Click **Open**.

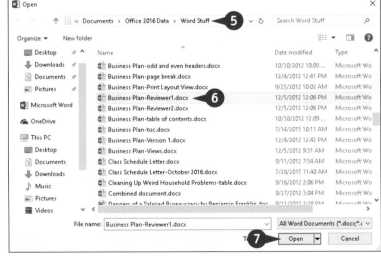

The Combine Documents dialog box reappears.

8 Repeat Steps **4** to **7**, clicking the **Open** button ( ) for the second document you want to combine.

Ⓐ You can type a label for changes to each document in these boxes.

9 Click **OK**.

Word displays four panes.

Ⓑ The left pane contains a summary of revisions.

Ⓒ The center pane contains the result of combining both documents.

Ⓓ The top right pane displays the document you selected in Step **6**.

Ⓔ The bottom right pane displays the document you selected in Step **8**.

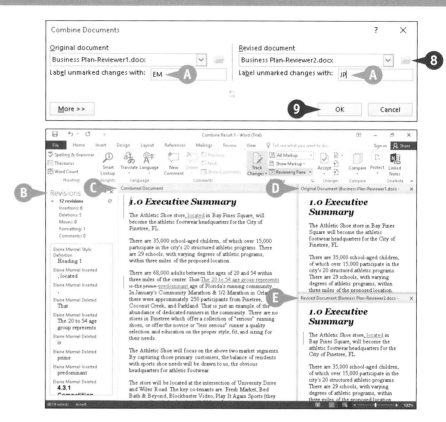

Two reviewers reviewed the same document but they forgot to track changes; can I somehow see their changes?
Yes. Follow the steps in this section, but, in Step **3**, click **Compare**. Word again displays four panes: the summary appears in the left pane; results of comparing the two documents appear in the center pane; the document you select in Step **6** appears in the top right pane; and the document you select in Step **8** appears in the bottom right pane.

How do I save the combined document?
The same way you save any Word document; see Chapter 2 for details.

CHAPTER 5

Formatting Text

You can format text to improve appearance, for emphasis, and for greater readability. And although the individual types of formatting are discussed separately, you can perform each of the tasks in this chapter on a single selection of text.

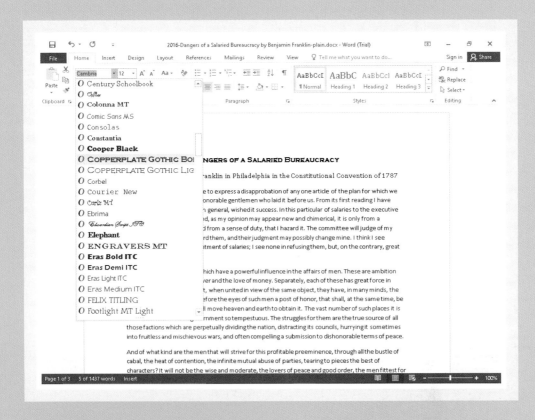

Change the Font

You can change the typeface that appears in your document by changing the font. Changing the font can help readers better understand your document.

Use *serif* fonts — fonts with short lines stemming from the bottoms of the letters — to provide a line that helps guide the reader's eyes along the line, making reading easier with less eyestrain. Most readers are not even aware that the short line along the bottom of the letters helps guide their eyes. Use *sans serif* fonts — fonts without short lines stemming from the bottoms of the letters — for headlines.

Change the Font

1 Select the text that you want to format.

Ⓐ If you drag to select, the Mini Toolbar appears, and you can use it by moving the mouse (⤵) toward the Mini Toolbar.

2 To use the Ribbon, click the **Home** tab.

3 Click the **Font** ▼ to display a list of the available fonts on your computer.

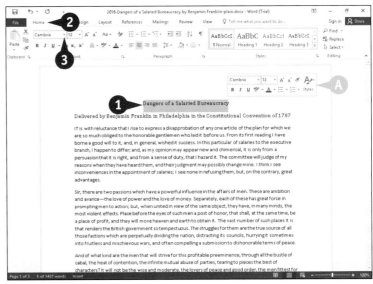

Note: Word displays a sample of the selected text in any font at which you point the mouse.

4 Click the font you want to use.

Ⓑ Word assigns the font to the selected text.

This example applies the **Copperplate Gothic** font to the text.

You can click anywhere outside the selection to continue working.

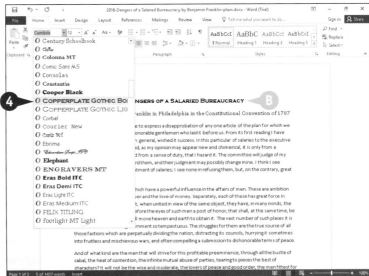

Change Text Size

You can increase or decrease the size of the text in your document. Increase the size to make reading the text easier; decrease the size to fit more text on a page.

Fonts are measured in *points*; the term originates in typography as a fraction of a pica, but desktop publishing redefined the point in the 1980s and 1990s as $\frac{1}{72}$ inch. In both typography and desktop publishing, 12 points equal a pica, the standard font size used for reading.

Change Text Size

1 Select the text that you want to format.

A If you drag to select, the Mini Toolbar appears in the background, and you can use it by moving the mouse (🖑) toward the Mini Toolbar.

2 To use the Ribbon, click the **Home** tab.

3 Click the **Font Size** ▼ to display a list of the possible sizes for the current font.

Note: Word displays a sample of the selected text in any font size at which you point the mouse.

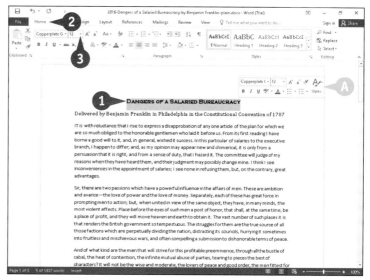

4 Click a size.

B Word changes the size of the selected text.

This example applies a **24**-point font size to the text.

Note: You also can change the font size using the **Increase Font Size** and **Decrease Font Size** buttons (A˄ and A˅) on the Home tab. Word increases or decreases the font size with each click of the button.

You can click anywhere outside the selection to continue working.

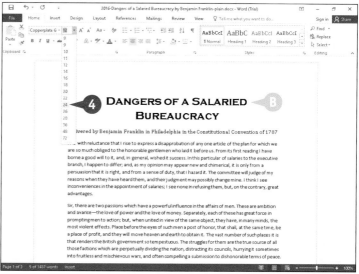

Emphasize Information with Bold, Italic, or Underline

You can apply italics, boldface, or underlining to add emphasis to text in your document. Each technique distinguishes text in a different way.

Boldface changes the brightness of the text, making the text darker than surrounding text. Italic applies a script-line appearance to text, slanting it the way handwriting slants. Underlining is not often used in printed material because it is considered to be too distracting to the reader; instead, you might find underlining appearing in handwritten materials to emphasize a point.

Emphasize Information with Bold, Italic, or Underline

1 Select the text that you want to emphasize.

A If you drag to select, the Mini Toolbar appears in the background, and you can use it by moving the mouse (⟲) toward the Mini Toolbar.

B If you want to use the Ribbon, click the **Home** tab.

2 Click the **Bold** button (**B**), the **Italic** button (*I*), or the **Underline** button (**U** ▾) on the Ribbon or the Mini Toolbar.

C Word applies the emphasis you selected.

This example shows the text after italic is selected.

You can click anywhere outside the selection to continue working.

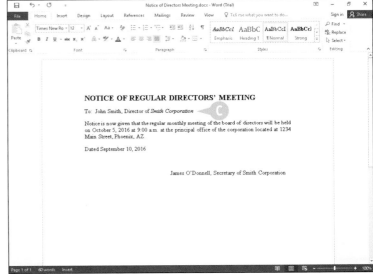

Superscript or Subscript Text

You can assign superscript or subscript notation to text. A superscript or subscript is a number, figure, or symbol that appears smaller than the normal line of type and is set slightly above or below it; superscripts appear above the baseline of regular text, whereas subscripts appear below the baseline. Subscripts and superscripts are perhaps best known for their use in formulas and mathematical expressions, but they are also used when inserting trademark symbols.

Superscript or Subscript Text

1 Type and select the text that you want to appear in superscript or subscript.

A If you drag to select, the Mini Toolbar appears in the background.

2 Click the **Home** tab.

3 Click the **Superscript** button (x^2) or the **Subscript** button (x_2).

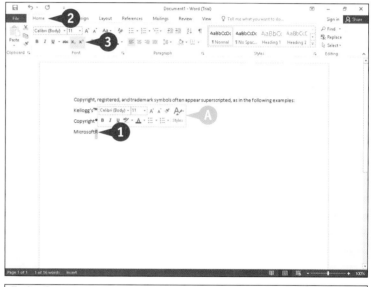

B Word adds superscripts or subscripts to the selected text.

You can click anywhere outside the selection to continue working.

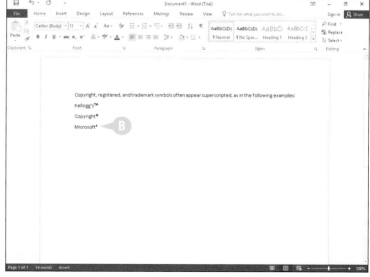

Change Text Case

You can change the case of selected text instead of retyping it with a new case applied. You can apply five types of case to your text. You can apply lowercase to selected text, which uses no capital letters. You can apply uppercase to selected text, which uses all capital letters. Using sentence case, you capitalize the first letter of the selected phrase while all other words in the phrase appear lowercase. You can capitalize each word in a selected phrase, or you can toggle case, which changes uppercase letters to lowercase and lowercase letters to uppercase in selected text.

Change Text Case

1 Select the text to which you want to assign a new case.

The Mini Toolbar appears in the background if you drag to select text.

2 Click the **Home** tab.

3 Click the **Change Case** button (Aa ▾).

4 Click the case you want to use.

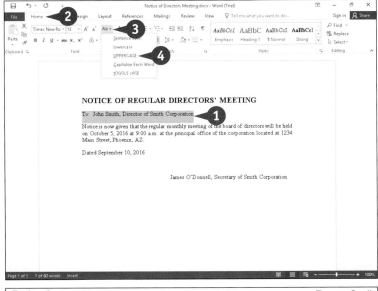

Ⓐ The selected text appears in the new case.

You can click anywhere outside the selection to continue working.

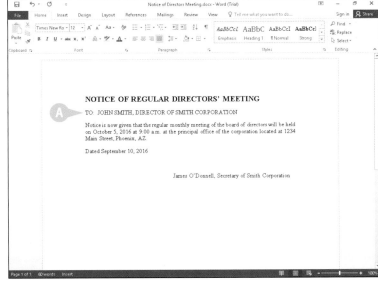

Change Text Color

You can change the color of selected text for emphasis. For example, if you are creating a report for work, you might make the title of the report a different color from the information contained in the report or even color-code certain data in the report.

Color is effective when you view your document on-screen, save it as a PDF or an XPS file, or print it using a color printer.

Change Text Color

1 Select the text that you want to change to a different color.

Ⓐ If you drag to select, the Mini Toolbar appears, and you can use it by moving the mouse (⧖) toward the Mini Toolbar.

2 To use the Ribbon, click the **Home** tab.

3 Click ▼ next to the **Font Color** button (**A** ▼), and point the mouse (⧖) at a color.

Word displays a preview of the selected text.

4 Click a color.

Ⓑ Word assigns the color to the text.

This example applies a blue color to the text.

You can click anywhere outside the selection to continue working.

Apply Text Effects

You can use a text effect to draw a reader's eye to the text. Text effects go beyond typical techniques you use for emphasis, such as boldface, italics, or underlining. (You can read about these emphasis techniques in the section "Emphasize Information with Bold, Italic, or Underline," earlier in this chapter.) Using text effects, you can apply outlines, shadows, reflections, and glows to text or WordArt. Text effects accomplish your goal of drawing the reader's eye most successfully if you apply them sparingly and limit your use of them to headlines or titles.

Apply Text Effects

1 Type and select the text to which you want to apply an effect.

2 Click the **Home** tab.

3 Click the **Text Effects** button ( ).

Ⓐ The Text Effects gallery appears.

4 Point the mouse ( ) at the type of text effect you want to apply.

Ⓑ Word displays a gallery of options available for the selected text effect; you can preview any text effect by pointing the mouse ( ) at it.

5 Click an option from the gallery to apply it.

Ⓒ Word applies your choice to the selected text.

You can click anywhere outside the selection to continue working.

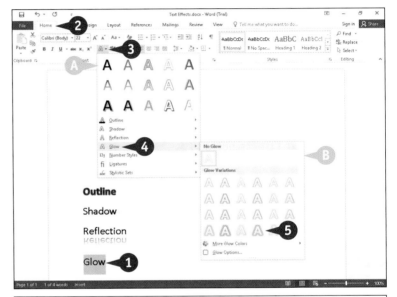

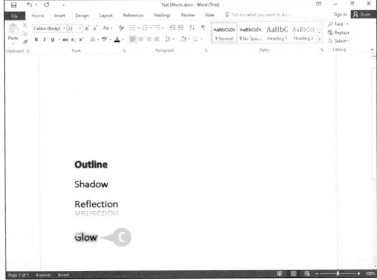

Apply a Font Style Set

You can use font style sets to enhance the appearance of OpenType fonts. Font style sets can add just the right mood to a holiday card by adding flourishes to the letters in the font set.

The OpenType font structure adds several options to its predecessor TrueType that enhance the OpenType font's typographic and language support capabilities. OpenType fonts use an extension of .otf or .ttf; the .ttf form typically includes PostScript font data. OpenType fonts store all information in a single font file and have the same appearance on Macs and PCs.

Apply a Font Style Set

1 Select an OpenType font.

This example uses **Gabriola**.

2 Type some text, and select it.

The Mini Toolbar appears if you drag to select text.

3 Click the **Text Effects** button (A ▾).

Ⓐ The Text Effects gallery appears.

4 Point the mouse (↳) at **Stylistic Sets**.

Ⓑ Word displays a gallery of options available for Stylistic Sets; you can preview any set by pointing the mouse (↳) at it.

5 Click an option from the gallery to apply it.

Ⓒ Word applies the font style set to the text you selected.

You can click anywhere outside the selection to continue working.

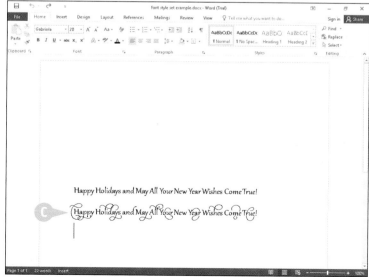

Apply Highlighting to Text

You can use color to create highlights in a document to draw attention to the text. You can help your reader be an active reader and understand and remember what you have written if you highlight a keyword or a small phrase. Highlighting is effective when viewing the document on-screen or when you print the document using a color printer.

Do not be tempted to overuse highlighting. If you highlight every other sentence or even all the headings in a document, your reader will learn to ignore the highlighting.

Apply Highlighting to Text

1 Select the text that you want to highlight.

The Mini Toolbar appears if you drag to select text, and you can use it by moving the mouse (⌖) toward the Mini Toolbar.

2 To use the Ribbon, click the **Home** tab.

3 Click ▼ beside the **Text Highlight Color** button (🖋 ▾) on the Ribbon or the Mini Toolbar.

A A palette of color choices appears.

You can point the mouse (⌖) at any color, and Word displays a sample of the selected text highlighted in that color.

4 Click a color.

B Word highlights the selected text using the color you choose.

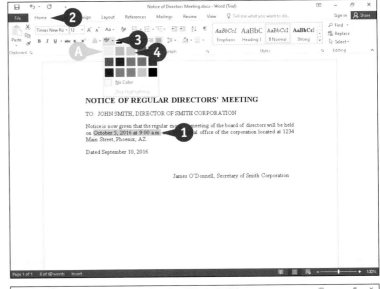

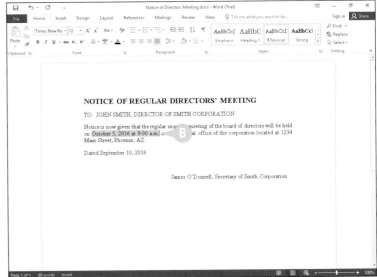

126

Apply Strikethrough to Text

You can use the Strikethrough feature to draw a line through text you propose to delete. Strikethrough formatting is often used in the legal community to identify text a reviewer proposes to delete; this formatting has developed a universal meaning and has been adopted by reviewers around the world. However, if you need to track both additions and deletions and want to update the document in an automated way, use Word's review tracking features as described in Chapter 4.

Apply Strikethrough to Text

1. Select the text to which you want to apply strikethrough formatting.

   The Mini Toolbar appears if you drag to select text.

2. Click the **Home** tab.

3. Click the **Strikethrough** button (abc).

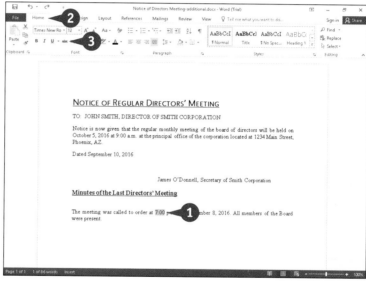

A. Word applies strikethrough formatting to the selected text.

You can click anywhere outside the selection to continue working.

You can repeat these steps to remove strikethrough formatting.

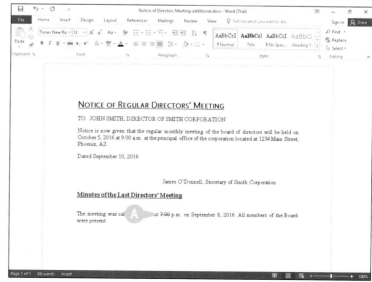

Copy Text Formatting

Suppose you have applied a variety of formatting options to a paragraph to create a certain look — for example, you changed the font, the size, the color, and the alignment. If you want to re-create the same look elsewhere in the document, you do not have to repeat the same steps as when you applied the original formatting, again changing the font, size, color, and alignment. Instead, you can use Word's Format Painter feature to "paint" the formatting to the other text.

Copy Text Formatting

1 Select the text containing the formatting that you want to copy.

The Mini Toolbar might appear in the background, and you can use it by moving the mouse (⇖) toward the Mini Toolbar.

2 To use the Ribbon, click the **Home** tab.

3 Click the **Format Painter** button (✔).

A The mouse (⇖) changes to ▲I when you move the mouse over your document.

4 Click and drag over the text to which you want to apply the same formatting.

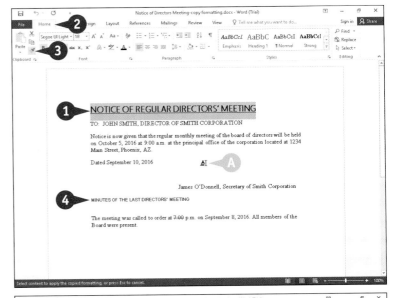

B Word copies the formatting from the original text to the newly selected text.

To copy the same formatting multiple times, you can double-click the **Format Painter** button (✔).

You can press **Esc** to cancel the Format Painter feature at any time.

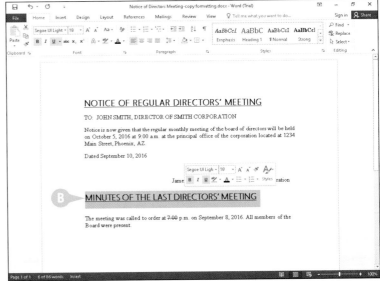

Remove Text Formatting

Sometimes, you may find that you have applied too much formatting to your text, making it difficult to read. Instead of undoing all your formatting changes by hand, you can use Word's Clear Formatting command to remove any formatting you have applied to the document text. When you apply the Clear Formatting command, which is located in the Home tab on the Ribbon, Word removes all formatting applied to the text and restores the default settings.

Remove Text Formatting

1 Select the text from which you want to remove formatting.

Note: If you do not select text, Word removes text formatting from the entire document.

2 Click the **Home** tab.

3 Click the **Clear Formatting** button (✤).

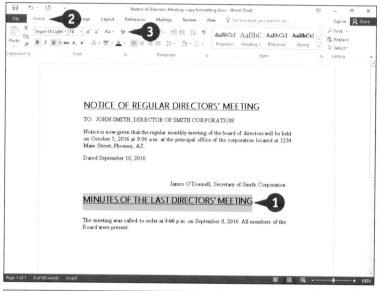

A Word removes all formatting from the selected text.

You can click anywhere outside the selection to continue working.

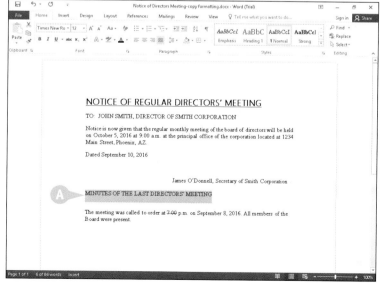

Set the Default Font for All New Documents

You can change the default font that Word uses for all new documents you create. Word's default font is Calibri, 11 point, a sans serif font. Suppose that most of the documents you create are report-like in nature. For these types of documents, you want to use a serif font, such as Cambria or Times New Roman, because the serifs on letters will help guide the reader's eye, making reading easier so that the reader can focus on your meaning.

Changing the default font does not affect documents you have already created.

Set the Default Font for All New Documents

Note: This example begins with the default Word font, Calibri, and size, 11. It changes the default font to Cambria and size to 12.

1 Click the **Home** tab.

2 Right-click the **Normal** style.

3 Click **Modify**.

The Modify Style dialog box appears.

4 Click ⌄ to select the font that you want to use for all new documents.

5 Click ⌄ to select the font size that you want to use for all new documents.

Ⓐ A preview of the new selections appears here.

6 Select **New documents based on this template** (○ changes to ●).

7 Click **OK**.

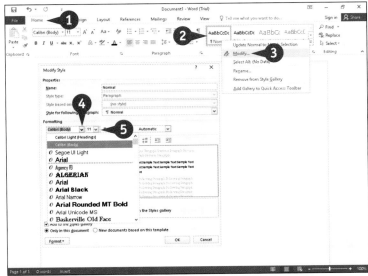

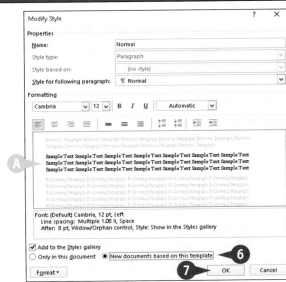

B When you open a new document, the default font and font size are the font and font size you selected in Steps **4** and **5**, respectively.

Note: To open a new document, see Chapter 2.

I like the default font, but I want to indent the first line of each paragraph by default. Can I do that?

Yes. Follow these steps:

1 Complete Steps **1** to **3** to open the Modify Style dialog box.

2 Click **Format** and, from the list that appears, click **Paragraph**.

The Paragraph dialog box appears.

3 In the Indentation section, click the **Special** ∨.

4 Click **First line**.

A By default, Word applies a .5" indentation, but you can change the value if you want.

5 Click **OK**.

6 Complete Steps **6** and **7**.

When you open a new document and begin typing text, the first line of each paragraph is indented by default.

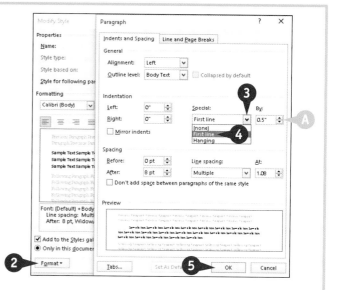

CHAPTER 6

Formatting Paragraphs

Instead of formatting individual words in your document, you can apply changes to entire paragraphs to help certain sections of your text stand out. You can apply formatting such as line spacing, bullets, or borders to the paragraphs in your document to enhance the appearance of the document.

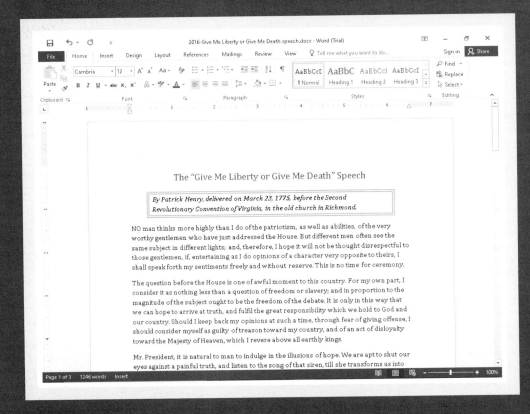

Change Text Alignment

You can use Word's alignment commands to change the way that your text is positioned horizontally on a page. By default, Word left aligns text. You can align text with the left or right margins, center it horizontally between both margins, or justify text between both the left and right margins. You can change the alignment of all the text in your document or change the alignment of individual paragraphs and objects. To align text vertically, see Chapter 7. The example in this section centers a headline between the left and right margins.

Change Text Alignment

1 Click anywhere in the paragraph that you want to align, or select the paragraphs and objects that you want to align.

2 Click the **Home** tab.

3 Click an alignment button.

The **Align Left** button (≡) aligns text with the left margin, the **Center** button (≡) centers text between the left and right margins, the **Align Right** button (≡) aligns text with the right margin, and the **Justify** button (≡) aligns text between the left and right margins.

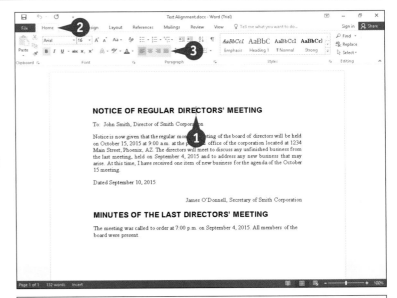

Word aligns the text.

Ⓐ This text is aligned with the left margin.

Ⓑ This text is centered between both margins.

Ⓒ This text is aligned with the right margin.

Ⓓ This text is justified between both margins.

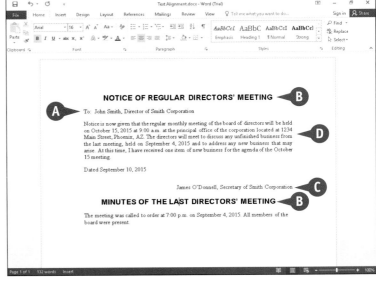

Set Line Spacing Within a Paragraph

You can change the amount of space Word places between the lines of text within a paragraph. For example, you might set 1.5 spacing to make paragraphs easier to read. By default, Word assigns single spacing within a paragraph for all new documents that you create.

Word can measure line spacing in inches, but, in keeping with typography tradition, line spacing is most often measured in points, specified as *pts*. Twelve pts equal approximately one line of space.

Set Line Spacing Within a Paragraph

1 Click in the paragraph for which you want to change line spacing.

2 Click the **Home** tab.

3 Click the **Line Spacing** button ($\updownarrow\equiv$ ▾).

Note: As you move the mouse ($\downarrow$) over line spacing options, Word previews the paragraph using each option.

4 Click a number.

A setting of **1** represents single spacing, **1.15** places a small amount of blank space between lines; **1.5** places half a blank line between lines of text; **2** represents double spacing; **2.5** places one and a half blank lines between lines of text; and **3** represents triple spacing.

A Word applies the line spacing you specified to the paragraph containing the insertion point.

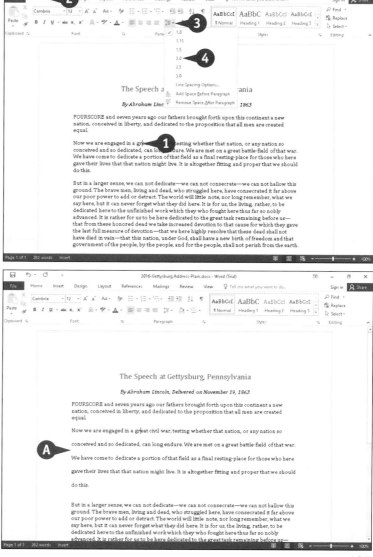

Set Line Spacing Between Paragraphs

In addition to changing the spacing between lines within a paragraph, you can change the amount of space Word places between paragraphs of text. For example, you can use this technique to set double spacing between paragraphs while maintaining single spacing within each paragraph.

You can set spacing before a paragraph or after a paragraph. Word measures spacing between paragraphs in points (pts), and one line equals approximately 12 pts. You can create one blank line between paragraphs by adding 6 pts before and 6 pts after the paragraph, or you can simply add 12 pts before or 12 pts after the paragraph.

Set Line Spacing Between Paragraphs

1 Select the paragraph or paragraphs for which you want to define spacing.

2 Click the **Home** tab.

3 Click the Paragraph group dialog box launcher (⌐).

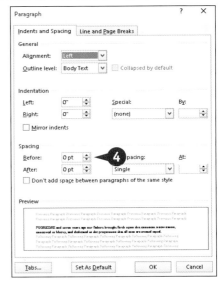

The Paragraph dialog box appears.

4 Click ‡ to increase or decrease the space before the selected paragraph.

5 Click ◆ to increase or decrease the space after the selected paragraph.

6 Click **OK**.

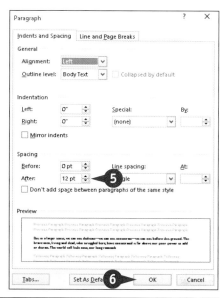

A Word applies the spacing before and after the selected paragraph.

You can click anywhere outside the selection to continue working.

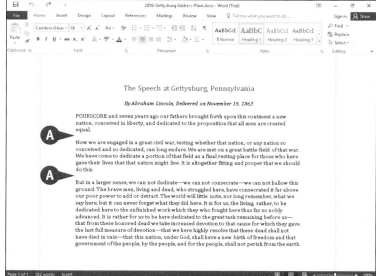

What does the Don't Add Space Between Paragraphs of the Same Style check box do?
As described later in this chapter, you can use styles to assign predefined sets of formatting information, such as font and paragraph information, including line spacing, to paragraphs. By default, Word assigns the Normal style to each paragraph of text. You can select **Don't add space between paragraphs of the same style** (☐ changes to ☑) to use the same spacing both within a paragraph and between paragraphs to which you have assigned the same style.

Create a Bulleted or Numbered List

You can draw attention to lists of information by using bullets or numbers. Bulleted and numbered lists can help you present your information in an organized way. You can create a list as you type it or after you have typed list elements.

A bulleted list adds dots or other similar symbols in front of each list item, whereas a numbered list adds sequential numbers or letters in front of each list item. As a general rule, use bullets when the items in your list do not follow any particular order, and use numbers when the items in your list follow a particular order.

Create a Bulleted or Numbered List

Create a List as You Type

1 Type **1.** to create a numbered list or ***** to create a bulleted list.

2 Press **Spacebar** or **Tab**.

A Word automatically formats the entry as a list item and displays the AutoCorrect Options button (🗲 ▾) so that you can undo or stop automatic numbering.

3 Type a list item.

4 Press **Enter** to prepare to type another list item.

B Word automatically adds a bullet or number for the next list item.

5 Repeat Steps **3** and **4** for each list item.

To stop entering items in the list, press **Enter** twice.

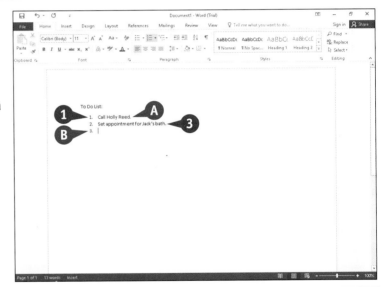

Create a List from Existing Text

1 Select the text to which you want to assign bullets or numbers.

2 Click the **Home** tab.

3 Click the **Numbering** button (☷ ▾) or the **Bullets** button (☷ ▾).

C Word applies numbers or bullets to the selection.

This example uses bullets.

You can click anywhere to continue working.

TIP

Can I create a bulleted or numbered list with more than one level, like the type of list you use when creating an outline?

Yes. You can use the Multilevel List button (⁀⁻).

1 Click the **Multilevel List** button (⁀⁻).

2 Click a format.

3 Type your list.

A You can press Enter to enter a new list item at the same list level.

B Each time you press Tab, Word indents a level in the list.

C Each time you press Shift+Tab, Word outdents a level in the list.

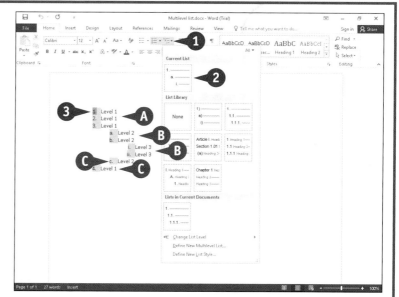

Display Formatting Marks

You can display formatting marks that do not print but help you identify formatting in your document. Displaying formatting marks can often help you identify problems in your documents. For example, if you display formatting marks, you can visibly see the difference between a line break and a paragraph mark. You also can see where spaces were used to attempt to vertically line up text when you should have used tabs, as described in the section "Set Tabs." Word can display formatting marks that represent spaces, tabs, paragraphs, line breaks, hidden text, and optional hyphens.

Display Formatting Marks

1 Open any document.

2 Click the **Home** tab.

3 Click the **Show/Hide** button (¶).

Word displays all formatting marks in your document.

A Single dots (·) represent the spaces you insert each time you press `Spacebar`.

B Paragraph marks (¶) appear each time you press `Enter`.

C Line breaks (↵) appear each time you press `Shift`+`Enter`.

D Arrows (→) appear each time you press `Tab`.

E Hidden text appears underlined with dots.

F Optional hyphens, inserted by pressing `Ctrl`+`-` appear as ¬.

You can click the **Show/Hide** button (¶) again to hide formatting marks.

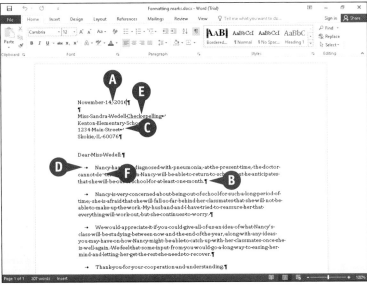

140

Hide or Display the Ruler

Y ou can hide or display horizontal and vertical rulers while you work on a Word document in Print Layout, Web Layout, or Draft views. Rulers can help you identify the position of text on the page both horizontally and vertically. You also can use the rulers to align tables and graphic objects and to indent paragraphs or set tabs in your document, as described in the sections "Indent Paragraphs" and "Set Tabs."

Hide or Display the Ruler

1 Click the **View** tab.

2 Select **Ruler** (☐ changes to ☑).

Ⓐ A ruler appears above your document.

Ⓑ A ruler appears on the left side of your document.

You can repeat Steps **1** and **2** (☑ changes to ☐) to hide the rulers.

Indent Paragraphs

Y ou can use indents as a way to control the horizontal positioning of text in a document. Indents are simply margins that affect individual lines or paragraphs. You might use an indent to distinguish a particular paragraph on a page — for example, a long quote.

You can indent paragraphs in your document from the left and right margins. You also can indent only the first line of a paragraph or all lines *except* the first line of the paragraph. You can set indents using buttons on the Ribbon, the Paragraph dialog box, and the Word ruler.

Indent Paragraphs

Set Quick Indents

1 Click anywhere in the paragraph you want to indent.

2 Click the **Home** tab on the Ribbon.

3 Click an indent button:

A You can click the **Decrease Indent** button (⬅≣) to decrease the indentation.

B You can click the **Increase Indent** button (➡≣) to increase the indentation.

C Word applies the indent change.

Set Precise Indents

1 Click in the paragraph or select the text you want to indent.

2 Click the **Home** tab.

3 Click the dialog box launcher (⌐) in the Paragraph group.

The Paragraph dialog box appears.

4 Use these boxes to specify the number of inches to indent the left and right edge of the paragraph or selection.

5 Click ⌄ to select an indenting option.

First line, shown in this example, indents only the first line of the paragraph, and **Hanging** indents all lines *except* the first line of the paragraph.

6 Click ⬍ to set the amount of the first line or hanging indent.

D The Preview area shows a sample of the indent.

7 Click **OK**.

E Word applies the indent to the paragraph containing the insertion point.

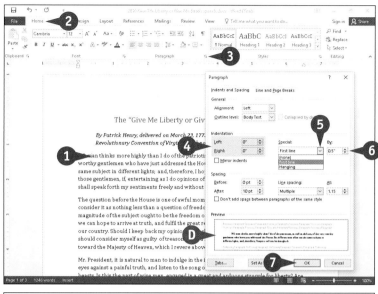

TIP

How do I set indents using the Word ruler?
The ruler contains markers for changing the left indent, right indent, first-line indent, and hanging indent. Click the **View** tab, and then click **Ruler** to display the ruler. On the left side of the ruler, drag the **Left Indent** button (☐) to indent all lines from the left margin, drag the **Hanging Indent** button (△) to create a hanging indent, or drag the **First Line Indent** button (▽) to indent the first line only. On the right side of the ruler, drag the **Right Indent** button (△) to indent all lines from the right margin.

Set Tabs

You can use tabs to create vertically aligned columns of text. Using tabs as opposed to spaces ensures that information lines up properly. To insert a tab, press [Tab]; the insertion point moves to the next tab stop on the page.

By default, Word creates tab stops every 0.5 inch across the page and left aligns the text on each tab stop. You can set your own tab stops using the ruler or the Tabs dialog box. You also can use the Tabs dialog box to change the tab alignment and specify an exact measurement between tab stops.

Set Tabs

Add a Tab

1 Click here until the type of tab you want to add appears.

L — Left tab, which sets the starting position of text that then appears to the right of the tab.

⊥ — Center tab, which aligns text centered around the tab.

⌐ — Right tab, which sets the starting position of text that then appears to the left of the tab.

⊥ — Decimal tab, which aligns values at the decimal point. Values before the decimal point appear to the left of the tab and values after the decimal point appear to the right of the tab.

I — Bar tab, which inserts a vertical bar at the tab stop.

2 Select the lines to which you want to add a tab.

3 Click the ruler where you want the tab to appear.

Word displays the type of tab you selected at the location you clicked on each selected line.

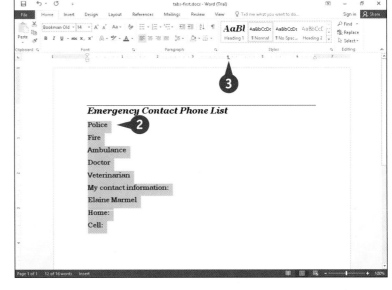

Using a Tab

1 Click to the left of the information you want to appear at the tab; in this example, immediately after the "e" in "Police" to add a tab followed by the phone number.

2 Press **Tab**.

A If you display formatting marks, Word displays an arrow (→) representing the tab character.

3 Type your text.

B The text appears aligned vertically with the tab.

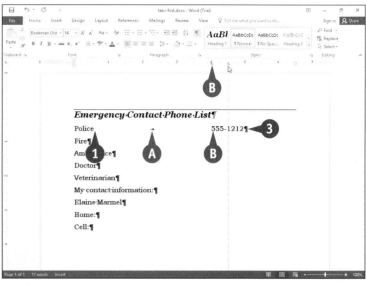

Move a Tab

1 Click the line using the tab or select the lines of text affected by the tab.

2 Drag the tab to the left or right.

C A vertical line marks its position as you drag.

When you click and drag a tab, the text moves to align vertically with the tab.

TIP

How can I delete a tab?

Perform the steps that follow: Click in or select the paragraphs containing the tab. Drag the tab off the ruler. When you delete a tab, text aligned at the tab moves to the first preset tab on the line (**A**).

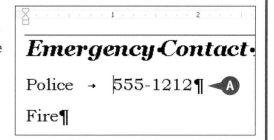

continued ▶

You can use dot leader tabs to help your reader follow information across a page. Dot leader tabs are often used in tables of contents to help the reader's eye follow the table of content entry across to its associated page number. Dot leader tabs also are helpful when you have a two-column list and the information in the second column is at least three inches away from the information in the first column. Three inches is not a rule, but simply a suggestion. Use your own judgment; if the second column material appears far away from the first column material, use dot leaders.

Set Tabs (continued)

Add Leader Characters to Tabs

1 Follow Steps **1** to **3** in the subsection "Add a Tab" to create a tab stop.

2 Select the text containing the tab to which you want to add dot leaders.

3 Click the **Home** tab.

4 Click the Paragraph group dialog box launcher (⌐).

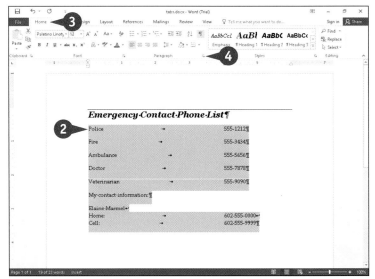

The Paragraph dialog box appears.

5 Click **Tabs**.

The Tabs dialog box appears.

6 Click the tab setting to which you want to add leaders.

7 Select a leader option (○ changes to ⦿).

8 Click **OK**.

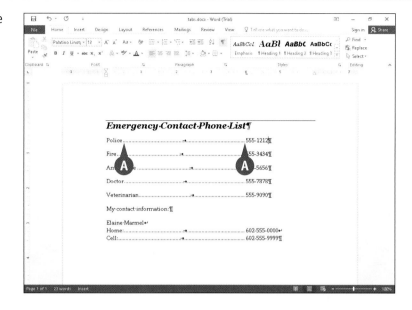

A Word adds leading characters from the last character before the tab to the first character at the tab.

You can click anywhere outside the selection to continue working.

TIP

Can I set tabs using the Tabs dialog box rather than the ruler?

Yes. Follow these steps:

1 Follow Steps **2** to **5** to display the Tabs dialog box.

2 Click here and type a tab stop position.

3 Select a tab alignment option (○ changes to ●).

4 Click **Set**.

5 Repeat Steps **2** to **4** for each tab stop you want to set.

6 Click **OK** to have the tabs you set appear on the ruler.

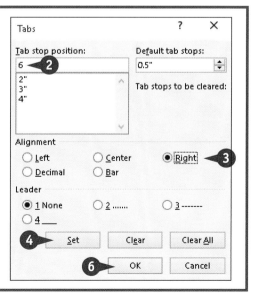

Add a Paragraph Border

The way that you communicate is just as important as the information you want to communicate: You want your important points to come through loud and clear. You can draw attention to a paragraph containing important information by adding a border to it. You can place a border around a paragraph or a page (see Chapter 7 for details on adding a border to a page), and you can control the color, weight, and style of the border. You also can add shading to a paragraph, as described in the section "Add Paragraph Shading," later in this chapter.

Add a Paragraph Border

1. Select the text that you want to surround with a border.

Note: To surround all lines in a paragraph by a border, select both the text and the paragraph mark (¶). To display paragraph marks, click the **Show/Hide** button (¶) on the Home tab in the Paragraph group.

2. Click the **Home** tab.

3. Click ▼ beside the **Borders** button (⊞ ▼).

4. Click **Borders and Shading**.

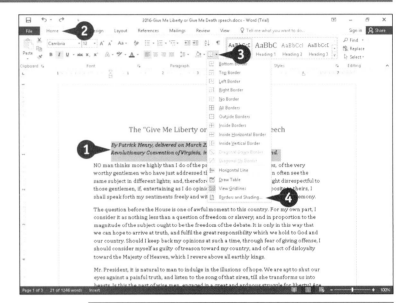

The Borders and Shading dialog box appears.

5. Click the **Borders** tab.

6. Click here to select a type of border.

   This example uses **Box**.

7. Click here to select the style for the border line.

8. Click ▼ and select a color for the border line.

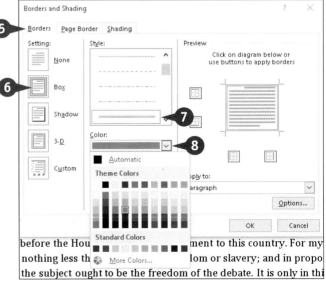

9 Click ⌄ and select a thickness for the border line.

A You can use this list to apply the border to an entire paragraph or to selected text.

B This area shows the results of the settings you select.

10 Click **OK**.

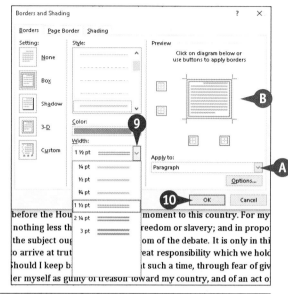

C The border appears around the text you selected in Step **1**.

You can click anywhere outside the selection to continue working.

Note: You can apply a border using the same color, style, and thickness you established in these steps to any paragraph by completing Steps **1** to **3** and clicking the type of border you want to apply in Step **6**.

TIP

How do I remove a border?
Click anywhere in the text surrounded by a border. Then, click the **Home** tab and click ⌄ beside the **Borders** button (▦ ⌄). From the menu that appears, click **No Border**, and Word removes the border.

Review and Change Formatting

You can review the formatting associated with text in your document to see the details that show the formatting applied to the text. When you reveal formatting for a selection, you can see, simultaneously, all formatting applied to the selected text; you do not need to open individual dialog boxes to view font and paragraph formatting. You also can compare the formatting of two selections to see their differences, as described in the next section, "Compare Formatting."

You also can have Word display wavy blue underlines to mark text you have formatted inconsistently in your document and supply suggestions to correct the formatting inconsistencies.

Review and Change Formatting

1 Select the text containing the formatting you want to review.

2 Click the **Home** tab.

3 Click the dialog box launcher (⌐) in the Styles group to display the Styles pane.

4 Click the **Style Inspector** button (⌐) to display the Style Inspector pane.

5 Click the **Reveal Formatting** button (⌐) to display the Reveal Formatting pane.

6 Click the **Close** buttons (✗) to close the Styles pane and the Style Inspector pane.

Ⓐ A portion of the selected text appears here.

Ⓑ Formatting details for the selected text appear here.

Ⓒ You can click an expand symbol (▷) to display links, or a collapse symbol (◢) to hide links.

7 Click the link for the type of change you want to make.

This example uses the **Alignment** link.

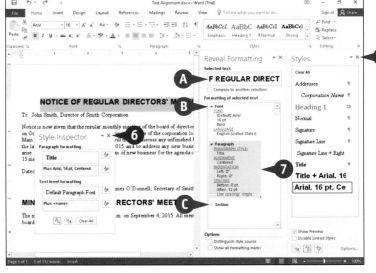

The Indents and Spacing tab of
the Paragraph dialog box appears.

⑧ Select the options you want to
change.

⑨ Click **OK**.

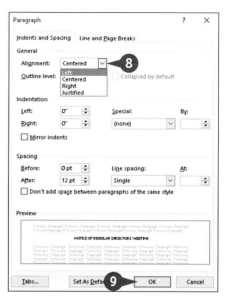

Ⓓ Word applies the formatting
changes.

Ⓔ The information in the Reveal
Formatting pane updates.

Ⓕ You can click ✖ to close the
Reveal Formatting pane.

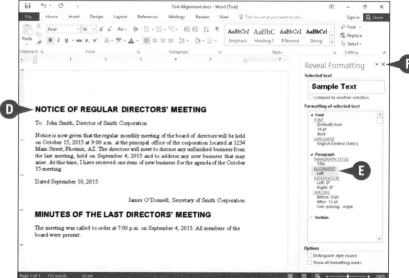

TIP

How can I view formatting inconsistencies?
To view wavy blue lines under formatting inconsistencies, click the **File** tab and then click **Options** to
display the Word Options dialog box. Click **Advanced** and, in the Editing Options section, select **Keep track
of formatting** (☐ changes to ✔) and **Mark formatting inconsistencies** (☐ changes to ✔). Then click
OK. You can repeat these steps to disable checking for formatting inconsistencies. For suggestions to
correct an inconsistency, right-click the underlined word.

Compare Formatting

You can compare the formatting of one selection to another. This feature is useful because it helps you ensure that you apply consistent manual formatting to multiple similar selections. Suppose, for example, that you have a few headings in a document and you do not use heading styles (for more information on using styles, see the next section, "Apply Formatting Using Styles") to format them; by comparing the formatting you apply, you can ensure that you apply formatting consistently. If you find discrepancies, Word can update the second selection so that it matches the first selection.

Compare Formatting

Select Text to Compare

1. Select the first text containing the formatting that you want to compare.

2. Click the **Home** tab.

3. Click the dialog box launcher (⬛) in the Styles group to display the Styles pane.

Ⓐ The Styles pane appears.

4. Click the **Style Inspector** button (⬛).

Ⓑ The Style Inspector pane appears.

5. Click the **Reveal Formatting** button (⬛).

Ⓒ The Reveal Formatting pane appears.

6. Click ✕ to close the Styles pane and the Style Inspector pane.

⑦ Select **Compare to another selection** (☐ changes to ☑).

Ⓓ A second box for selected text appears.

⑧ Select the text that you want to compare to the text you selected in Step **1**.

Ⓔ Formatting differences between the selections appear here.

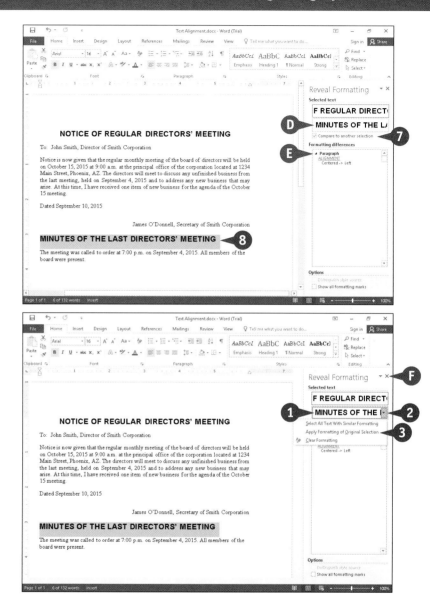

Match Formatting

① Slide the mouse (↳) over the sample box for the second selection; ▼ appears.

② Click ▼.

③ Click **Apply Formatting of Original Selection**.

Word applies the formatting of the first selection to the second selection.

You can click anywhere to continue working.

Ⓕ You can click ✖ to close the Reveal Formatting pane.

What kind of formatting differences does Word identify in the Reveal Formatting pane?
For any two selections, Word identifies differences in font, paragraph style, alignment, outline level, spacing before and after the paragraphs, line and page breaks, and bullets and numbering. You can make changes to any of these formatting differences by following the steps in the section "Review and Change Formatting."

What happens if I select the Show All Formatting Marks option below the Reveal Formatting pane?
When you select this option, Word displays formatting marks in your document that represent tabs, spaces, paragraphs, line breaks, and so on.

Apply Formatting Using Styles

You can quickly apply formatting and simultaneously maintain formatting consistency to different selections in your document by using styles to format text. *Styles* are predefined sets of formatting that can include font, paragraph, list, and border and shading information. For example, by using heading styles to format headings in your document, you can ensure that all headings use the same formatting and therefore look the same. You can store styles you use frequently in the Styles gallery, but you also can easily use styles not stored in the Styles gallery.

Apply Formatting Using Styles

Using the Styles Gallery

1 Select the text to which you want to apply formatting.

2 Click the **Home** tab.

3 In the Styles group, click ▲ and ▼ to scroll through available styles.

4 Click the **More** button (▼).

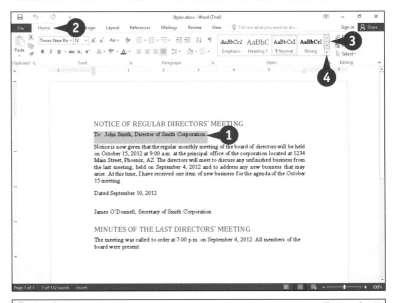

Ⓐ Word displays the Styles gallery.

Ⓑ The style of the selected text appears highlighted.

Ⓒ As you position the mouse (⬚) over various styles, Live Preview shows you the way the selected text would look in each style.

You can click a style to apply it to the selected text.

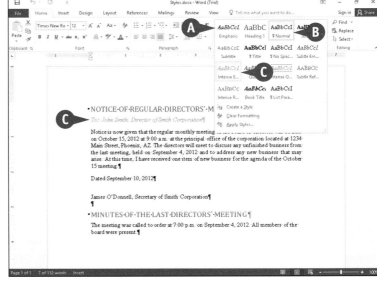

Using Other Styles

1 Select the text to which you want to apply formatting.

2 Click the **Home** tab.

3 In the Styles group, click the **More** button (⏷) to display the Styles gallery.

4 Click **Apply Styles**.

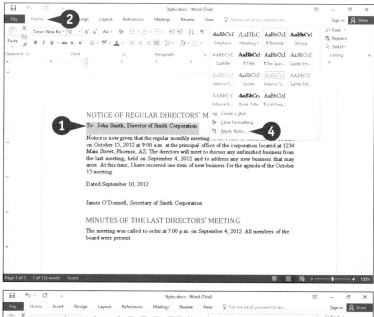

The Apply Styles pane appears.

5 Click ⏷ to open the Style Name list.

6 Select a style.

D Word applies the style to the selected text.

7 Click ✕ to close the Apply Styles dialog box.

You can click anywhere to continue working.

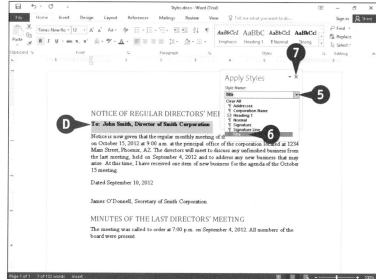

<hr/>

TIP

How can I easily view styles as they would appear in my document?

Perform the steps that follow: In the Styles group, click the dialog box launcher (⌂) to display the Styles pane. In the Styles pane, select **Show Preview** (☐ changes to ☑). Word displays styles using their formatting in the Styles pane.

Switch Styles

Y ou can easily change all text that is formatted in one style to another style. Using this technique can help you maintain formatting consistency in your documents.

For example, suppose that you have been working for a while on a document, and you have been using one particular style for headings. You then decide that you do not like the style you chose to use for headings. Although you could select each heading and change its style, that approach would be tedious and time-consuming — and unnecessary. You can, instead, switch all text in the document formatted in one style to a different style.

Switch Styles

1 Place the insertion point in or select one example of text containing the formatting that you want to change.

2 Click the **Home** tab.

3 Click the dialog box launcher ( ) in the Styles group to display the Styles pane.

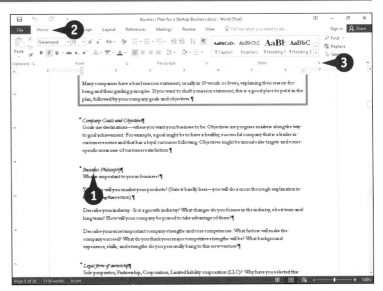

Word displays the Styles pane.

Note: If the Styles pane appears floating on-screen, you can dock it at the right side of the screen if you drag it past the right edge of the screen. If the pane appears docked as it does in this section, you can, if you want, drag it to the left to float it on-screen.

A The style for the selected text appears highlighted.

B You can position the mouse ( ) over any style to display its formatting information.

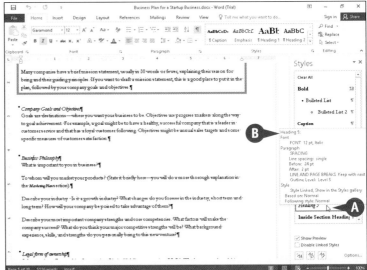

4 Position the mouse (⬚) over a style until ⬚ appears.

5 Click ⬚ to display a list of options.

6 Click **Select All Instance(s)**.

⒞ Word selects all text in your document formatted using the style of the text you selected in Step **1**.

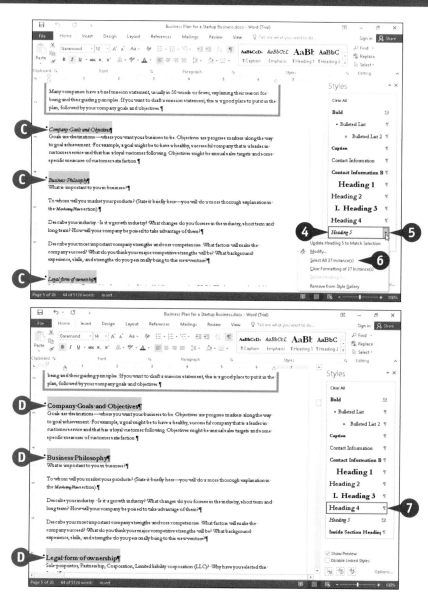

7 Click the style you want to apply to all selected text.

⒟ Word changes all selected text to the style you selected in Step **7**.

You can click anywhere to continue working.

TIP

Can I sort styles alphabetically in the Styles pane?
Yes. By default, Word sorts styles using the As Recommended setting, but sorting in alphabetical order is a useful alternative. At the bottom of the Styles pane, click the **Options** link to display the Style Pane Options dialog box. Click the **Select how list is sorted** ⬚ and select **Alphabetical**. Then click **OK**.

Save Formatting in a Style

In addition to the styles Word provides for you in the Styles gallery for headings, normal text, quotes, and more, you can easily create your own styles to store formatting information. Creating your own styles is particularly useful if you cannot find a built-in style that suits your needs.

You can create a new style by formatting text the way you want it to appear when you apply the style. You then use the example text to create the style and store it in the Styles gallery. You also can modify the style settings at the same time that you create the style.

Save Formatting in a Style

1. Format text in your document using the formatting you want to save in a style.

2. Select the text containing the formatting you want to save.

3. In the Styles group, click the **More** button (⩒).

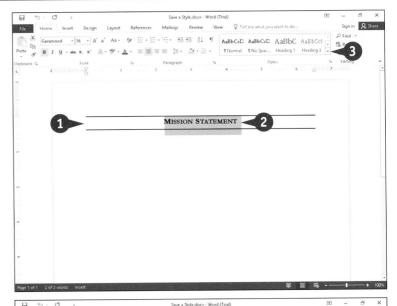

Ⓐ The Styles gallery appears.

4. Click **Create a Style**.

The Create New Style from Formatting dialog box appears.

⑤ Type a name for the style.

⑥ Click **Modify**.

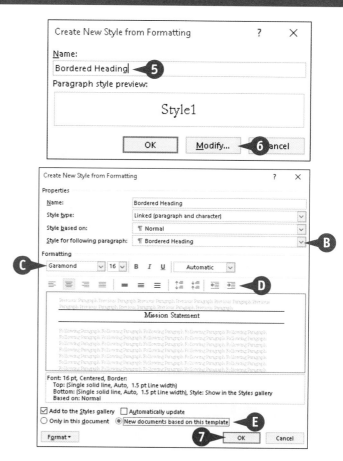

Word displays additional options you can set for the style.

Ⓑ You can click ❯ and select the style for the following paragraph when you use the style you are creating.

Ⓒ Use these options to select font formatting for the style.

Ⓓ Use these options to set paragraph alignment, spacing, and indentation options.

Ⓔ Select this option to make your style available in new documents (◯ changes to ◉).

⑦ Click **OK**.

Word saves your newly created style.

TIPS

What happens if I click Format?
A menu appears that you can use to specify additional formatting. Select the type of formatting, and Word displays a dialog box where you can add more formatting characteristics to the style.

What does the Style Based On option do?
Every style you create is based on a built-in Word style. Changing a built-in style can result in many styles changing. For example, many styles are based on the Normal style. If you change the font of the Normal style, you change the font of all styles based on the Normal style.

Expand or Collapse Document Content

You can hide or display document content by expanding or collapsing headings. Hiding or displaying content can be particularly beneficial if you are working on a long, complicated document. For example, you can hide everything except the portion on which you want to focus your attention. If you send the document to others to review, you can help your reader avoid information overload if you display only the headings and let your reader expand the content of the headings of interest.

To use this feature, you must apply heading styles to text in your document.

Expand or Collapse Document Content

1 In a document, apply heading styles such as Heading 1 or Heading 2.

2 Slide the mouse (I) toward a heading.

A collapse button (▲) appears beside the heading.

3 Click ▲.

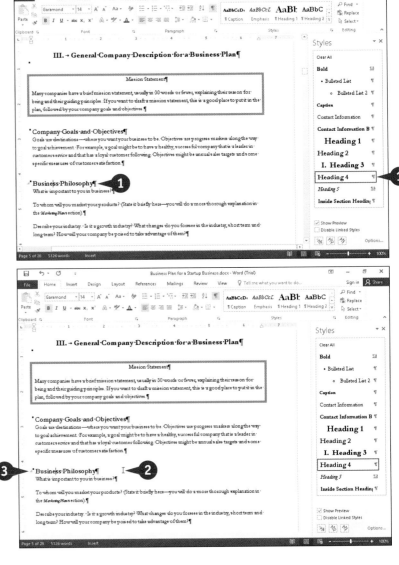

A All text following the heading that is not styled as a heading disappears from view.

An expand button (▷) replaces ◢ .

4 Click ▷ .

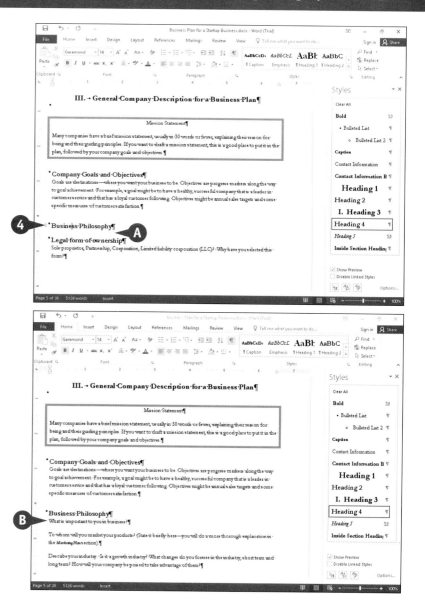

B The hidden text reappears.

TIP

How can I expand or collapse all headings?
Perform the steps that follow: Right-click any heading. From the menu that appears, point the mouse (▷) at **Expand/Collapse**. Click **Expand All Headings** or **Collapse All Headings** (**A**). Collapsing all headings hides all text and headings except text formatted as Heading 1.

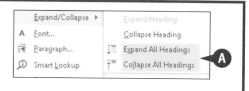

Modify a Style

At some point, you may decide that the formatting of a style is close to but not exactly what you want. For example, you might want to change the size of the font used in a heading style. You do not need to create a new style; you can modify the existing one.

When you change a style, you can add the style to the Styles gallery, and you can ensure that the style changes appear in new documents you create. You also can have Word update all text in your document that currently uses the style you are modifying.

Modify a Style

1. Open a document containing the style you want to change.

2. Click the **Home** tab.

3. Click the dialog box launcher (⬚) in the Styles group to display the Styles pane.

4. Right-click the style you want to change.

5. Click **Modify**.

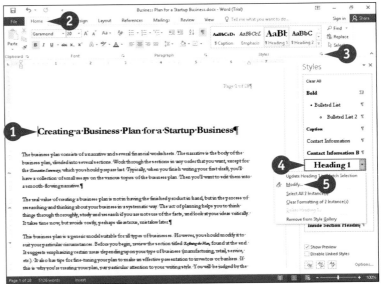

The Modify Style dialog box appears.

6. Make font or paragraph formatting changes.

7. Select the option to make the modified style available in new documents (○ changes to ●).

8. Select the option to add the style to the Styles gallery (☐ changes to ☑).

9. Click **OK**.

Word updates all text in the document formatted with the style you changed.

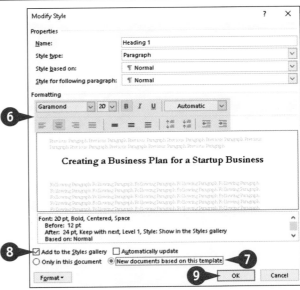

Add Paragraph Shading

Shading is another technique you can use to draw your reader's attention. Shading appears on-screen and when you print your document; if you do not use a color printer, paragraph shading will be most effective if you select a shade of gray for your shading.

Add Paragraph Shading

1 Select the paragraph(s) that you want to shade.

2 Click the **Home** tab.

3 Click ▼ beside the **Borders** button (▦ ▼).

4 Click **Borders and Shading**.

The Borders and Shading dialog box appears.

5 Click the **Shading** tab.

6 Click ▼.

7 Click a fill color.

8 Click **OK**.

You can click anywhere outside the paragraph(s) you selected in Step **1**.

Ⓐ Word shades the selection you made in Step **1**.

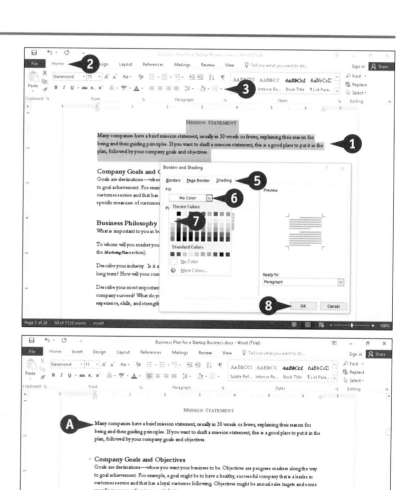

CHAPTER 7

Formatting Pages

In addition to applying formatting to characters and paragraphs, you can apply formatting to pages of your Word document. Find out how to make your pages look their best in this chapter.

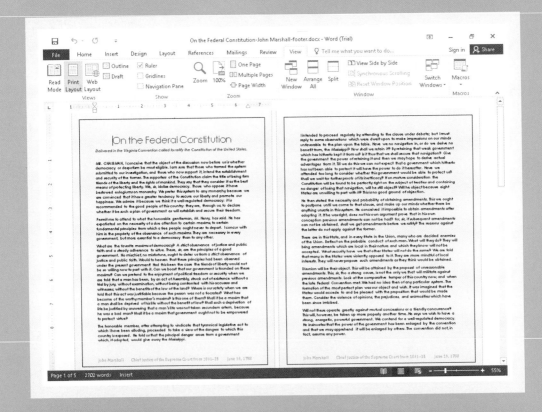

Adjust Margins

By default, Word assigns a 1-inch margin all the way around the page in every new document that you create. You can change these margin settings, however. For example, you can set wider margins to fit more text on a page or set smaller margins to fit less text on a page. You can apply your changes to the current document only or set them as the new default setting, to be applied to all new Word documents you create. When you adjust margins, Word sets the margins from the position of the insertion point to the end of the document.

Adjust Margins

Set Margins Using Layout Tools

① Click anywhere in the document or section where you want to change margins.

② Click the **Layout** tab on the Ribbon.

③ Click **Margins**.

Ⓐ The Margins gallery appears.

④ Click a margin setting.

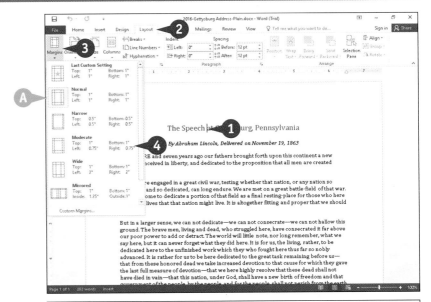

Ⓑ Word applies the new setting.

166

Set a Custom Margin

1. In the document or section you want to change, click the **Layout** tab on the Ribbon.

2. Click **Margins**.

   Ⓒ The Margins gallery appears.

3. Click **Custom Margins**.

   The Page Setup dialog box appears, displaying the Margins tab.

4. Type a specific margin in the **Top**, **Bottom**, **Left**, and **Right** boxes.

   Ⓓ You can also click ⬍ to set a margin measurement.

5. Choose a page orientation.

   Ⓔ Preview the margin settings here.

6. Click ⌄ and specify whether the margin should apply to the whole document or from this point forward.

7. Click **OK**.

   Word immediately adjusts the margin in the document.

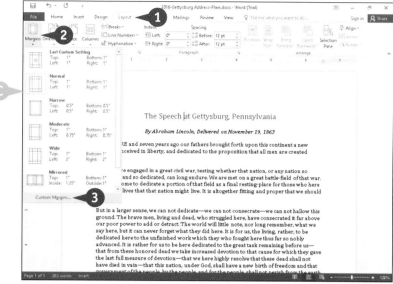

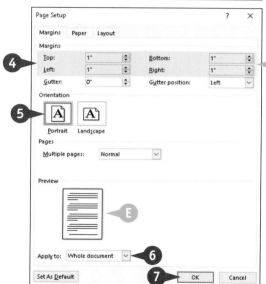

TIPS

How do I set new default margins?
To establish a different set of default margins for every new document that you create, make the desired changes to the Margins tab of the Page Setup dialog box, and click **Set As Default** before clicking **OK**.

Why is my printer ignoring my margin settings?
Some printers have a minimum margin setting, and in most cases, that minimum margin is 0.25 inch. If you set your margins smaller than your printer's minimum margin setting, you place text in an unprintable area. Be sure to test the margins or check your printer documentation for more information.

Insert a Page Break

A dding page breaks can help you control where text appears. By default, Word automatically starts a new page when the current page becomes filled with text. But you can insert a page break to force Word to start text on a new page, for example, at the end of a chapter. You can insert page breaks using the Ribbon or using your keyboard.

You can insert a page break in all views except Read Mode. Page breaks are visible in Print Layout view and, if you display formatting information as described in Chapter 6, page breaks are also visible in Draft, Web Layout, and Outline views.

Insert a Page Break

Using Ribbon Buttons

1 Click in the document where you want to insert a page break.

2 Click the **Insert** tab.

3 Click **Pages**.

4 Click **Page Break**.

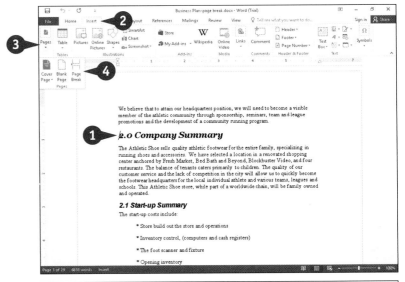

A Word inserts a page break and moves all text after the page break onto a new page.

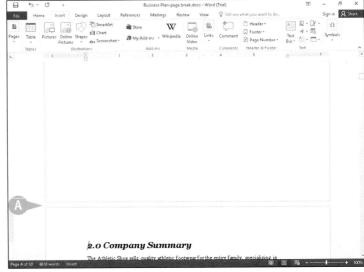

Using the Keyboard

Note: Steps **1** to **3** display formatting information and change your document to Draft view; you can skip these steps and insert a page break in any view except Read Mode.

1 On the Home tab, click the **Show/Hide** button (¶) to display formatting information.

2 Click the **View** tab.

3 Click **Draft**.

4 Position the insertion point immediately before the text that you want to appear on a new page.

5 Press Ctrl + Enter.

B Word inserts a page break and moves all text after the page break onto a new page.

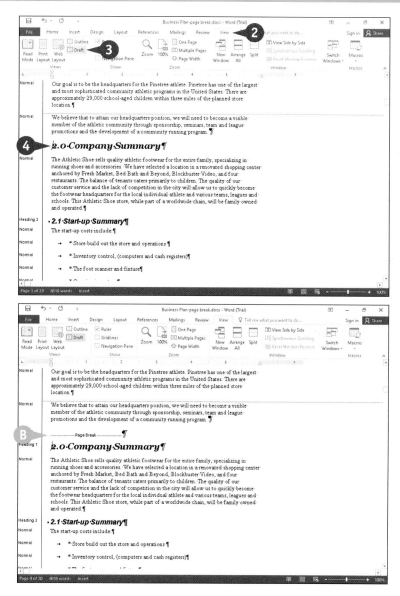

Can I delete a page break?

Yes. You can delete manually inserted page breaks. With formatting information visible, you can identify these pages breaks in Draft view; they appear as dotted lines containing the words "Page Break." Page breaks that Word inserts automatically also appear as dotted lines but do not contain the words "Page Break." Perform Steps **1** to **3** in the subsection "Using the Keyboard." Click anywhere on a manually inserted page break line and press Delete.

Control Text Flow and Pagination

Although you cannot delete automatic page breaks that Word inserts when you fill a page with text, you can control the placement of page breaks in a number of ways to help your reader more easily understand the document's content.

You can eliminate widows and orphans. You can keep selected lines of a paragraph together on the same page; similarly, you can keep selected paragraphs together, forcing the paragraphs to appear on the same page. You also can force Word to insert a page break before a selected paragraph. The benefits of these controls appear most obviously in Draft view (see Chapter 3).

Control Text Flow and Pagination

Note: To switch to Draft view, click **View** and then click **Draft**.

1 Select the text whose flow you want to affect.

Note: To control widows and orphans, you do not need to select any text.

2 Click the **Home** tab.

3 Click the Paragraph group dialog box launcher (□).

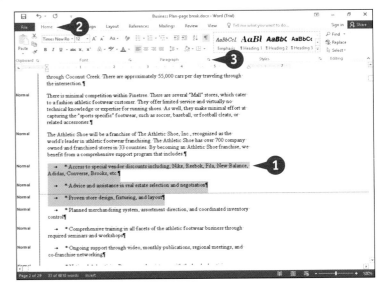

The Paragraph dialog box appears.

4 Click the **Line and Page Breaks** tab.

Ⓐ This area contains the options you can use to control text flow and automatic pagination.

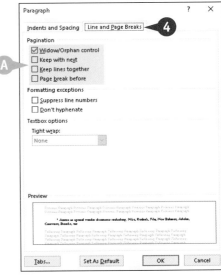

5 Select an option (☐ changes to ☑).

Note: This example keeps lines together on a page.

6 Repeat Step **5** as needed.

7 Click **OK**.

Ⓑ Word groups the selected text in the manner you specified; in this example, Word inserts a page break before the selected text to keep it together on a page.

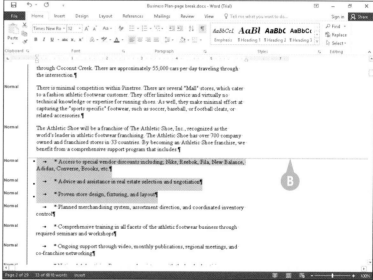

What is a widow?

Widow is the term used to describe text grouped so that the first line of a paragraph appears at the bottom of a page and subsequent lines appear on the following page. Widows are distracting to reading comprehension.

What is an orphan?

Orphan is the term used to describe text grouped so that the last line of a paragraph appears at the top of a new page and all preceding lines appear at the bottom of the previous page. Like widows, orphans are distracting to reading comprehension.

Align Text Vertically on the Page

You can align text between the top and bottom margins of a page if the text does not fill the page. For example, you might want to center text vertically on short business letters or report cover pages to improve their appearance.

By default, Word applies vertical alignment to your entire document, but you can limit the alignment if you first divide the document into sections. You will need to use this technique to vertically align the cover page of a report; otherwise, you will align all pages of the report vertically. See the section "Insert a Section Break" for more information.

Align Text Vertically on the Page

Note: To align a report cover page, insert a Next Page section break after the cover page and click anywhere on the cover page.

1. In the document you want to align, click the **Layout** tab.

2. Click the Page Setup group dialog box launcher (⛶).

   The Page Setup dialog box appears.

3. Click the **Layout** tab.

4. Click the **Vertical alignment** ⌄ and select a vertical alignment choice.

   Ⓐ To align a cover page, click the **Apply to** ⌄ and select **This section**.

5. Click **OK**.

   Ⓑ Word applies vertical alignment.

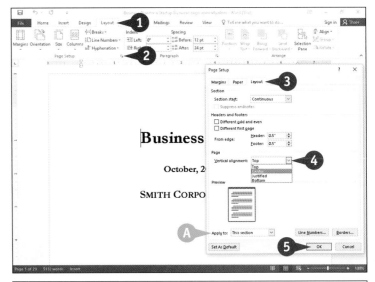

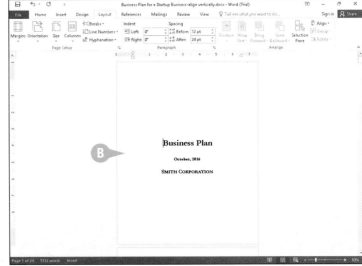

Change Page Orientation

You can change the direction that text prints from the standard portrait orientation of 8½ inches x 11 inches to the landscape orientation of 11 inches x 8½ inches. Changing orientation is particularly helpful on pages containing tables with many columns; using a landscape orientation might help you fit all columns on a single page.

Change Page Orientation

Note: To change the page orientation of a single page in a multipage document, first insert a Next Page section break before and after the page and click anywhere on the page.

1. Click anywhere in the document or on the page whose orientation you want to change.

2. Click the **Layout** tab.

3. Click **Orientation**.

Ⓐ The current orientation appears highlighted.

4. Click an option.

Ⓑ Word changes the orientation.

Note: The document in this example appears zoomed out to show orientation changes more clearly.

Note: By default, Word changes the orientation for the entire document. To limit orientation changes, divide the document into sections. See the next section, "Insert a Section Break."

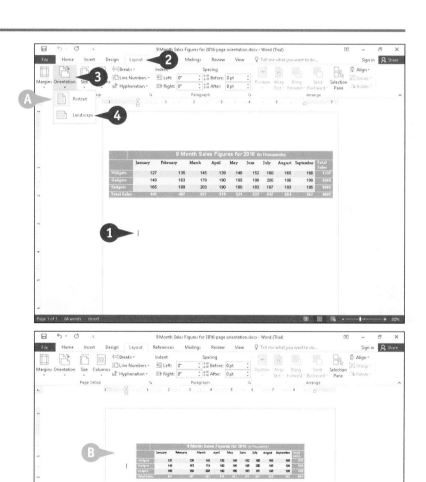

Insert a Section Break

You can use section breaks in a document to establish separate margins, headers, footers, vertical page alignment, and other page formatting settings within a single document.

You can start a new section on a new page or anywhere on a page. For example, to establish separate page numbers for chapters, your break should start a new page. But suppose that your document includes a table that will fit on a portrait-oriented page if you can establish narrower margins to accommodate the table. In this case, you can insert continuous section breaks before and after the table and establish margins for the table between the breaks.

Insert a Section Break

1 Click in the location where you want to start a new section in your document.

2 Click the **Layout** tab.

3 Click **Breaks**.

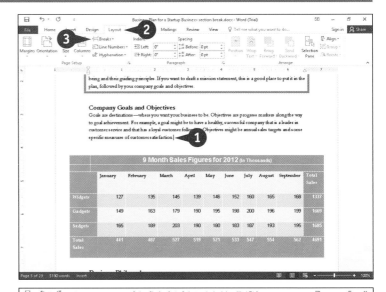

A The Breaks gallery appears, organized by type of page breaks and type of section breaks.

4 Click an option to select the type of section break you want to insert.

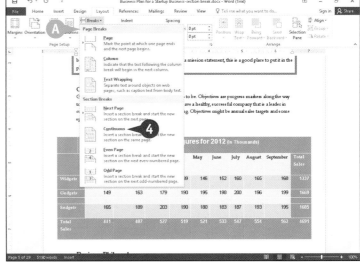

Word inserts the type of break you selected.

5 Click the **View** tab.

6 Click **Draft** to display the document in Draft view.

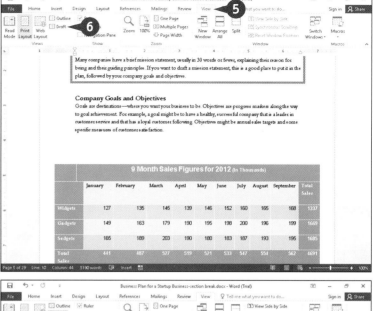

B A section break line appears.

You can remove the section break by clicking the section break line and pressing Delete.

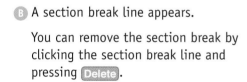

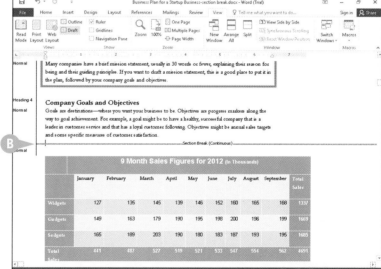

TIPS

How does Word handle printing when I insert a section break?
Section breaks are formatting marks that do not print; instead, the effects of the section break are apparent when you print. If you insert a Next Page section break, Word starts the text that immediately follows the section break on a new page. But if you insert a Continuous section break as shown in this section, text flows continuously.

What happens if I select Even Page or Odd Page?
Word starts the next section of your document on the next even or odd page. If you insert an Even Page section break on an odd page, Word leaves the odd page blank.

Add Page Numbers to a Document

You can add page numbers to make your documents more manageable. You can choose to add page numbers to the header or footer area at the top or bottom of a page or in the page margins, or you can add a single page number at the current position of the insertion point.

Page numbers in headers and footers appear on-screen only in Print Layout view. A single page number at the current position of the insertion point also appears in Read Mode view. As you edit your document to add or remove text, Word adjusts the document and the page numbers accordingly.

Add Page Numbers to a Document

Note: To place a single page number at a specific location in the document, click that location.

1 Click the **Insert** tab.

2 Click **Page Number**.

Ⓐ Page number placement options appear.

3 Click a placement option.

Note: If you choose **Current Position**, Word inserts a page number only at the current location of the insertion point — and nowhere else in the document.

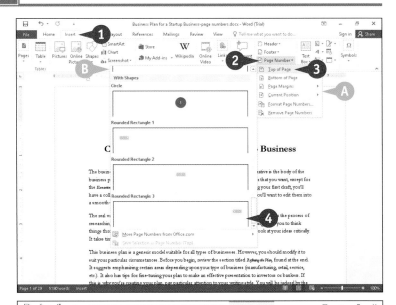

Ⓑ A gallery of page number alignment and formatting options appears.

4 Click an option.

Ⓒ The page number appears in the location and using formatting you selected.

176

D For page numbers placed anywhere *except* at the current position of the insertion point, Word opens the header or footer pane.

E Header & Footer Tools appear on the Ribbon.

F If you do not see the page number, click the **Print Layout** button (▤) on the status bar to display the document in Print Layout.

5 Click **Close Header and Footer** to continue working in your document.

Note: In Print Layout view, all page numbers *except* those placed at the current position of the insertion point appear gray and unavailable for editing. To work with these page numbers, you must open the header or footer pane. See the section "Add a Header or Footer," later in this chapter.

TIP

How can I start each section of my document with page 1?
You can break the document into sections as described in the previous section, "Insert a Section Break," and then use these steps to start each section on page 1:

1 Complete the steps in this section to insert page numbers in your document.

2 Place the insertion point in the second section of your document, and repeat Steps **1** to **3**, selecting **Format Page Numbers** in Step **3**.

The Page Number Format dialog box opens.

3 In the Page Numbering section, select **Start at** (○ changes to ●) and type **1** in the box.

4 Click **OK**.

5 Repeat these steps for each subsequent section of your document.

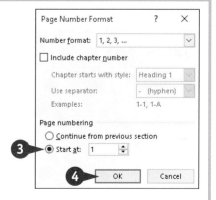

Add Line Numbers to a Document

You can add numbers to the left edge of every line of your document. Line numbers are particularly useful for proofreading; proofreaders can refer to locations in the document by their line numbers. You can number lines in your document continuously, or you can have numbering restart on each page or at each new section. And you can suppress line numbers for selected paragraphs. Line numbers appear on-screen only in Print Layout view.

By default, line numbers appear beside every line in your document, but using line numbering options, you can display lines at intervals you establish.

Add Line Numbers to a Document

Add Line Numbers

1. Click ▤ to display the document in Print Layout view.

2. Click the **Layout** tab.

3. Click **Line Numbers**.

4. Click a line numbering option.

   This example shows **Continuous**.

Ⓐ Word assigns line numbers to each line of your document.

Note: To remove line numbers, complete Steps **1** to **4**, clicking **None** in Step **4**.

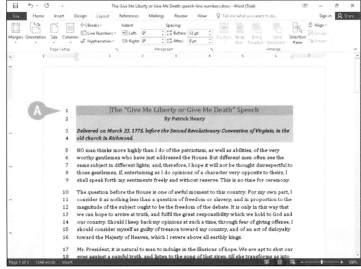

Number in Unusual Increments

1 Repeat Steps **1** to **4**, selecting **Line Numbering Options** in Step **4**.

The Layout tab of the Page Setup dialog box appears.

2 Click **Line Numbers** to display the Line Numbers dialog box.

3 Click the **Count by** ↕ to specify an increment for line numbers.

4 Click **OK** to close the Line Numbers dialog box.

5 Click **OK** to close the Page Setup dialog box.

B Line numbers in the increment you selected appear on-screen.

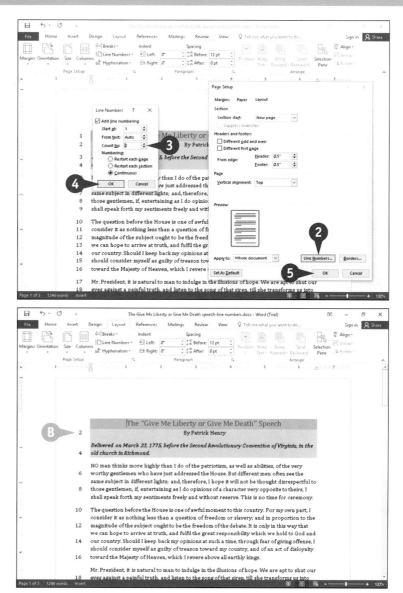

TIP

How can I skip numbering certain lines?

To skip numbering certain lines, such as a page title or introductory text, follow Steps **1** to **4** in the subsection "Add Line Numbers." Then perform the steps that follow: Select the paragraphs for which you do not want to display line numbers. Click the **Layout** tab and click **Line Numbers**. In the Line Numbers dialog box, click **Suppress for Current Paragraph**. Word removes line numbers from the selected paragraph and renumbers subsequent lines.

Using the Building Blocks Organizer

*B*uilding blocks are preformatted text and graphics that you can use to quickly and easily add a splash of elegance and pizzazz to your documents. Some building blocks appear by default as gallery options in Word. And some building blocks provide placeholder text that you replace to customize the building block in your document.

Word organizes building blocks into different galleries, such as cover pages, headers, footers, tables, and text boxes, so that you can sort the building blocks by gallery to easily find something to suit your needs. This section adds a header building block to a document.

Using the Building Blocks Organizer

1 Open a document to which you want to add a building block.

Note: Depending on the type of building block you intend to use, you may need to position the insertion point where you want the building block to appear.

2 Click the **Insert** tab.

3 Click the **Quick Parts** button (▤ ▾).

4 Click **Building Blocks Organizer**.

The Building Blocks Organizer window appears.

Ⓐ Building blocks appear here.

Ⓑ You can preview a building block here.

5 Click a column heading to sort building blocks by that heading.

Sorting by Gallery is most useful to find a building block for a specific purpose.

6 Click a building block.

7 Click **Insert**.

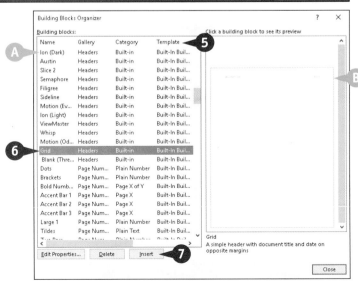

C The building block appears in your document.

This example incorporates a place for a title and date in the header.

8 Click in the building block and fill in any required information.

D For header and footer building blocks, you can make the building block appear on all pages of your document if you do not select **Different First Page**.

E You can click **Close Header and Footer** to continue working in your document.

TIP

How do I know where in my document Word will insert a building block?

Word places a building block in your document based on the building block's properties. Complete Steps **1** to **4** in this section to display the Building Blocks Organizer window. Click a building block and click **Edit Properties** to display the Modify Building Block dialog box. Click the **Options** ∨ (**A**) to determine where a particular building block will appear in your document: in its own paragraph or in its own page.

Add a Header or Footer

I̲f you want to include text at the top or bottom of every page, such as the title of your document, your name, or the date, you can use headers and footers. Header text appears at the top of the page above the margin; footer text appears at the bottom of the page below the margin.

To view header or footer text, you must display the document in Print Layout view. To switch to this view, click the **View** tab and click the **Print Layout** button. Then double-click the top or bottom of the page, respectively, to view the header or footer.

Add a Header or Footer

1 Click the **Insert** tab.

2 Click the **Header** button to add a header, or click the **Footer** button to add a footer.

This example adds a footer.

A The header or footer gallery appears.

3 Click a header or footer style.

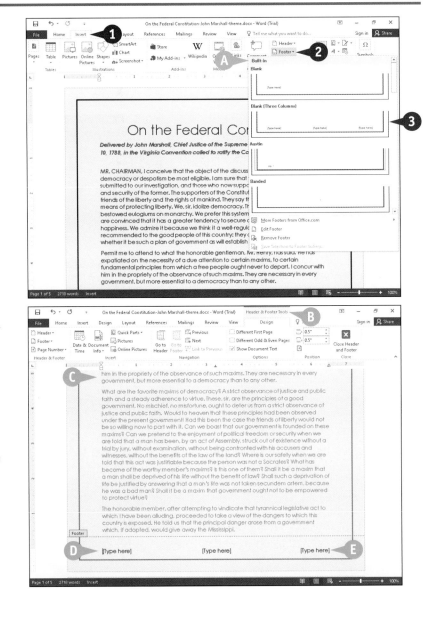

B Word adds the header or footer and displays the Header & Footer Tools tab.

C The text in your document appears dimmed.

D The insertion point appears in the footer area.

E Some footers, like the one shown here, contain information prompts.

④ Click or select an information prompt.

⑤ Type footer information.

⑥ Click **Close Header and Footer**.

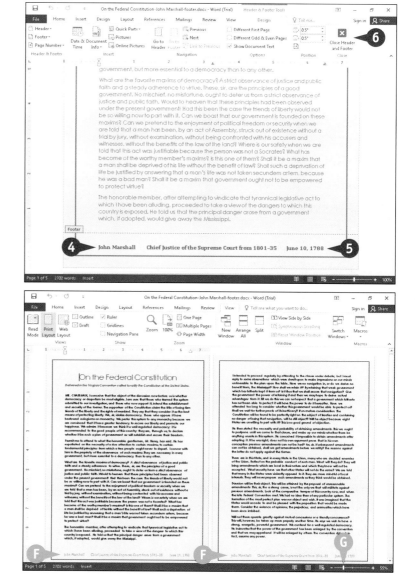

Ⓕ Word closes the Header & Footer Tools tab and displays the header or footer on the document page.

Ⓖ You can zoom out to view the header or footer on multiple pages of your document.

Note: To edit a header or footer, click the **Insert** tab on the Ribbon, click the **Header** or **Footer** button, and click **Edit Header** or **Edit Footer** to redisplay the Header & Footer Tools tab.

Can I format text in a header or footer?
Yes. You can apply boldface, italics, underlining, and other character formatting the same way that you apply them in the body of a document, and you can use styles. Also, the header area and footer area each contain two predefined tabs so that you can center or right-align text you type.

How do I remove a header or footer?
Click the **Insert** tab, click the **Header** or **Footer** button, and click the **Remove Header** or **Remove Footer** command. Word removes the header or footer from your document.

183

Using Different Headers or Footers Within a Document

Y ou can use different headers or footers in different portions of your document. For example, suppose that you are preparing a business plan and you intend to divide it into chapters. You could create separate headers or footers for each chapter. If you plan to use more than one header or footer in your document, insert section breaks before you begin. See the section "Insert a Section Break" for details.

This section shows how to create different headers in your document, but you can use the steps to create different footers by substituting "footer" wherever "header" appears.

Using Different Headers or Footers Within a Document

1 Click in the first section for which you want to create a header.

2 Click the **Insert** tab.

3 Click **Header**.

The Header gallery appears.

4 Click a header.

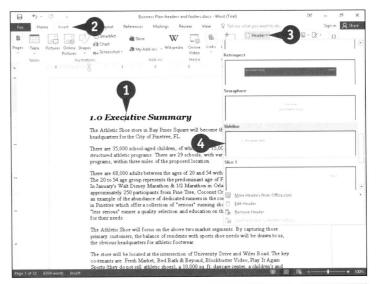

A Word inserts the header in the First Page Header-Section 1 box.

B The text in your document appears dimmed.

C The insertion point appears in the header.

D To make all headers for a section the same, you can deselect **Different First Page** (☑ changes to ☐).

Note: This example uses different first page headers.

5 Type any necessary text in the header.

6 Click **Next** to move the insertion point to the next page of the first section, Header-Section 1.

7 Click **Next** again.

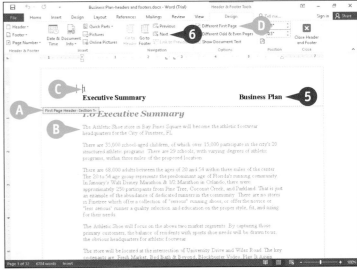

(E) Word moves the insertion point into the header for Section 2.

(F) The First Page Header-Section 2 box appears.

(G) Word identifies the header or footer as "Same as Previous."

8 Click **Link to Previous** to deselect it and unlink the headers of the two sections.

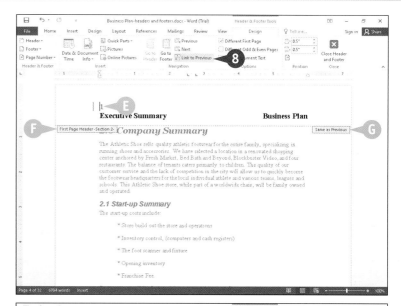

(H) Word removes the "Same as Previous" marking from the right side of the header box.

9 Repeat Steps **2** to **5** to insert a new header in the second section.

This example displays new text on the left side of the header.

10 Repeat these steps for each section for which you want a different header.

11 Click **Close Header and Footer**.

Can I create different headers or footers for odd or even pages?
Yes, and you do not need to insert section breaks. Complete Steps **2** to **5**. Then, on the Design tab of the Header & Footer Tools, click **Different Odd & Even Pages**. Each header or footer box is renamed to Odd Page or Even Page. Click **Next** to switch to the Even Page Header box or the Even Page Footer box and type text.

Add a Footnote

You can include footnotes in your document to identify sources or references to other materials or to add explanatory information. When you add a footnote, a small number appears alongside the associated text, and footnote text appears at the bottom of a page. As you add, delete, and move text in your document, Word also adds, deletes, moves, or renumbers associated footnotes.

Footnotes appear within your document in Print Layout view and Read Mode view. Footnote references appear in the body of your document in all views.

Add a Footnote

1 Click where you want to insert the footnote reference.

2 Click the **References** tab.

3 Click **Insert Footnote**.

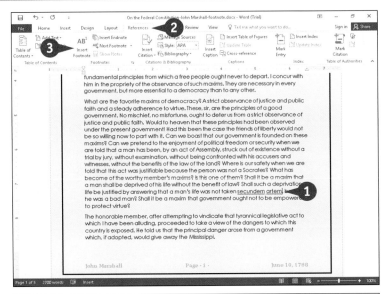

A Word displays the footnote number in the body of the document and in the note at the bottom of the current page.

4 Type the footnote text.

You can double-click the footnote number or press Shift+F5 to return the insertion point to the place in your document where you inserted the footnote.

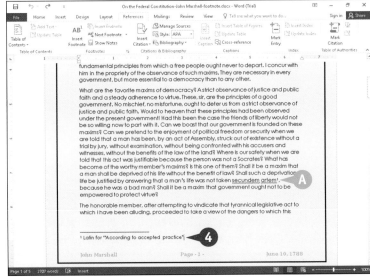

Add an Endnote

You can include endnotes in your document to identify sources or references to other materials or to add explanatory information. Endnotes are automatically numbered i, ii, iii, and so on and, as you add, delete, and move text in your document, Word adds, deletes, moves, or renumbers any associated endnotes. Endnote content appears at the end of your document in Print Layout view and Read Mode view. Endnote references appear in the body of your document in all views.

Add an Endnote

1 Click where you want to insert the endnote reference.

A In this example, the endnote number appears on page 1.

2 Click the **References** tab.

3 Click **Insert Endnote**.

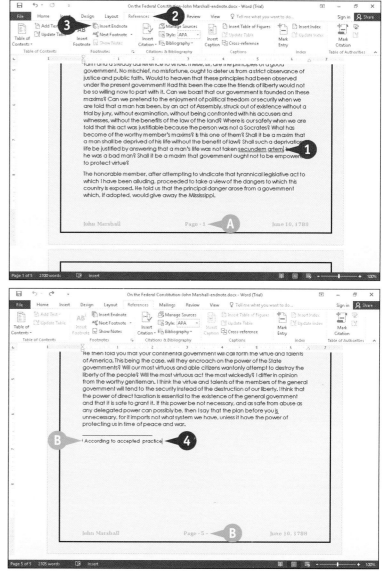

Word inserts the endnote number in the body of your document.

B Word inserts the endnote number at the end of your document and displays the insertion point in the endnote area at the bottom of the last page of the document.

4 Type your endnote text.

You can double-click the endnote number or press Shift + F5 to return the insertion point to the place in your document where you inserted the endnote.

Find, Edit, or Delete Footnotes or Endnotes

As you work, you might find that you need to edit or delete the content of a footnote or an endnote. To make changes to a footnote or an endnote, you must first find the footnote or endnote reference and the associated footnote or endnote text.

You can work in any view to find, edit, or delete a footnote or an endnote. Remember that you do not need to worry about renumbering or moving footnotes or endnotes because Word handles those functions for you automatically. Although you can include both footnotes and endnotes, most documents typically have only one type of note.

Find, Edit, or Delete Footnotes or Endnotes

Find Footnotes or Endnotes

1 Press **Ctrl**+**Home** to move the insertion point to the top of the document.

2 Click **References**.

3 Click ▼ beside the **Next Footnote** button.

4 Click an option to find the next or previous footnote or endnote.

Word moves the insertion point to the reference number of the next or previous note.

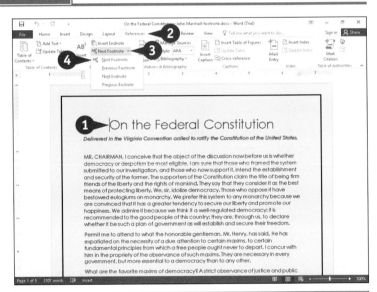

Edit Footnotes or Endnotes

Note: To easily edit endnotes, skip Steps **1** and **2**. Instead, press **Ctrl**+**End** to move the insertion point to the end of the document.

1 Select the footnote reference number in your document.

2 Double-click the selection.

Ⓐ In Print Layout view, Word moves the insertion point into the footnote.

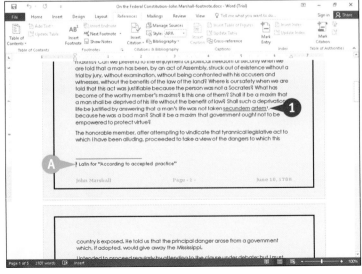

B In Draft view, Word displays footnotes in the Footnotes pane.

3 Edit the text of the note as needed.

4 In Draft view, click the **Close** button (✖) when you finish editing.

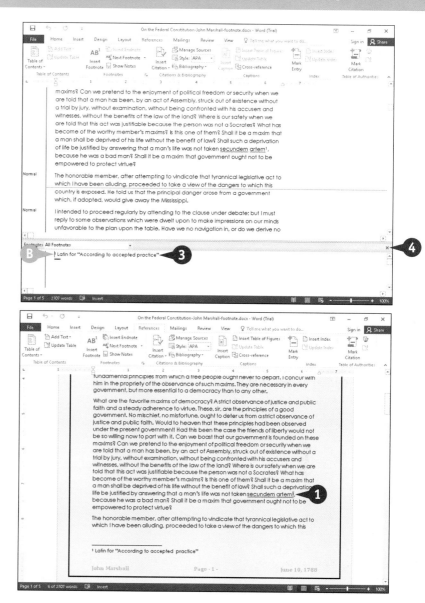

Delete a Footnote or Endnote

1 Select the reference number of the footnote or endnote you want to delete.

2 Press Delete.

Word removes the footnote or endnote number and related information from the document and automatically renumbers subsequent footnotes or endnotes.

Can I print endnotes on a separate page?
Yes. Click in your document before the first endnote. Then, click the **Insert** tab and click **Page Break**. Word inserts a page break immediately before the endnotes, placing them on a separate page at the end of your document.

Convert Footnotes to Endnotes

You can convert endnotes to footnotes or footnotes to endnotes. Converting footnotes to endnotes or endnotes to footnotes gives you the flexibility to try one type of note and then decide that you prefer the other type of note. Converting notes also helps if you accidentally enter one type of note when you meant to enter the other type. You do not need to delete existing notes of one type and then reenter them as the other type of note. Instead, you can save time by converting footnotes or endnotes.

Although you can include both footnotes and endnotes, people typically use only one type of note.

Convert Footnotes to Endnotes

1 Click the **References** tab.

2 Click the Footnotes group dialog box launcher (⌐).

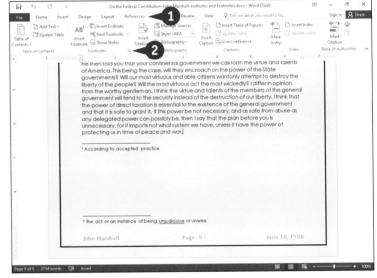

The Footnote and Endnote dialog box appears.

3 Click **Convert**.

The Convert Notes dialog box appears.

4 Select the option that describes what you want to do (○ changes to ◉).

5 Click **OK** to redisplay the Footnote and Endnote dialog box.

In the Footnote and Endnote dialog box, Cancel changes to Close.

6 Click **Close**.

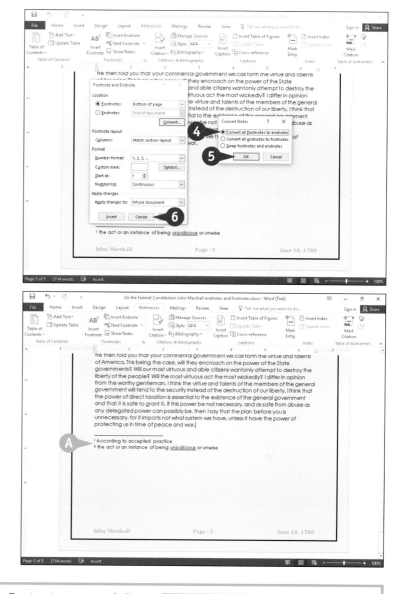

A Word makes the conversion and renumbers footnotes and endnotes appropriately.

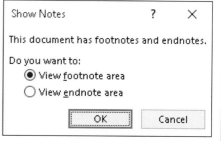

TIP

What does the Show Notes button in the Footnotes group do?
If your document contains only footnotes or only endnotes, Word jumps to the footnote section on the current page or the endnote section at the end of the document. If your document contains both footnotes and endnotes, Word displays this dialog box so that you can select an option to view.

Show Notes   ?   ✕

This document has footnotes and endnotes.

Do you want to:
◉ View footnote area
○ View endnote area

OK   Cancel

Generate a Table of Contents

You can use Word to generate a table of contents (TOC) for your document that automatically updates as you change your document. You select from Word's gallery of TOC styles to establish the TOC's look and feel. You can most easily create a TOC if you apply heading styles — Heading 1, Heading 2, and Heading 3 — to text that should appear in the TOC. Word searches for text that you format using a heading style and includes that text in the TOC.

You can create a table of contents at any time, continue working, and update the table of contents automatically with new information whenever you want.

Generate a Table of Contents

Insert a Table of Contents

1 Place the insertion point in your document where you want the table of contents to appear.

A This example places the table of contents on a blank page after the cover page of a report.

2 Click the **References** tab.

3 Click **Table of Contents**.

The Table of Contents gallery appears.

4 Click a table of contents layout.

B Word inserts a table of contents at the location of the insertion point.

The information in the table of contents comes from text to which Heading styles 1, 2, and 3 are applied.

You can continue working in your document, adding new text styled with heading styles.

Note: Do not type directly in the table of contents; make corrections in the document.

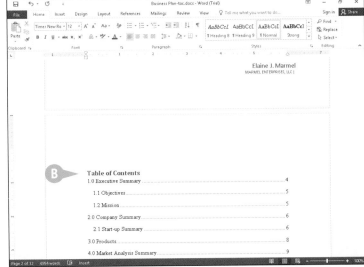

Update the Table of Contents

1. Add or change text styled with heading styles or remove heading styles from text in your document.

2. Click anywhere in the table of contents.

3. Click **Update Table**.

   The Update Table of Contents dialog box appears.

4. Select **Update entire table** (○ changes to ◉).

5. Click **OK**.

C. Word updates the table of contents to reflect your changes.

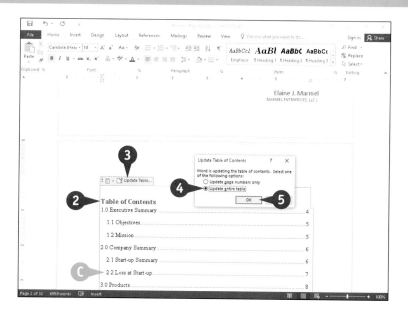

TIP

Can I include additional heading styles, such as Heading 4, in the table of contents?
Yes. Simply follow these steps:

1. Complete Steps **2** to **4** in the subsection "Insert a Table of Contents," selecting **Custom Table of Contents** in Step **4** to display the Table of Contents dialog box.

2. Click the **Show levels** ↕ to change the number of heading styles included in the table of contents.

3. Click **OK**.

   Word prompts you to replace the current table of contents.

4. Click **Yes** to update the table of contents.

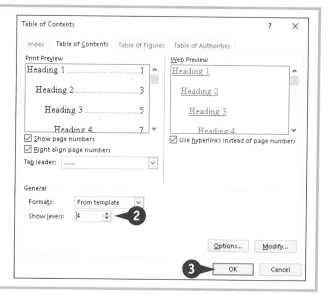

Add a Watermark

You can add a watermark to your document to add interest or convey a message. A watermark is faint text that appears behind information in a document. For example, you can place a watermark on a document that marks it confidential or urgent. Or you can place a watermark on a document to mark it as the original or as a copy. Using a "Draft" watermark can help distinguish a final copy from a review copy. And for material that should not be reproduced, you can apply a "Do Not Copy" watermark.

Watermarks are visible in Print Layout view and when you print your document.

Add a Watermark

1. Click 📄 to display your document in Print Layout view.

2. Click the **Design** tab.

3. Click **Watermark**.

Ⓐ If you see the watermark you want to use in the Watermark gallery, you can click it and skip the rest of the steps in this section.

4. Click **Custom Watermark**.

The Printed Watermark dialog box appears.

5. Select **Text watermark** (○ changes to ◉).

6. Click ❤ and select the text to use as a watermark or type your own text.

Ⓑ You can use these options to control the font, size, color, intensity, and layout of the watermark.

7. Click **OK**.

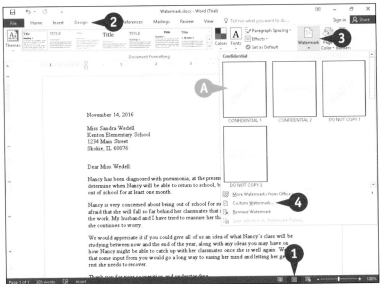

C Word displays the watermark on each page of your document.

TIP

What happens if I select the Picture Watermark option in the Printed Watermark dialog box?

Word enables you to select a picture stored on your hard drive or to search online using Bing to select a picture as the watermark in your document. Follow these steps:

1 Follow Steps **1** to **5**, selecting **Picture watermark** in Step **5**.

2 In the Printed Watermark dialog box, click **Select Picture**.

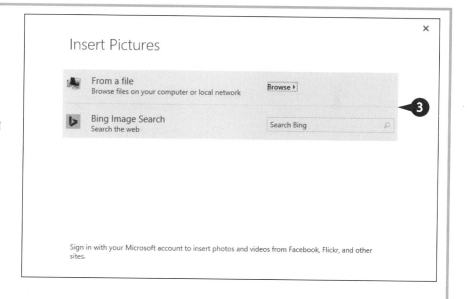

3 In the Insert Picture dialog box, navigate to and insert the picture you want to use as a watermark.

4 Click **OK** in the Printed Watermark dialog box to add the picture watermark to your document.

Add a Page Border

You can add a border around each page of your document to add interest or make the document aesthetically appealing. You also can add borders around single or multiple paragraphs, as described in Chapter 6, but be careful not to use too many effects; you risk making your document difficult to read. For example, do not use both paragraph and page borders.

You can apply one of Word's predesigned borders to your document, or you can create your own custom border — for example, bordering only the top and bottom of each page.

Add a Page Border

① Click ▤ to display your document in Print Layout view.

② Click the **Design** tab.

③ Click **Page Borders**.

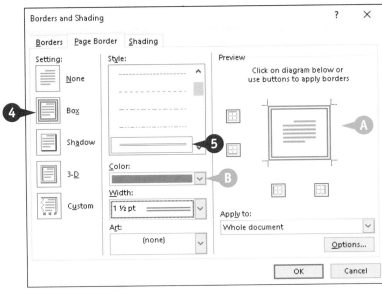

The Borders and Shading dialog box appears, displaying the Page Border tab.

④ Click the type of border you want to add to your document.

⑤ Click a style for the border line.

Ⓐ This area shows a preview of the border.

Ⓑ You can click ⌄ to select a color for the border from the palette that appears.

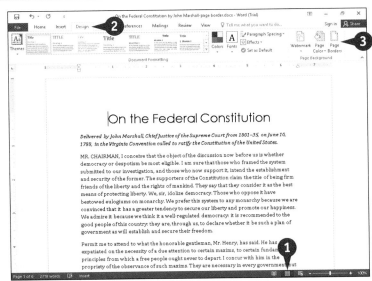

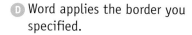 You can click ✔ to select a width for the border.

6 Click ✔ to specify the pages on which the border should appear.

7 Click **OK**.

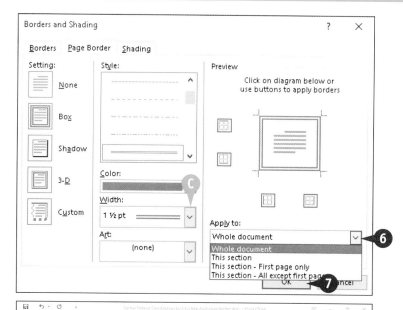

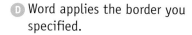 Word applies the border you specified.

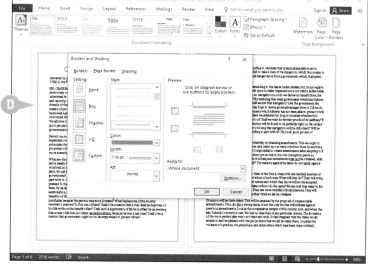

TIP

Can I add a border that does not surround the page?
Yes. Complete Steps **1** to **6** to select the border you want to apply. In the Preview area, click the border lines that you do not want to appear in your document (Ⓐ). Click **OK**, and Word applies the modified page border.

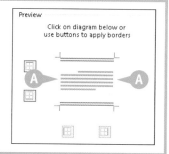

Apply Document Formatting

Y ou can give a professional look to a document using document formatting. You can apply a document *theme*, which consists of a set of theme colors that affect fonts, lines, and fill effects. Applying a theme to a document is a quick way to add polish to it. And once you apply a theme, you also can apply *style sets*, which vary the fonts.

The effect of applying a theme is more obvious if you have assigned styles such as headings to your document. The effects of themes are even more pronounced when you assign a background color to a page.

Apply Document Formatting

Apply a Theme

1 Open a document.

The document uses the default Office theme colors and styles for its fonts, lines, page color, and fill effects.

2 Click the **Design** tab.

3 Click **Themes**.

Note: You can point at a theme, and Live Preview will show you how the document would look using that theme.

4 Click a theme.

Your document appears using the theme you selected.

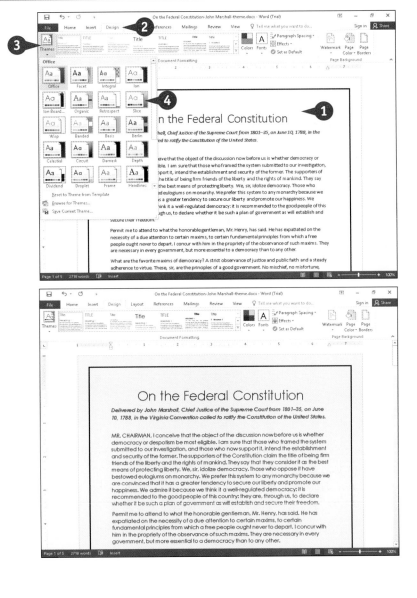

Apply a Style Set

1. Complete Steps **1** to **4** in the previous subsection.

2. Click the **Design** tab.

3. Point the mouse (⬉) at various style sets.

Note: Live Preview shows you how the document would look using that style set.

4. Click a style set.

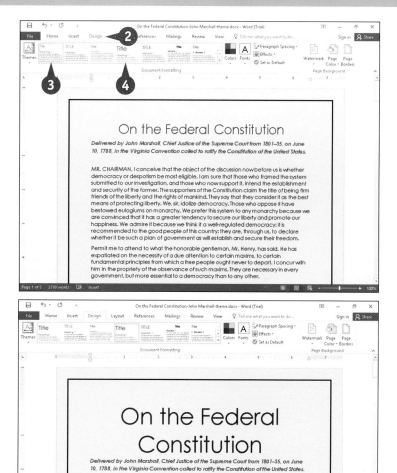

Your document appears using the style set you selected.

How can I make the effects of my theme more obvious?

The effects of applying a theme become more obvious if you have applied heading styles and a background color to your document. To apply a background color, click the **Design** tab, click **Page Color** (Ⓐ), and click a color in the palette (Ⓑ); Word applies the color you selected to the background of the page. For help applying a style, see Chapter 6.

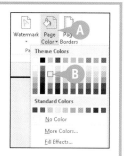

Create Newspaper Columns

You can create columns in Word to present your text in a format similar to a newspaper or magazine, where columnar information runs from the bottom of one column to the top of the next column. For example, if you are creating a brochure or newsletter, you can use columns to make text flow from one block to the next.

If you simply want to create a document with two or three columns, you can use one of Word's preset columns. Alternatively, you can create custom columns, choosing the number of columns you want to create in your document, indicating the width of each column, and more.

Create Newspaper Columns

Create Quick Columns

Note: If you want to apply columns to only a portion of your text, select that text.

① Click the **Layout** tab.

② Click the **Columns** button.

③ Click the number of columns that you want to assign.

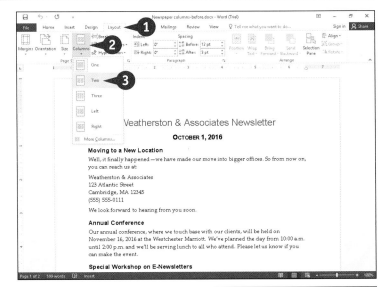

Word displays your document in the number of columns that you specify.

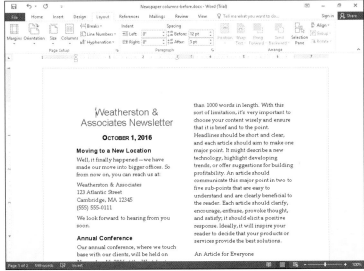

Create Custom Columns

Note: If you want to apply columns to only a portion of your text, select that text.

1 Click the **Layout** tab.

2 Click **Columns**.

3 Click **More Columns**.

The Columns dialog box appears.

4 Click ↕ to select the number of columns you want.

A You can select this option (☐ changes to ☑) to include a vertical line separating the columns.

5 Deselect this option to set exact widths for each column (☑ changes to ☐).

6 Set an exact column width and spacing here.

B You can click ⌄ to specify whether the columns apply to the selected text or the entire document.

7 Click **OK**.

Word applies the column format to the selected text.

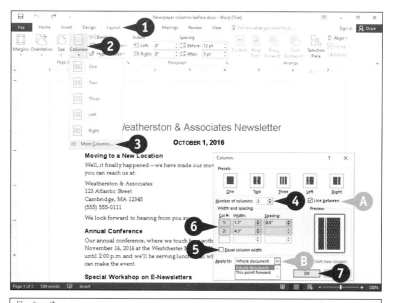

How do I wrap column text around a picture or other object?

Click the picture or other object that you want to wrap, click the **Format** tab, click the **Wrap Text** button, and then click the type of wrapping that you want to apply.

Can I create a break within a column?

Yes. To add a column break, click where you want the break to occur and then press Ctrl+Shift+Enter. To remove a break, select it and press Delete. To return to a one-column format, click the **Columns** button on the Layout tab, and then select the single-column format.

CHAPTER 8

Printing Documents

After your document looks the way you want it to look, you are ready to distribute it. In this chapter, you learn how to preview and print documents, print envelopes, and print labels.

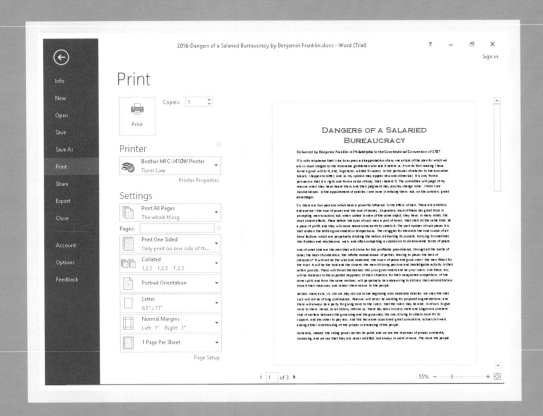

Preview and Print a Document

If your computer is connected to a printer, you can print your Word documents. For example, you might print a document to look for layout errors and other possible formatting inconsistencies or to distribute it as a handout in a meeting.

When you print a document, you have two options. You can send a document directly to the printer using the default settings, or you can change these settings. For example, you might opt to print just a portion of the document or print using a different printer. You can preview your document before you print it.

Preview and Print a Document

1 Open the document you want to print.

Note: To print only selected text, select that text.

2 Click the **File** tab.

Backstage view appears.

3 Click **Print**.

Ⓐ A preview of your document appears here.

4 Click these arrows (◀ and ▶) to page through your document.

5 To magnify the page, drag the **Zoom** slider.

6 To print more than one copy, type the number of copies to print here or click ⏶.

7 Click ▼ to select a printer.

8 Click ▼ to select what to print.

Ⓑ You can print the entire document, text you selected, or only the current page.

Ⓒ You can click ▲ and ▼ to select document elements to print, such as document properties or a list of styles used in the document.

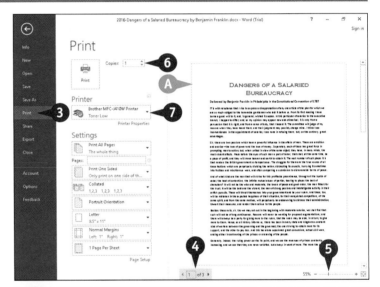

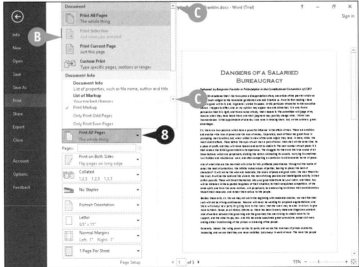

9 To print noncontiguous pages, type the pages you want to print, such as **1,5,6-9** or **1,3-4** in the **Pages** box.

10 To print the document, click the **Print** button.

D If you change your mind and do not want to print, click the **Back** button (⊙) to return to the document window.

What other print options can I set?

In the Settings section, click buttons to select options:

Option	Purpose
Print on Both Sides — Flip pages on long edge	Determine whether to print on one or both sides of the paper.
Collated — 1,2,3 1,2,3 1,2,3	When printing multiple copies, specify whether to collate the copies or print multiple copies of each page at the same time.
Portrait Orientation	Choose to print in Portrait or Landscape orientation.
Letter — 8.5" x 11"	Select a paper size.
Normal Margins — Left: 1" Right: 1"	Select page margins.
1 Page Per Sheet	Specify the number of pages to print on a single sheet of paper.

Print on Different Paper Sizes

You can print one part of your document on one size of paper and another part on a different size of paper. For example, you may want to print one portion of your document on legal-sized paper to accommodate a particularly long table and then print the rest of the document on letter-sized paper.

You must insert section breaks in your document for each portion of the document that you want to print on different paper sizes. To learn how to insert section breaks, see Chapter 7.

Print on Different Paper Sizes

1 After dividing your document into sections, place the insertion point in the section that you want to print on a different paper size.

2 Click the **Layout** tab.

3 Click the Page Setup group dialog box launcher (⌐).

The Page Setup dialog box appears, displaying the Margins tab.

4 Click the **Paper** tab.

5 Click ∨, and select the paper size you want to use.

A The width and height of the paper size you select appear here.

B A preview of your selection appears here.

6 Click a paper tray for the first page in the section.

7 Click a paper tray for the rest of the section.

8 Click the **Apply to** ⌄.

9 Click **This section**.

10 Repeat Steps **1** to **9** for other sections of the document.

11 Click **OK** to save your changes.

TIP

What happens when I click Print Options in the Page Setup dialog box?
The Display tab of the Word Options dialog box appears. In the Printing Options section, you can select check boxes to control the printing of various Word elements.

Printing options

- ☑ Print drawings created in Word ⓘ
- ☐ Print background colors and images
- ☐ Print document properties
- ☐ Print hidden text
- ☐ Update fields before printing
- ☐ Update linked data before printing

Print an Envelope

If your printer supports printing envelopes, Word can print a delivery and return address on an envelope for you. You also can have Word automatically fill in the recipient's name and address. Word checks the currently open document for information that appears to be an address; if Word finds an address, Word fills in the address automatically. To save yourself time and typing, open the letter you intend to mail before you follow the steps in this section to print the envelope.

Consult your printer manual to determine whether your printer supports printing envelopes.

Print an Envelope

1 Click the **Mailings** tab.

2 Click **Envelopes**.

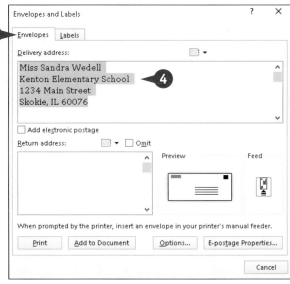

The Envelopes and Labels dialog box appears.

3 Click the **Envelopes** tab.

Note: If Word finds an address near the top of your document, it displays and selects that address in the Delivery Address box.

4 You can type a delivery address.

You can remove an existing address by pressing Delete.

By default, Word displays no return address in the Return Address box.

5 Click here to type a return address.

6 Click **Print**.

A dialog box appears if you supplied a return address.

Note: If you save the return address, Word displays it each time you print an envelope and does not display this dialog box.

7 Click **Yes**.

Word saves the return address as the default return address and prints the envelope.

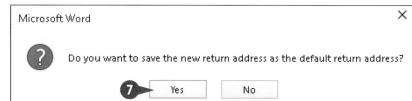

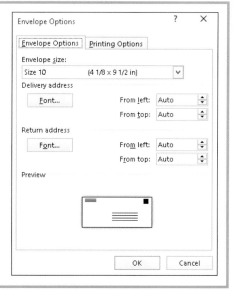

TIP

What happens if I click Options in the Envelopes and Labels dialog box?

Word displays the Envelope Options dialog box. On the Envelope Options tab, you can set the envelope size, include a delivery bar code, and set fonts for the delivery and return addresses. On the Printing Options tab, you can set the feed method and tray for your printer.

Set Up Labels to Print

You can format a Word document so that you can use it to type and print labels using an assortment of standard labels from a variety of vendors, including Avery, 3M, Microsoft, Office Depot, and Staples, to name just a few. Printing address labels is useful when you need to mail packages or envelopes that are not letter size. You also are not limited to printing address labels; for example, you can create name tag and file folder labels. This section demonstrates how to create a blank page of address labels onto which you can type address label information.

Set Up Labels to Print

1 Click the **Mailings** tab.

2 Click **Labels**.

The Envelopes and Labels dialog box appears.

3 Click the **Labels** tab.

Ⓐ This area shows the label currently selected.

4 Click **Options**.

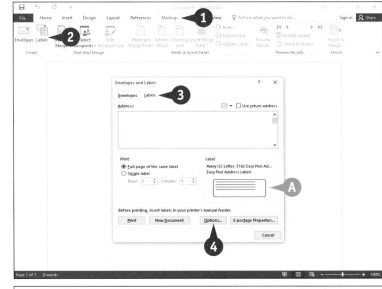

The Label Options dialog box appears.

5 In this area, select the type of printer and printer tray to print labels (○ changes to ●).

6 Click ∨ to select the vendor that makes your labels.

7 Click the product number of your labels.

8 Click **OK**.

9 Click **New Document** in the Envelopes and Labels dialog box.

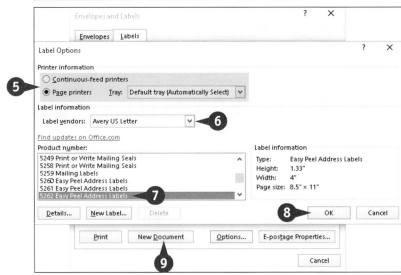

Word displays a blank document, set up for label information.

10 If you do not see gridlines separating labels, click the **Table Tools Layout** tab.

11 Click **View Gridlines**.

12 Type a label.

13 Press `Tab` to move to the next label and type an address.

Note: To print labels, see the section "Preview and Print a Document," earlier in this chapter.

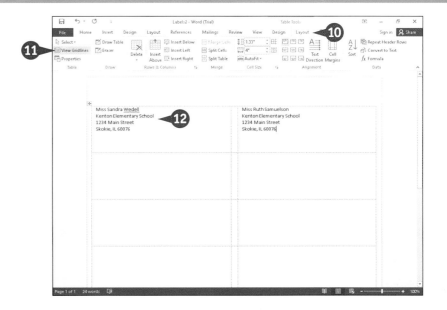

TIP

Can I print a single label?

1 Complete Steps **1** to **3** in this section to display the Labels tab in the Envelopes and Labels dialog box.

2 Select **Single label** (○ changes to ●).

3 Type the row and column of the label on the label sheet that you want to use.

4 Click here to display the Label Options dialog box and select the label you use (refer to Steps **5** to **8**).

5 Type the label information here.

6 Click **Print**, and Word prints the single label.

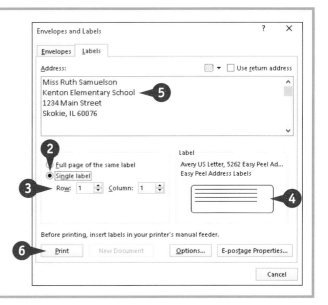

CHAPTER 9

Working with Tables and Charts

Do you want to keep the information in your Word document easy to read? The answer may very well be to add a table to contain your data. In this chapter, you learn how to create and work with tables in Word.

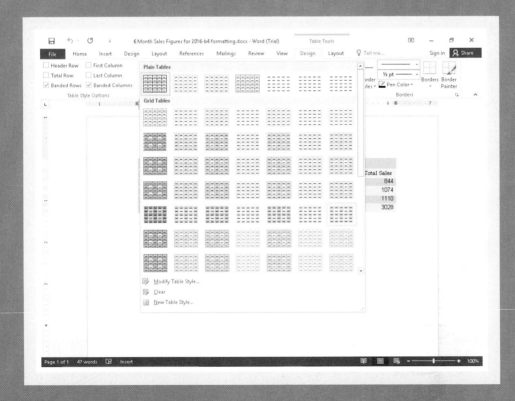

Create a Table

You can use tables to present data in an organized fashion. For example, you might add a table to your document to display a list of items or a roster of classes. Tables contain columns and rows, which intersect to form *cells*. You can insert all types of data in cells, including text and graphics.

To enter text in cells, click in the cell and then type your data. As you type, Word wraps the text to fit in the cell. Press Tab to move from one cell to another. You can select table cells, rows, and columns to perform editing tasks and apply formatting.

Create a Table

Insert a Table

1. Click in the document where you want to insert a table.

2. Click the **Insert** tab.

3. Click the **Table** button.

Ⓐ Word displays a table grid.

4. Slide the mouse (⬚) across the squares that represent the number of rows and columns you want in your table.

Ⓑ Word previews the table as you drag over cells.

5. Click the square representing the lower right corner of your table.

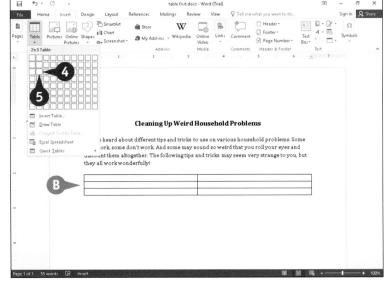

The table appears in your document.

C Table Tools appear on the Ribbon.

6 Click in a table cell and type information.

D If necessary, Word expands the row height to accommodate the text.

You can press `Tab` to move the insertion point to the next cell.

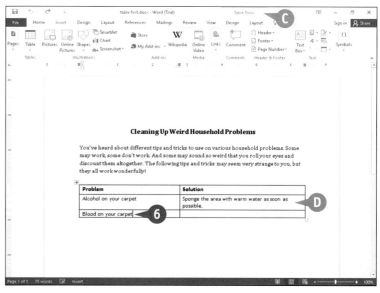

Delete a Table

1 Click anywhere in the table you want to delete.

2 Click the **Table Tools Layout** tab.

3 Click **Delete**.

4 Click Delete Table.

Word removes the table and its contents from your document.

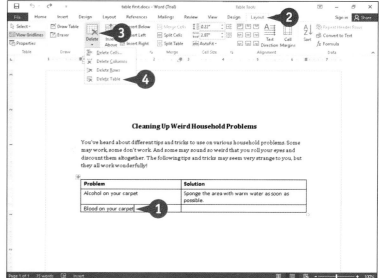

TIPS

Can I add rows to a table?
Yes. To add a row to the bottom of the table, place the insertion point in the last cell and press `Tab`. To add a row anywhere else, use the buttons in the Rows & Columns section of the Layout tab.

What, exactly, is a table cell?
Cell refers to the intersection of a row and a column. In spreadsheet programs, columns are named with letters, rows are named with numbers, and cells are named using the column letter and row number. For example, the cell at the intersection of Column A and Row 2 is called A2.

Change the Row Height or Column Width

You can change the height of rows or the width of columns to accommodate your table information. Be aware that Word changes row height automatically to accommodate information but leaves column width unchanged unless you take action to change a column's width. Most people change row height or column width to improve the appearance of their table.

You cannot change either row height or column width unless you work in Print Layout view or Web Layout view, so use the buttons on the status bar to switch to one of these views before you try to change row height or column width.

Change the Row Height or Column Width

Change the Row Height

1 Click the **Print Layout** button (▤) or the **Web Layout** button (▨).

2 Position the mouse over the bottom of the row you want to change (I changes to ↕).

3 Drag the row edge up to shorten or down to lengthen the row height.

Ⓐ A dotted line marks the proposed bottom of the row.

4 When the row height suits you, release the mouse button.

Ⓑ Word adjusts the row height.

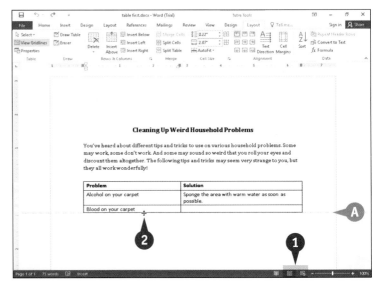

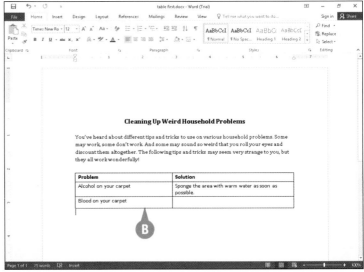

Change the Column Width

1 Position the mouse over the right side of the column you want to change (I changes to +‖+).

2 Drag the column edge right to widen or left to narrow the column width.

C A dotted line marks the proposed right side of the column.

3 Release the mouse.

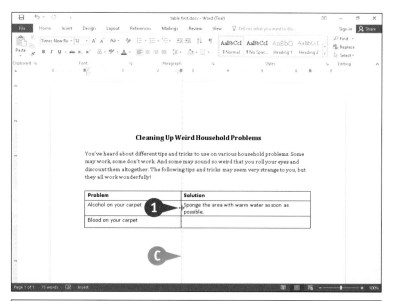

D Word adjusts the column width.

Note: For any column except the rightmost column, changing a column's width also changes the width of the column to its right, but the overall table size remains constant. When you change the width of the rightmost column, you change the width of the entire table.

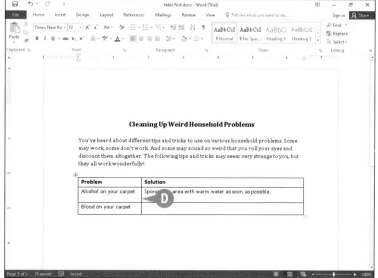

TIPS

I tried to change the row height, but the mouse pointer did not change, and I could not drag the row. What did I do wrong?

You can change row height only when displaying your document in either Print Layout view or Web Layout view. Make sure you select one of those views by clicking ▤ or ▥. See Chapter 3 for more on understanding document views and switching between them.

Can I easily make a column the size that accommodates the longest item in it?

Yes. Double-click the right edge of the column. Word widens or narrows the column based on the longest entry in the column and adjusts the overall table size.

Move a Table

You can move a table to a different location in your document. You might discover, for example, that you inserted a table prematurely in your document and, as you continue to work, you decide that the table would better help you make your point if you move it to a location farther down in your document. You do not need to reinsert the table and reenter its information; instead, move it.

Make sure that you are working from Print Layout or Web Layout view; you can use the buttons on the status bar or on the View tab to switch views if necessary.

Move a Table

1 Click the **Print Layout** button (▤) or the **Web Layout** button (▥).

2 Position the mouse (I) over the table.

A A table selection handle (⊞) appears in the upper left corner of the table.

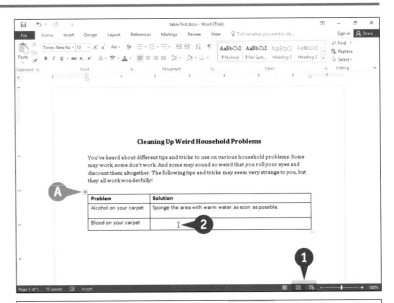

3 Position the mouse over the table selection handle (⊞); (I changes to ⇲).

4 Drag the table to a new location (⇲ changes to ✛).

B A dashed line represents the proposed table position.

5 Release the mouse button.

The table appears in the new location.

To copy the table, perform these steps but press and hold Ctrl in Step **3**.

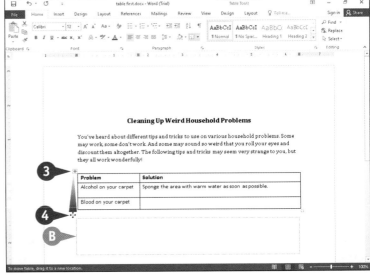

Resize a Table

I f your table dimensions do not suit your purpose, you can resize the table from Print Layout view or Web Layout view. For example, you may want to resize a table to make it longer and narrower, especially if your table is small; in that case, you could reduce the space occupied by the table and wrap text in your document around it using the Table Properties box.

Resize a Table

1 Click the **Print Layout** button (▤) or the **Web Layout** button (▦).

2 Position the mouse (I) over the table.

Ⓐ A handle (□) appears in the lower right corner of the table.

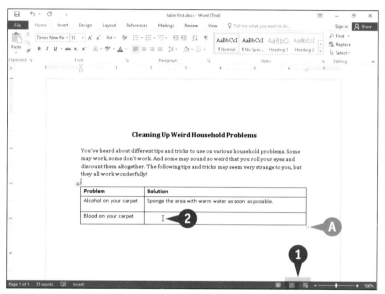

3 Position the mouse over the handle (I changes to ⬉).

4 Drag up, down, left, right, or diagonally to adjust the table's size (⬉ changes to +).

Note: Dragging diagonally simultaneously changes the table width and height.

Ⓑ The table outline displays the proposed table size.

5 Release the mouse button to change the table's size.

Note: On the Table Tools Layout tab, you can click **Properties** to control how text wraps around the outside of your table.

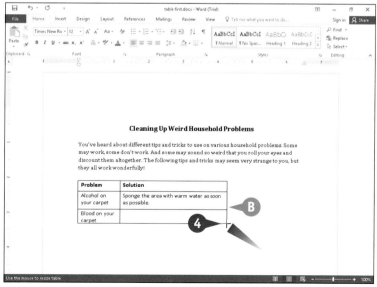

Add or Delete a Row

You can easily add rows to accommodate more information or remove rows of information you do not need. Word automatically adds rows to the bottom of a table if you place the insertion point in the last table cell and press **Tab**. If you accidentally insert an extra row at the bottom of the table, you can delete it. If you need additional rows in the middle of your table to accommodate additional information, you can insert extra rows.

To add a new first row to your table, see the first tip at the end of this section.

Add or Delete a Row

Add a Row

1 Slide I outside the left edge of the row below where you want a new row to appear.

A I changes to ⬈ and a plus sign (⊕) attached to a pair of horizontal lines that span the width of the table appears.

2 Click ⊕.

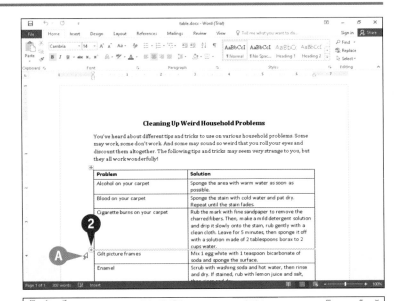

B Word inserts a row above the row you identified in Step **1** and selects it.

When you slide the mouse away from the row, ⊕ disappears. You can click in the row to add information to the table.

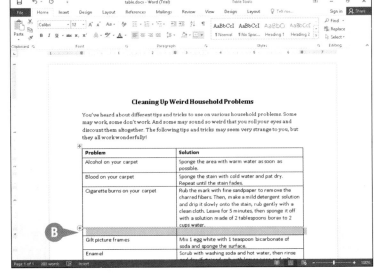

Delete a Row

1 Click anywhere in the row you want to delete.

2 Click the **Table Tools Layout** tab.

3 Click **Delete**.

4 Click **Delete Rows**.

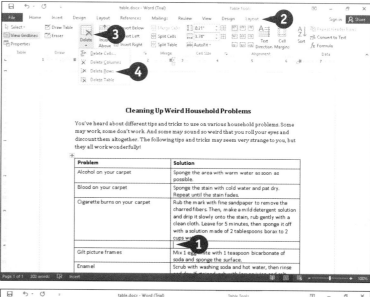

C Word removes the row and any text it contained from the table.

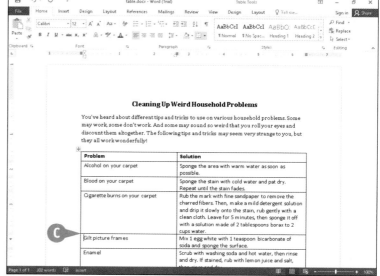

How can I insert a new first row in my table?

Place the insertion point anywhere in the first table row. Click the **Layout** tab and then click **Insert Above**.

Can I delete more than one row at a time?

Yes. Select the rows you want to delete and perform Steps **2** to **4** in the subsection "Delete a Row." To select the rows, position the mouse (⇗) outside the left side of the table. Drag to select the rows you want to delete. The same approach works for inserting rows; select the number of rows you want to insert before you begin.

Add or Delete a Column

You can add or delete columns to change the structure of a table to accommodate more or less information. If you need additional columns in the middle of your table, you can insert extra columns. If you insert too many extra columns, you can delete those columns, too. When you add columns, Word decreases the size of the other columns to accommodate the new column but retains the overall size of the table.

Add or Delete a Column

Add a Column

Note: If you need to add a column to the left side of your table, click anywhere in the first column and, on the Table Tools Layout tab, click the **Insert Left** button.

1 Slide the mouse (I) outside the top edge of the column to the left of the column you want to add.

A I changes to ⬚ and a plus sign (⊕) attached to a pair of vertical lines that span the height of the table appears.

2 Click ⊕.

B Word inserts a new column in the table to the right of the column you identified in Step **1** and selects the new column.

Note: Word maintains the table's overall width.

You can click in the column to add text to it.

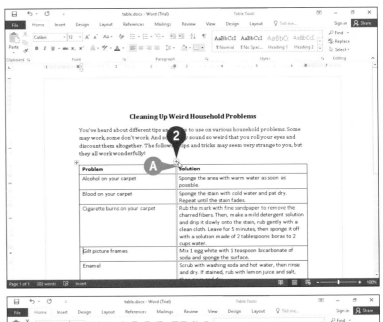

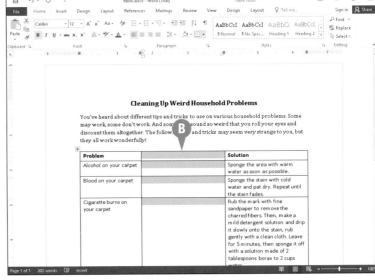

Delete a Column

1 Click anywhere in the column you want to delete.

2 Click the **Table Tools Layout** tab.

3 Click **Delete**.

4 Click **Delete Columns**.

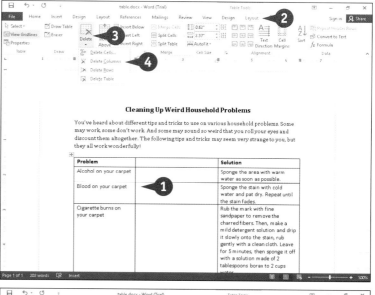

C Word removes the column and any text it contained from the table.

D The insertion point appears in the column to the right of the one you deleted.

Word does not resize existing columns to use the space previously occupied by the deleted column.

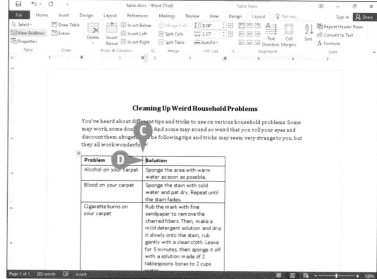

TIP

Is there a way I can easily enlarge a table to fill up the space between the left and right margins after deleting a column?

Yes. Click anywhere in the table. Then, click the **Table Tools Layout** tab, click **AutoFit** in the Cell Size group, and then click **AutoFit Window** (**A**). The table content and columns readjust to fill the space.

Set Cell Margins

You can set margins in table cells to make table information more legible. For example, you might want to use the top and bottom margins of table cells to add space above and below text in the cells of your table. When you increase top and bottom cell margins, you create more space between rows of the table, making table information easier to read. You also can adjust left and right cell margins to add more space vertically between cells, again creating an easier-to-read table. When you adjust cell margins, you can have Word automatically adjust the cell contents within the margins.

Set Cell Margins

1 Click anywhere in the table.

2 Click the **Table Tools Layout** tab.

3 Click Cell Margins.

The Table Options dialog box appears.

4 Type margin settings here.

5 Click **OK**.

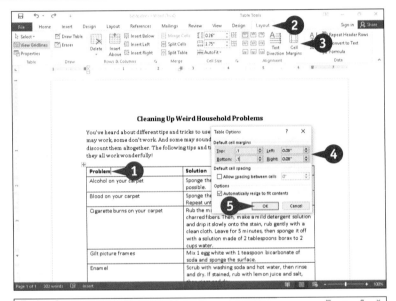

Ⓐ Word applies cell margin settings.

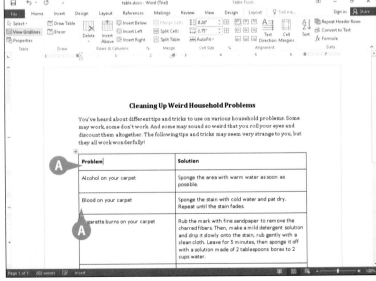

Add Space Between Cells

You can set spacing between table cells. When you allow additional spacing between cells, Word applies the spacing both horizontally and vertically; you cannot allow additional space in only one direction. To adjust space in only one direction, adjust cell margins as described in the previous section, "Set Cell Margins." When you adjust cell margins, you can have Word automatically adjust the cell contents within the margins.

Add Space Between Cells

1 Click anywhere in the table.

2 Click the **Table Tools Layout** tab.

3 Click Cell Margins.

The Table Options dialog box appears.

4 Select **Allow spacing between cells** (☐ changes to ☑) and type a setting for space between cells.

5 Click **OK**.

Ⓐ Word adds space between cells.

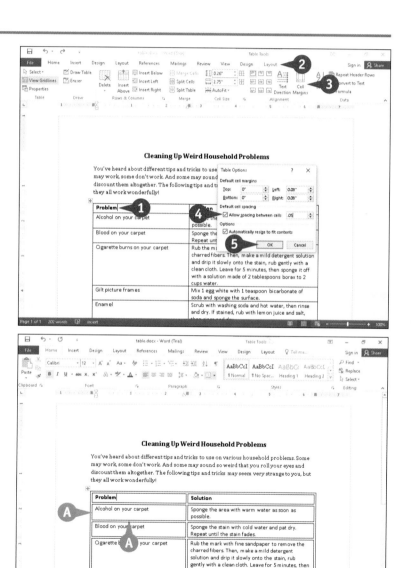

Combine Cells

You can combine two or more cells to create one large cell in which you can store, for example, a table title. Word uses the term *merge* for this function.

You cannot add a single cell to a table; you must add either a row or a column. To create a single cell that stores a table title, insert a table row as described in the section "Add or Delete a Row," earlier in this chapter. Then use the steps in this section to combine the cells of that row into a row that contains one cell that spans the width of the table.

Combine Cells

1 Slide the mouse inside and at the left edge of the first cell you want to merge (I changes to ➚).

2 Drag the mouse (➚) across the cells you want to merge to select them.

3 Click the **Table Tools Layout** tab.

4 Click **Merge Cells**.

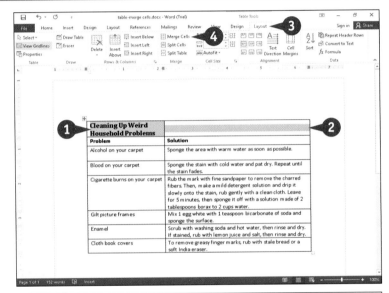

A Word combines the cells into one cell and selects that cell.

To center a table title, see the section "Align Text in Cells," later in this chapter.

You can click anywhere to cancel the selection.

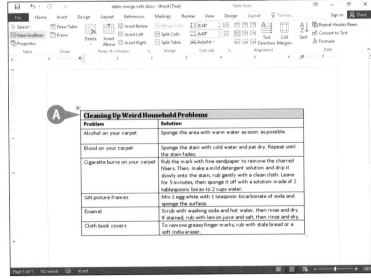

Split Cells

You can split one cell into two or more cells. Splitting a cell can be advantageous if you find that you have more information in one cell than you want. By splitting the cell, you can make room for additional information.

You can split any cell; you are not limited to splitting a cell that you previously merged. When you split a cell, the new cells that you create can span one row, one column, or multiple rows and columns.

Split Cells

1 Click anywhere in the cell you want to split.

2 Click the **Table Tools Layout** tab.

3 Click **Split Cells**.

The Split Cells dialog box appears.

4 Type the number of columns and rows into which you want to split the cell here.

5 Click **OK**.

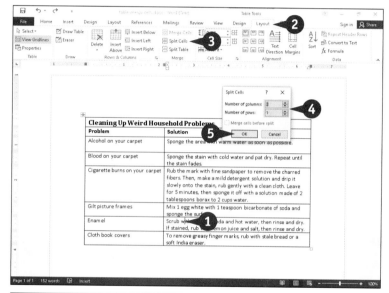

A Word splits and selects the cell.

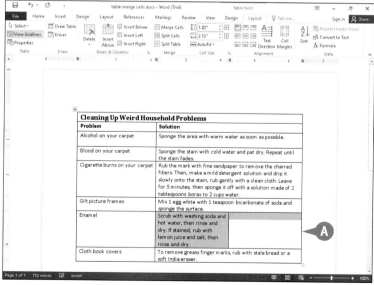

Split a Table

You can split one table into two. This feature is useful if you discover, after entering information in a table, that you should have created separate tables.

Suppose, for example, that you are putting together a table of methods one can use to clean up common household stains. Initially, you create one table for all the stains, but after working awhile, you realize that the information might be more useful if you create one table that covers cleaning up liquid stains and another table that addresses cleaning up dry stains. You can split the table.

Split a Table

1 Position the insertion point anywhere in the row that should appear as the first row of the new table.

2 Click the **Table Tools Layout** tab.

3 Click **Split Table**.

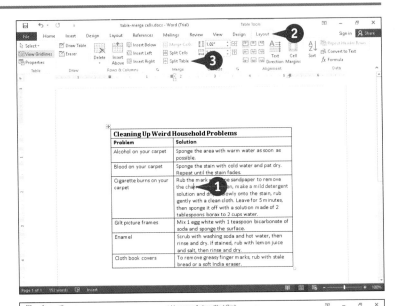

A Word separates the table into two tables.

B The insertion point appears between the tables.

C Because the insertion point is not resting in a table cell, Table Tools no longer appear on the Ribbon.

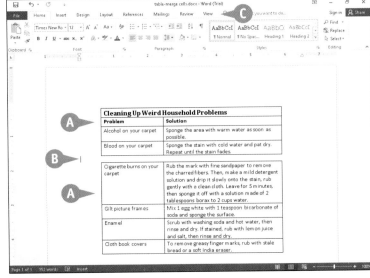

228

Add a Formula to a Table

You can place a formula in a cell and let Word automatically do the math for you. Word generally suggests the correct formula for the situation and can calculate a variety of values. For example, Word can sum or average values, identify a maximum or minimum value, and count the number of values in a selected range, among other functions.

Add a Formula to a Table

1 In a table containing numbers, click in a cell that should contain a formula.

2 Click the **Table Tools Layout** tab.

3 Click **Formula**.

The Formula dialog box appears, suggesting a formula.

A You can click ∨ to select a number format.

B You can click ∨ to select a different formula.

4 Click **OK**.

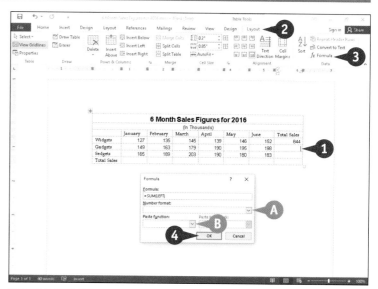

C Word places the formula in the cell containing the insertion point and displays the calculated result of the formula.

If you change any of the values in the row or column that the formula calculates, you can click in the cell containing the formula and press F9 to update the formula result.

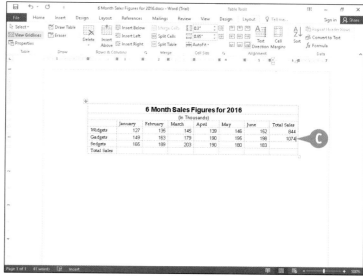

Align Text in Cells

To make your text look more uniform, you can align text or numbers with the top, bottom, left, right, or center of cells. By default, Word aligns table entries at the top left edge of each cell. But, in some cases, Word's default alignment is not appropriate for the data you are presenting.

For example, many people prefer to center the title of a table in its cell. And most people want values to align along the right side of the cell, especially if the total of the values appears in the table.

Align Text in Cells

① Click in the cell you want to align.

You can position the mouse over the left edge of the cell whose alignment you want to change (I changes to ➴) and drag to select multiple cells.

② Click the **Table Tools Layout** tab.

③ Click an alignment button.

This example uses the **Align Center** button (▤) to align a title vertically and horizontally in a cell.

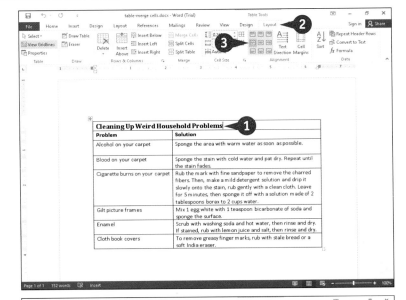

Ⓐ Word selects the text and aligns it accordingly in the cell.

You can click anywhere to cancel the selection.

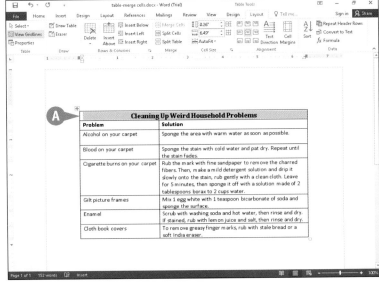

Add Shading to Cells

You can add shading to cells to call attention to them. Shading adds depth to drawings, and can improve the appearance of a table if you apply it properly. For example, you might want to shade a table title or table column or row headings, or both title and headings to help ensure that the reader will notice them and better understand the table content.

Be careful not to apply too much shading or too dark a shade, which can make text unreadable.

Add Shading to Cells

1 Click anywhere in the cell to which you want to add shading.

A You can position the mouse over the left edge of any cell (I changes to ➚) and drag to select multiple cells.

2 Click the **Table Tools Design** tab.

3 Click ▼ on the **Shading** button.

B The Shading gallery appears.

You can position the mouse (I) over a color, and Live Preview displays a sample of the selected cells shaded in the proposed color.

4 Click a color.

C Word applies the shading to the selected cells.

You can click anywhere outside the cells to continue working.

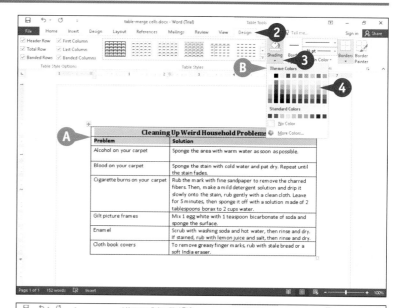

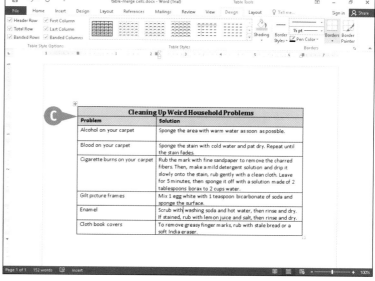

Change Cell Borders

You can change the appearance of cell borders. By default, Word displays the borders that separate each cell to help you enter information into a table and to help your reader read the table's information. You might want to change the appearance of the borders surrounding selected cells to call attention to them.

You can select a border style, which applies a predetermined line style, weight, and color, or you can manually select these characteristics. And you can apply your selection to individual borders using the Border Painter tool or to an entire cell using the Borders tool.

Change Cell Borders

Paint a Border Style

1 Click anywhere in the table to display Table Tools tabs on the Ribbon.

2 Click the **Table Tools Design** tab.

3 Click ▼ on the **Border Styles** button.

A The Theme Borders gallery appears.

4 Click a color and style.

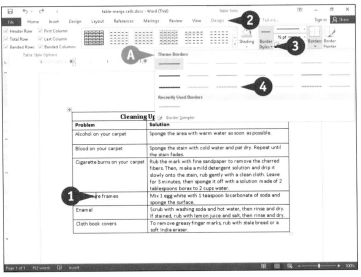

B ⌖ changes to ✎.

5 Slide the mouse (✎) over the table border to which you want to apply the border style you chose in Step **4**, and click the border.

Word applies the selected border style.

6 Repeat Step **5** for each border you want to change.

C You can click **Border Painter** or press Esc to stop applying the border.

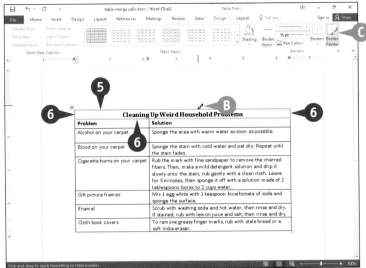

232

Manually Change Cell Borders

1 Click in the cell whose borders you want to change.

2 Click the **Table Tools Design** tab.

3 Click the **Line Style** ▼ to display the Line Style gallery, and click the line style you want to apply.

D You can repeat Step **3** using the **Line Weight** ▼ and the **Pen Color** ▼ to select the weight and color of the border line.

Word selects the Border Painter button.

4 Click the **Border Painter** button to deselect it.

5 Click ▼ on the **Borders** button to display the Borders gallery.

6 Click the type of border to apply.

This example uses **Outside Borders**.

E Word applies the border using the selected line style, weight, and pen color to the selected cells.

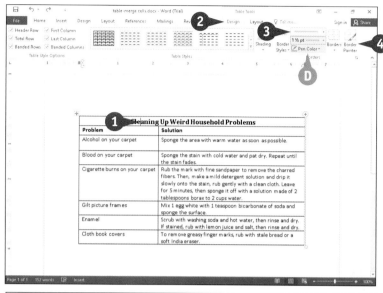

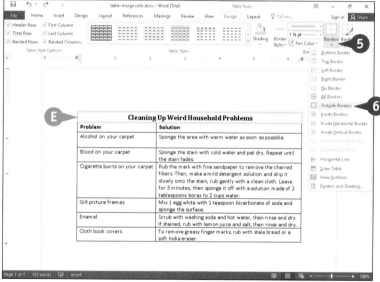

TIP

How can I remove borders from table cells?

Click in the cell whose borders you want to remove. Click the **Design** tab. Click ▼ on the **Borders** button and then click **No Border**. Word removes the borders from the table cells and replaces them with dotted gridlines, which do not print.

Format a Table

You can easily apply formatting to your tables by using the table styles found in the Table Styles gallery on the Design tab. Earlier sections in this chapter show you how to apply shading and borders to your table. Each table style in the Table Styles gallery contains its own unique set of formatting characteristics, and when you apply a table style you simultaneously apply shading, color, borders, and fonts to your table. You also can set table style options that add a header row or a total row, emphasize the table's first column, and more.

Format a Table

1 Click anywhere in the table.

2 Click the **Table Tools Design** tab.

3 Click the **More** button (⟱) in the Table Styles group.

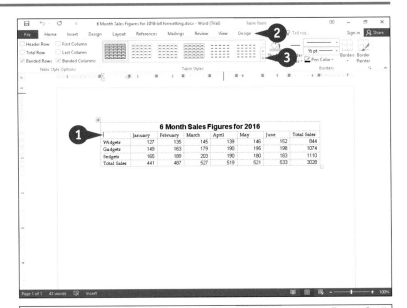

A The Table Styles gallery appears.

4 Position the mouse (⇗) over a table style.

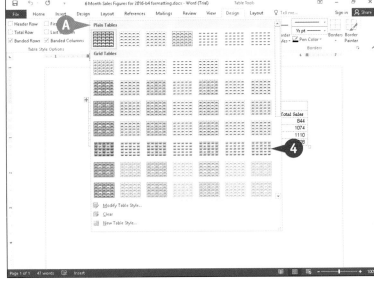

B Live Preview displays the table in the proposed table style, using the style's fonts, colors, and shading.

5 Repeat Step **4** until you find the table style you want to use.

6 Click the table style you want to use.

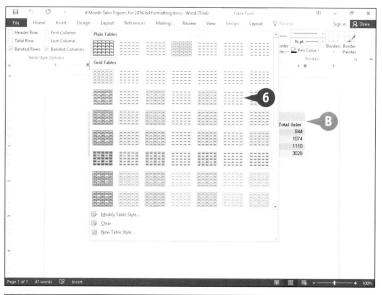

C Word displays the table in the style you selected.

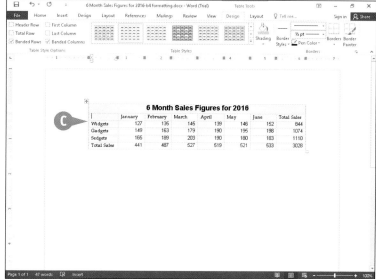

Add a Chart

You can chart data stored in a Microsoft Word 2016 document using Microsoft Excel 2016. When you create a chart in a Word document, you supply all data for the chart in Excel. Although you might have a table containing the information in Word, you do not use the information in that table to create the chart.

If your Word document contains a table and you choose to chart that data, remember that the chart you create is completely independent of the table. You could easily delete either the chart or the table and the other element remains unaffected.

Add a Chart

1 Click in the document where you want a chart to appear.

2 Click the **Insert** tab.

3 Click **Chart**.

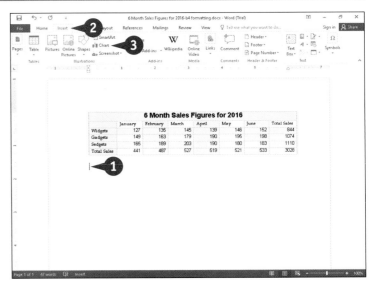

The Insert Chart dialog box appears.

Ⓐ Chart types appear here.

4 Click a chart type.

Ⓑ You can click a variation within a given chart type.

5 Click **OK**.

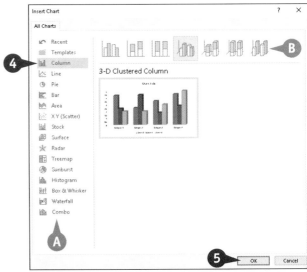

C Microsoft Excel opens, displaying sample data in the chart in a Microsoft Word window.

D A sample chart of the data appears in Word.

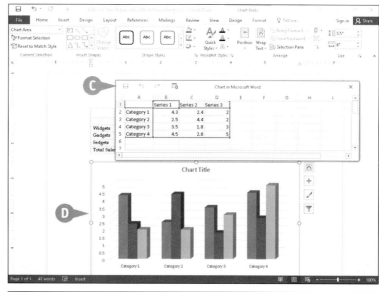

6 Change the data in Excel.

E The chart in Word updates to reflect the changes in Excel.

F You can close Excel without saving by clicking the **Close** button (✖). The chart retains the changes you made in the Excel window.

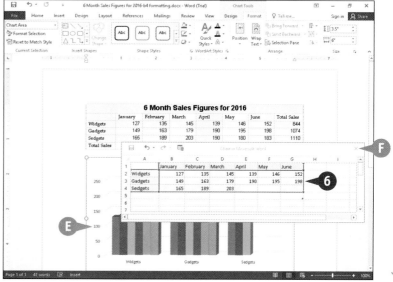

TIP

Can I format the chart in Word?

Yes. When you select the chart, Word displays Chart Tools on the Ribbon and, beside the chart, formatting buttons: the **Layout Options** button (⬚), the **Chart Elements** button (➕), the **Chart Styles** button (🖌), and the **Chart Filters** button (▽). Using either Ribbon tools or formatting buttons, you can select a layout and style, add and format shape styles and WordArt styles, set up chart and axis titles, add data labels and a data table, and modify the legend. You also can control how text wraps around your chart, change the color and style of your chart, and filter data from your chart to highlight select values.

Chart Concepts

When creating a chart, you have a wide variety of choices to communicate information in different ways. In addition to the commonly used charts listed below, you can create treemap, sunburst, box and whisker, and waterfall charts. A *treemap* chart presents data in a hierarchical fashion. A *sunburst* chart is a variation of a pie chart. A *box and whisker* chart focuses on the middle half of your data points. A *waterfall* chart is a variation of a stock chart.

Column Charts

A column chart shows data changes over a period of time and can compare different sets of data. A column chart contains vertically oriented bars.

Line Charts

Line charts help you see trends. A line chart connects many related data points; by connecting the points with a line, you see a general trend.

Pie Charts

Pie charts demonstrate the relationship of a part to the whole. Pie charts are effective when you are trying to show, for example, the percentage of total sales for which the Midwest region is responsible.

Bar Charts

Bar charts typically compare different sets of data and can also show data changes over time. A bar chart closely resembles a column chart, but the bars are horizontally oriented.

Area Charts

Area charts show data over time, but an area chart helps you see data as broad trends, rather than individual data points.

XY (Scatter) Charts

Statisticians often use an XY chart, also called a scatter chart, to determine whether a correlation exists between two variables. Both axes on a scatter chart are numeric, and the axes can be linear or logarithmic.

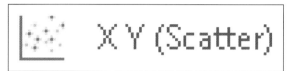

Stock Charts

Also called High-Low, Open-Close charts, stock charts are used for stock market reports. This chart type is very effective for displaying data that fluctuates over time. Waterfall charts are similar to stock charts and focus on showing increases and decreases in sequentially introduced positive or negative values.

Surface Charts

Topographic maps are surface charts, using colors and patterns to identify areas in the same range of values. A surface chart is useful when you want to find the best-possible combination between two sets of data.

Radar Charts

You can use a radar chart to compare data series that consist of several variables. Each data series on a radar chart has its own axis that "radiates" from the center of the chart — hence the name radar chart. A line connects each point in the series.

Histogram Charts

A histogram groups numeric data into bins; these charts are often used by teachers to depict the distribution of grades in a grading curve.

Combo

You can use a combination of charts to help make your point. Word provides three predefined combination charts: a clustered column–line chart, a clustered column–line on a secondary axis chart, and a stacked area–clustered column chart. If none of these meets your needs, you can create your own custom combination chart.

CHAPTER 10

Working with Graphics

You can spruce up documents by inserting a variety of graphics; the technique to insert graphics varies, depending on the type of graphic. You can edit graphics in a variety of ways using the tools that appear when you select the graphic. In this chapter, you learn how to edit a picture, clipart image, screenshot, WordArt drawing, shape, and text box.

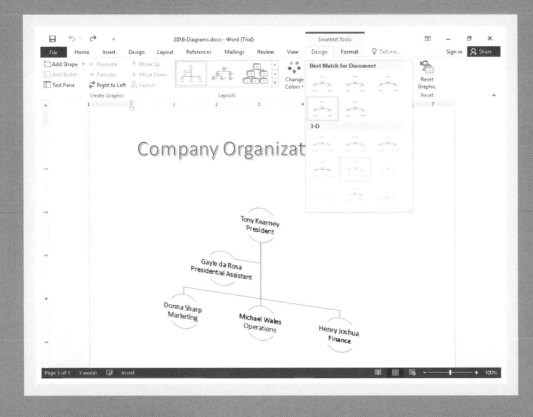

Add WordArt

ordArt is decorative text that you can add to a document as an eye-catching visual effect. You can create text graphics that bend and twist or display a subtle shading of color. You find the various WordArt options on the Insert tab of the Ribbon.

You can create WordArt text at the same time that you create a WordArt graphic, or you can apply a WordArt style to existing text. After you convert text into a WordArt object, you can resize, move, or modify the graphic in the ways described in the section "Understanding Graphics Modification Techniques," later in this chapter.

Add WordArt

1 Click in the document where you want to add WordArt or select existing text and apply WordArt to it.

2 Click the **Insert** tab.

3 Click the **WordArt** button (A ▾).

Ⓐ The WordArt gallery appears.

4 Click the WordArt style you want to apply.

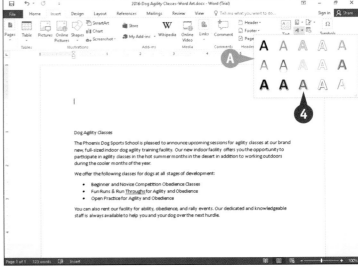

CHAPTER

10

Working with Graphics

B If you selected text in Step **1**, your text appears selected in the WordArt style you applied; otherwise, the words "Your Text Here" appear selected at the location you selected in Step **1**.

C Handles (○) surround the WordArt graphic.

D Drag the rotate handle (⟳) to rotate the graphic.

E The Layout Options button (▣) controls text flow as described in the section "Wrap Text Around a Graphic."

F The Drawing Tools Format tab appears on the Ribbon; you can use tools on this tab to format WordArt.

5 If necessary, type text.

G Word converts the text to a WordArt graphic.

You can click anywhere outside the WordArt to continue working.

Note: You can move, resize, or rotate the WordArt; see the section "Move or Resize a Graphic."

Note: You can change the size of the WordArt font by selecting the WordArt text and, on the Home tab, selecting a different font size from the Font list in the Font group.

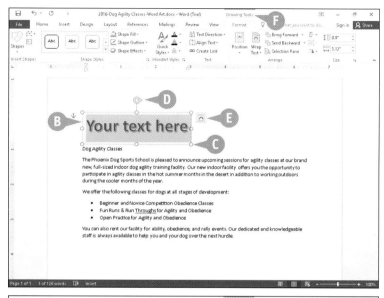

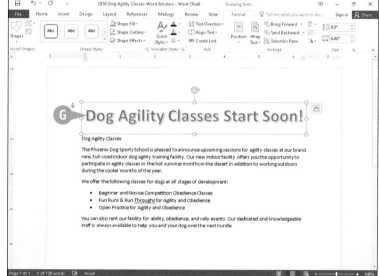

TIPS

Can I edit the WordArt drawing?
Yes. Click inside the WordArt drawing. Handles (○) appear around the WordArt. Edit the text the way you would edit any text, deleting and changing as needed. Use the rotate handle (⟳) to rotate the WordArt drawing.

Can I delete a WordArt drawing?
Yes, but be aware that deleting the drawing also deletes the text. Click near the edge of the drawing or, if you click inside the drawing, click any handle (○) to select the drawing; then press Delete.

243

Add a Picture

You can include a picture stored on your computer to add punch to your Word document. For example, if you have a photo or graphic file that relates to the subject matter in your document, you can insert it into the document to help the reader understand your subject. After you insert a picture, you can resize, move, or modify the graphic in a variety of ways. The section "Understanding Graphics Modification Techniques," later in this chapter, describes the many ways you can edit an image or add effects to an image.

Add a Picture

1 Click in your document where you want to add a picture.

2 Click the **Insert** tab.

3 Click **Pictures**.

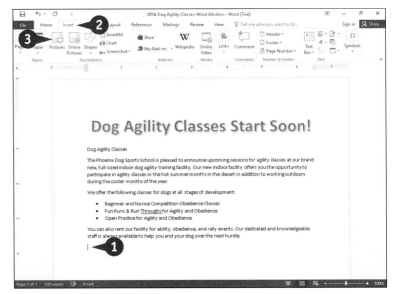

The Insert Picture dialog box appears.

Ⓐ The folder you are viewing appears here.

Ⓑ You can click in the folder list to navigate to commonly used locations where pictures may be stored.

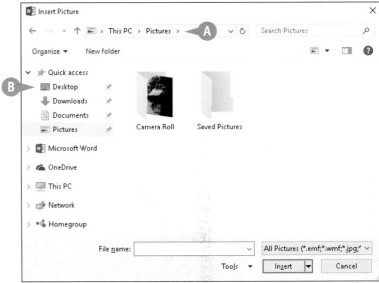

④ Navigate to the folder containing the picture you want to add.

⑤ Click the picture you want to add to your document.

⑥ Click **Insert**.

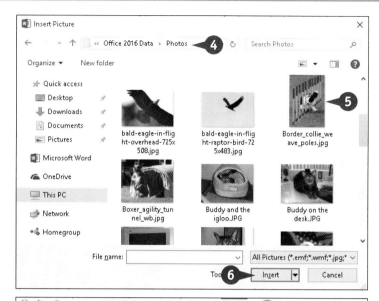

Ⓒ The picture appears in your document, selected and surrounded by handles (○).

Ⓓ Drag the rotate handle (◉) to rotate the picture.

Ⓔ The Layout Options button (▣) controls text flow around the picture as described in the section "Wrap Text Around a Graphic."

Ⓕ The Picture Tools Format tab appears on the Ribbon; you can use tools on this tab to format pictures.

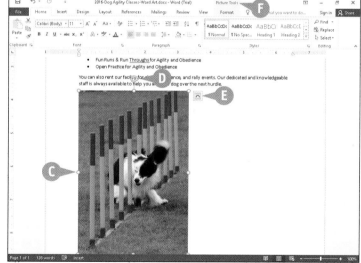

TIP

How can I delete a picture?

① Move the mouse over the picture.

Ⓐ ☌ changes to ⭧.

② Click the picture to select it.

③ Press Delete.

Insert an Online Picture

In addition to pictures stored on your computer's hard drive, you can insert a picture from an online source into a Word document.

The online picture search uses Bing Image Search by default; all images you find are licensed under Creative Commons. To avoid violating copyright laws, exercise care in choosing online pictures. Make sure that they fall into the public domain or that you have written permission to use the picture. You can search all websites rather than just Bing Image Search.

Insert an Online Picture

1 Click in your document where you want to add a picture.

2 Click the **Insert** tab.

3 Click **Online Pictures**.

The Insert Pictures window appears.

4 Click here and type a description of the type of image you want.

Note: If you sign in using your Microsoft account, additional search locations appear.

5 Click the **Search** button (🔍).

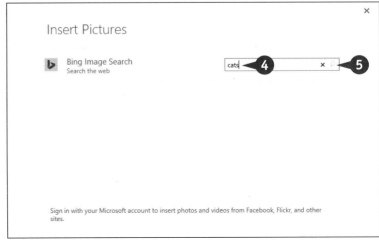

The results of your search appear.

Ⓐ You can click the arrows (∧ and ∨) to navigate through the search results.

Ⓑ You can click **Show all web results** to search all websites.

Ⓒ You can click **Back to Sites** to return to the Insert Picture window and search for a different image.

⑥ Click the picture you want to add to your document.

⑦ Click **Insert**.

Ⓓ The picture appears in your document, selected and surrounded by handles (○).

Ⓔ Drag the rotate handle (⟳) to rotate the picture.

Ⓕ The Layout Options button (⬚) controls text flow around the picture as described in the section "Wrap Text Around a Graphic."

Ⓖ The Picture Tools Format tab appears on the Ribbon; you can use tools on this tab to format the picture.

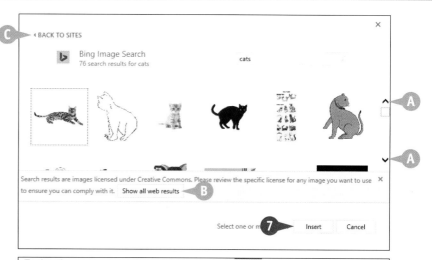

TIP

Why must I make sure that the image I choose falls into the public domain?
Images that are privately owned are often available for use only if you agree to pay a fee and/or give credit to the owner of the image. To use a public domain image, you do not need to pay a royalty or get permission from an image owner to use the image.

Insert an Online Video

You can insert a video available on the Internet into a Word document. After you have inserted the video, you can play it directly from the Word document.

You can insert videos you find using Bing Search or videos available on YouTube, or you can insert a video embed code — an HTML code that uses the `src` attribute to define the video file you want to embed. Most videos posted on the Internet are public domain, but if you are unsure, do some research to determine if you can use the video freely.

Insert an Online Video

1 Click in your document where you want to add a video.

2 Click the **Insert** tab.

3 Click **Online Video**.

The Insert Video window appears.

4 In one of the search boxes, type a description of the video you want to insert.

Note: This example searches YouTube.

5 Click the **Search** button (🔎).

The results of your search appear.

Ⓐ You can click the arrows (⋀ and ⋁) to navigate through the search results.

Ⓑ You can click **Back to Sites** to return to the Insert Video window and search for a different video.

6 Click the video you want to add to your document.

7 Click **Insert**.

Ⓒ The video appears in your document, selected and surrounded by handles (○).

Ⓓ Drag the rotate handle (⟲) to rotate the video.

Ⓔ The Layout Options button (▣) controls text flow around the video as described in the section "Wrap Text Around a Graphic."

Ⓕ The Picture Tools Format tab appears on the Ribbon; you can use tools on this tab to format the appearance of the video in your document.

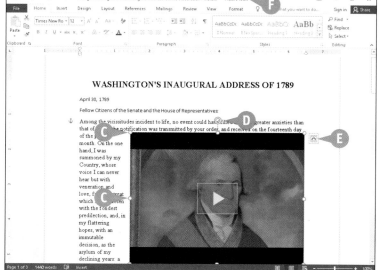

How do I play an inserted video?

From Print Layout view or Read Mode view, click the video **Play** button (▶). The video appears in its own window, the document appears behind a shaded, translucent background, and the Play button changes from black to red. Click anywhere on the video — not just on the Play button — to start the video. To stop the video and return to the document, click anywhere outside the video on the shaded translucent background of the document window or press `Esc`.

Add a Screenshot

Y ou can insert an image called a *screenshot* into a Word document. You can capture a screenshot of another document open in Word or of a document open in another program.

Screenshots are exact pictures of the open document at the moment you take the screenshot. In addition to including a screenshot in a Word document, if you are having a problem on your computer, you can use a screenshot to help capture the problem so that you can provide accurate and detailed information to the technical support person who helps you.

Add a Screenshot

1 Open the document you want to capture.

A This example shows a chart in Excel.

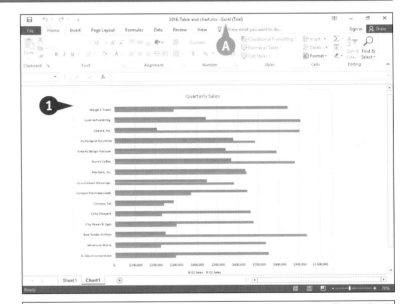

2 Open the Word document in which you want to insert a screenshot of the document you opened in Step **1**.

3 Position the insertion point where you want the screenshot to appear.

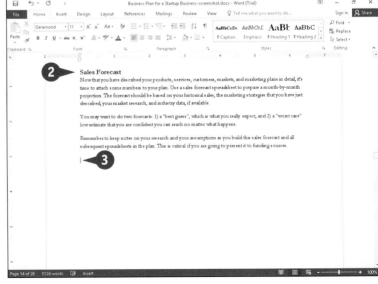

④ Click **Insert**.

⑤ Click **Screenshot**.

Ⓑ The Screenshot gallery shows open programs and available screenshots of those programs.

Note: You can open as many programs and documents as your computer permits. In this example, in addition to the chart in Excel and Word, another Excel workbook is also open.

⑥ Click the screenshot you want to insert in your Word document.

Ⓒ The screenshot appears in your Word document, selected and surrounded by handles (○).

Ⓓ Drag the rotate handle (⟳) to rotate the screenshot.

Ⓔ The Layout Options button (⬜) controls text flow around the screenshot as described in the section "Wrap Text Around a Graphic."

Ⓕ The Picture Tools Format tab appears on the Ribbon; you can use tools on this tab to format the screenshot.

You can click anywhere outside the screenshot to continue working.

TIP

Can I take a picture of my desktop?
You cannot use the Screenshot feature to take a picture of your desktop. But here is a workaround: While viewing your desktop, press the Print Screen key. Then, switch to Word and position the insertion point where the screenshot should appear. Press Ctrl+V to paste the image into your Word document.

Add a Shape

To give your Word document pizzazz, you can add graphic shapes such as lines, arrows, stars, and banners. Suppose, for example, that you are part of a barbershop quartet that wants to sell and deliver singing telegrams for Valentine's Day — the perfect fun way to raise money to support your hobby. You can create a flyer that advertises your unique gift offering, suitable not only for lovers, but for anyone who occupies a special place in the life of the sender — a grandparent, parent, child, or longtime friend.

Shapes are visible in Print Layout, Web Layout, and Read Mode views.

Add a Shape

1 In the document where you want to include a shape, click the **Insert** tab.

2 Click **Shapes**.

The Shapes gallery appears.

3 Click a shape.

The Shapes gallery closes and the mouse (I) changes to ✛.

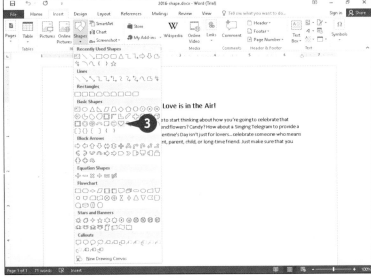

4 Position the mouse at the upper left corner of the place where you want the shape to appear.

5 Drag the mouse (+) down and to the right until the shape is the size you want.

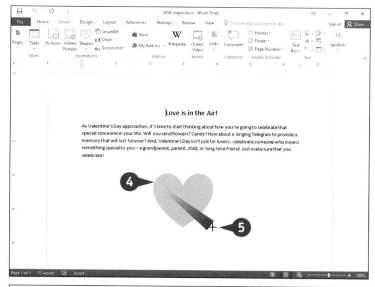

A When you release the mouse button, the shape appears in your document, selected and surrounded by handles (○).

B Drag the rotate handle (⟳) to rotate the shape.

C The Layout Options button (⬚) controls text flow around the shape as described in the section "Wrap Text Around a Graphic."

D The Drawing Tools Format tab appears on the Ribbon.

You can press Esc or click anywhere to continue working in your document.

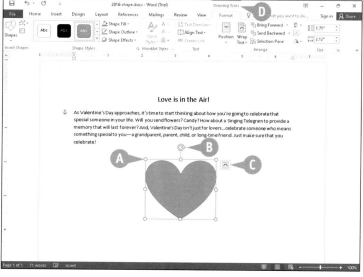

TIP

Can I change the color of a shape?
Yes, you can change the color inside a shape as well as the shape's outline color using tools on the Drawing Tools Format tab. Click the shape to select it. On the Ribbon, in the Shape Styles group, click the **Shape Fill** button (**A**) to display the color gallery. Move the mouse (⍾) over the color gallery; Live Preview displays the outline of the shape in the proposed color. Click a theme color or a standard color. Repeat these steps, clicking **Shape Outline** instead of **Shape Fill**.

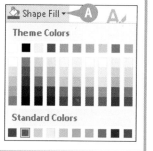

Add a Text Box

You can add a text box graphic to your document to control the placement and appearance of the text that appears in the box. Use text boxes to help you draw attention to specific text, to easily move text around within a document, or to display text vertically instead of horizontally.

Word inserts your text box near the insertion point, but you can move the text box the same way you move any graphic element; see the next section, "Move or Resize a Graphic," for details. Text boxes are visible only in Print Layout, Web Layout, and Read Mode views.

Add a Text Box

1 Click near the location where you want the text box to appear.

2 Click the **Insert** tab.

3 Click **Text Box**.

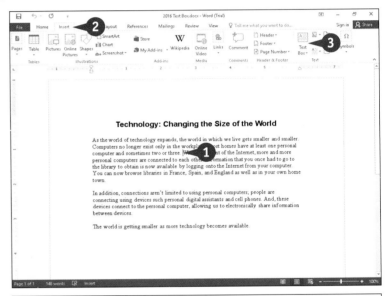

The Text Box gallery appears.

4 Click a text box style.

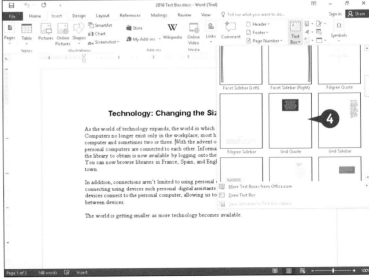

A The Text Box gallery closes and Word places a text box in your document.

Sample text appears inside a text box, and Word selects the sample text.

B Existing text flows around the box.

C Drag the rotate handle (⟳) to rotate the text box as described in the section "Wrap Text Around a Graphic."

D The Drawing Tools Format tab appears on the Ribbon; you can use tools on this tab to format the text box.

5 To replace the sample text, start typing.

E The Layout Options button (▣) appears; use it to control text flow around the shape as described in the section "Wrap Text Around a Graphic."

6 Click outside the text box.

Note: You can format the text using the techniques described in Chapter 5.

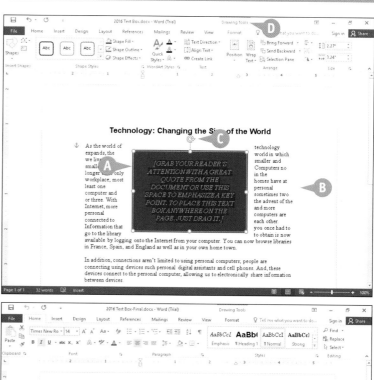

What should I do if I do not like any of the predefined text box formats?
You can examine additional styles available from Office.com, or you can draw your own text box and format it. Complete Steps **1** to **3** in this section. Click **More Text Boxes from Office.com** to view some additional text box styles. If you still do not see a style you like, click **Draw Text Box** (I changes to +). Drag the mouse (+) from the upper left to the lower right corner of the place where you want the text box to appear; the text box appears.

Move or Resize a Graphic

If you find that a graphic — a picture, shape, text box, or WordArt graphic — is not positioned where you want it or it is too large or too small, you can move or resize it. Alignment guides — green lines — appear as you move a graphic to help you determine where to place the graphic. After you have picked the spot for the graphic, the alignment guides disappear. Text automatically reflows around a graphic wherever you place it or however you size it; see the section "Wrap Text Around a Graphic," later in this chapter, to control the way text flows.

Move or Resize a Graphic

Move a Graphic

1 Click the graphic.

A Handles (○) surround the graphic.

2 Position the mouse over the WordArt image, picture, video, or shape, or over the edge of the text box (I changes to ⁺⟨).

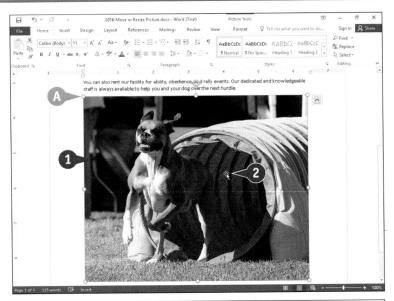

3 Drag the graphic to a new location.

B Green alignment guides help you position the graphic.

4 Release the mouse button.

The graphic appears in the new location, and the alignment guides disappear.

5 Click outside the graphic to cancel its selection.

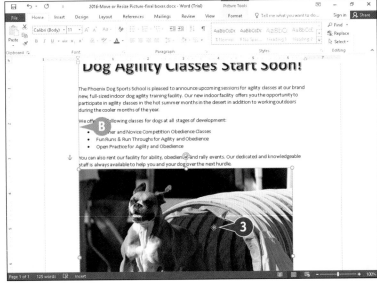

Resize a Graphic

1 Click the graphic.

C Handles (○) surround the graphic.

2 Position the mouse over one of the handles (I changes to ↘, ↕, ↗, or ⟷).

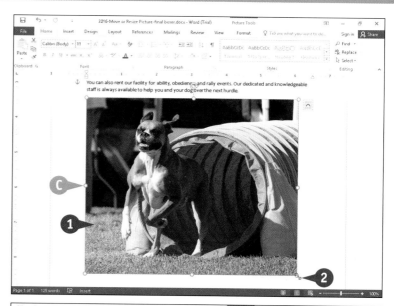

3 Drag the handle inward or outward until the graphic is the appropriate size (↘, ↕, ↗, or ⟷ changes to +).

4 Release the mouse button.

The graphic appears in the new size.

5 Click outside the graphic to cancel its selection.

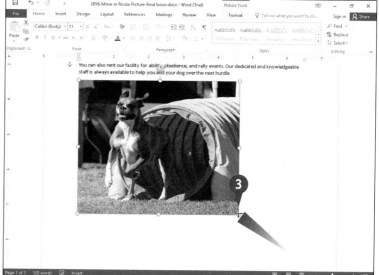

TIP

Does it matter which handle I use to resize a graphic?
If you click and drag any of the corner handles, you maintain the proportion of the graphic as you resize it. The handles on the sides, top, or bottom of the graphic resize the width or the height only of the graphic, so using one of them can make your graphic look distorted, especially if you resize a picture, video, or screenshot using any handle except a corner handle.

Understanding Graphics Modification Techniques

In addition to moving or resizing graphics, you can modify their appearance using a variety of Ribbon buttons. When you select a graphic, Word displays additional tabs specific to the graphic you select. These tabs contain the buttons you can use to modify the appearance of the selected image. You can adjust the size, brightness or contrast, and color of a picture. You can rotate a graphic or make it three-dimensional. You also can add a shadow or apply a color outline or style to a graphic. And you can change the color of a graphic.

Crop a Picture

You can use the Crop tool to create a better fit, to omit a portion of the image, or to focus the viewer on an important area of the image. You can crop a picture, screenshot, or clipart image. When you crop an object, you remove vertical and/or horizontal edges from the object. The Crop tool is located on the Format tab on the Ribbon, which appears when you click the object you want to crop.

Rotate or Flip a Graphic

After you insert an object such as a piece of clipart or a photo from your hard drive into a Word document, you may find that the object appears upside down or inverted. Or maybe you want to rotate or flip pictures, clipart images, and some shapes for dramatic effect. For example, you might flip a clipart image to face another direction or rotate an arrow object to point elsewhere on the page. You cannot rotate text boxes.

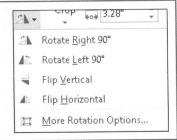

Correct Images

You can change the brightness and contrast of a picture, clipart image, or screenshot to improve its appearance, and you can sharpen or soften an image. Suppose the image object you have inserted in your Word file is slightly blurry or lacks contrast. You find the image-correction tools on the Picture Tools Format tab on the Ribbon, which appears when you click to select the object to which you want to apply the effect.

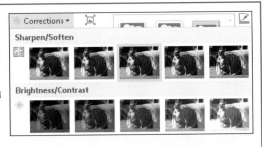

Make Color Adjustments

You can adjust the color of a picture, screenshot, or clipart image by increasing or decreasing color saturation or color tone. You also can recolor a picture, screenshot, or clipart image to create an interesting effect.

Color saturation controls the intensity of a color, expressed as the degree to which it differs from white in a photo. Color tone controls the appearance of a photo as the result of mixing a pure color with any grayscale color.

Remove the Background of an Image

You can remove the background of a picture, screenshot, or clipart image. Suppose that you inserted a screenshot of an Excel chart in a Word document; the screenshot would, by default, include the Excel Ribbon. You can use the Remove Background tool in the Adjust group on the Picture Tools Format tab to remove the Excel Ribbon and focus the reader's attention on the chart.

Add a Picture or Shape Effect

You can use tools to assign unique and interesting special effects to objects. For example, you can apply a shadow effect, create a mirrored reflection, apply a glow effect, soften the object's edges, make a bevel effect, or generate a 3-D rotation effect. You can find these tools on the Format tab of the Ribbon, which appears when you click to select the object to which you want to apply the effect.

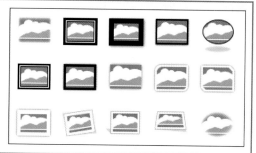

Apply a Style to a Graphic

You can apply a predefined style to a shape, text box, WordArt graphic, picture, or clipart image. Styles contain predefined colors and effects and help you quickly add interest to a graphic. Applying a style removes other effects that you may have applied, such as shadow or bevel effects. Sample styles appear on the Picture Tools Format or Drawing Tools Format tab when you click the **More** button ([▾]) in the Picture Styles or Shape Styles group.

Add a Picture Border or Drawing Outline

You can add a border to a picture, shape, text box, WordArt graphic, clipart image, or screenshot. Using the Picture Border or Shape Outline tool, which appears on the Picture Tools Format or Drawing Tools Format tab, you can control the thickness of the border, set a style for the border (a solid line or dashed line), and change the color of the border.

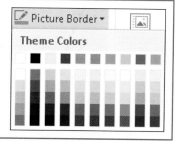

Apply Artistic Effects

You can apply artistic effects to pictures, screenshots, and clipart images in order to liven them up. For example, you can make an image appear as though it was rendered in marker, pencil, chalk, or paint. Other artistic effects might remind you of mosaics, film grain, or glass. You find the Artistic Effects button on the Picture Tools Format tab, which appears when you click to select the object to which you want to apply the effect.

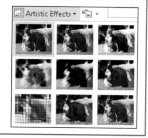

Understanding Text Wrapping and Graphics

When you insert graphics into a Word document, you can control the way text wraps around the graphic. For example, you can wrap text around a graphic, force text to skip a graphic and leave its left and right sides blank, or place a graphic on top of or underneath text. By default, most graphics have a relatively square boundary, even if the graphic is not a square, and most text wrapping options relate to that relatively square boundary. By editing a graphic's wrap points, you can change the square boundary to more closely match the graphic's shape and wrap text more closely around the shape.

Button	Function
In Line with Text	Text does not wrap around the graphic. Word positions the graphic exactly where you placed it. The graphic moves to accommodate added or deleted text, but no text appears on the graphic's right or left.
Square	This option wraps text in a square around your graphic regardless of its shape. You can control the amount of space between text and all your graphic's sides.
Tight	This option wraps text around the graphic's outside edge. The difference between this option and Square becomes apparent with a nonsquare shape; with Tight, you can control the space between the text and the graphic's right and left sides. Word leaves no space between text and the graphic's top and bottom sides.
Through	With this option, if you edit a graphic's wrap points by dragging them to match the shape of the graphic, you can wrap text to follow the graphic's shape.
Top and Bottom	Wraps text around the graphic's top and bottom but leaves the space on either side of a graphic blank.
Behind Text	With this option, the text runs over the graphic, as if the graphic were not there.
In Front of Text	With this option, the graphic appears to block the text underneath the graphic's location.
Edit Wrap Points	Displays handles that represent an image's wrap points. You can drag the handles to change the position of the wrap points. Changing a wrap point does not change the image's appearance but affects the way text wraps around the image.
✓ Move with Text / Fix Position on Page	Choose one of these options to determine the way Word positions an image. It can move as you add text or it can remain on the page exactly where you placed it.

Wrap Text Around a Graphic

You can control the way that Word wraps text around a graphic image in your document. Controlling the way text wraps around a graphic becomes very important when you want to place graphics in a document where space is at a premium, such as a two-columned newsletter. See the previous section for details on text wrapping methods. The information in this section shows text wrapping for a picture but applies to text wrapping for any kind of graphic.

Wrap Text Around a Graphic

① Click a graphic.

Ⓐ Handles (○) appear around the image.

② Click the **Format** tab.

③ Click **Wrap Text**.

④ Point the mouse (↳) at each wrapping style to see how it affects the text and the image.

⑤ Click the wrapping style you want to apply.

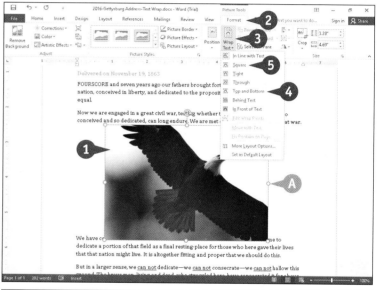

Word wraps text around the graphic using the text wrapping option you selected.

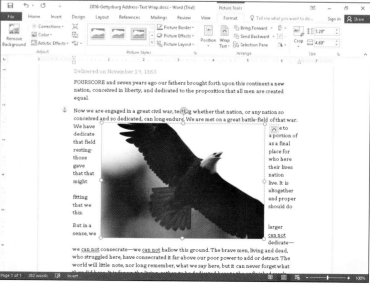

Work with Diagrams

You can use the SmartArt feature to create all kinds of diagrams to illustrate concepts and processes. For example, you might insert a diagram in a document to show the hierarchy in your company or to show the workflow in your department. SmartArt offers predefined diagram types, including list, process, cycle, hierarchy, relationship, matrix, pyramid, and picture. In addition, you can choose from several diagram styles within each type. For example, if you choose to create a hierarchy diagram, you can choose from several different styles of hierarchy diagrams.

The example in this section demonstrates adding an organizational chart.

Work with Diagrams

Add a Diagram

1 Click in your document where you want the diagram to appear.

2 Click the **Insert** tab.

3 Click **SmartArt**.

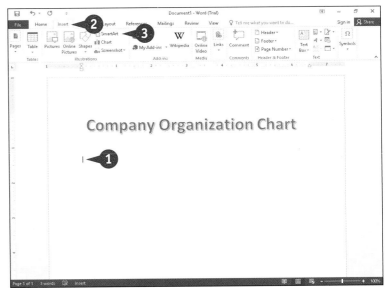

The Choose a SmartArt Graphic dialog box appears.

4 Click a diagram category.

5 Click the type of diagram you want to add.

Ⓐ A description of the selected diagram appears here.

6 Click **OK**.

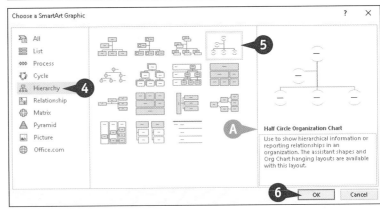

Word adds the diagram.

Ⓑ The handles (○) surrounding the diagram indicate that the diagram is selected; the border will not print.

Ⓒ SmartArt Tools tabs appear.

Ⓓ If you do not see the text pane, click **Text Pane**. Each bullet in the text pane matches a text block in the diagram.

Each object within the diagram is called a *shape*.

Add Text to the Diagram

① If the Text pane is not visible, on the SmartArt Tools Design tab, click **Text Pane**.

② Click a bullet in the Text pane and type the text you want to add.

Ⓔ Text you add appears both in the Text pane and on the diagram.

Note: You do not need to use the Text pane; you can click and type directly in a shape.

③ Repeat Step **2** for each shape in the diagram. When you finish, click ✖ to close the Text pane and click a blank spot on the diagram.

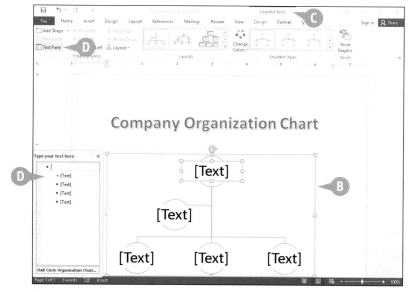

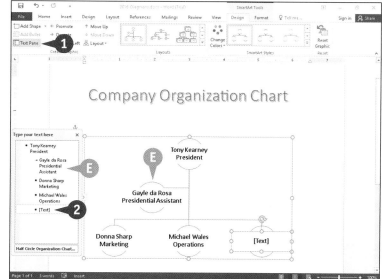

How can I add two lines of text to a shape?
After you type the first line of the text in the text pane, press Shift + Enter. Then type the second line. Word adjusts the font size of the text to fit the shape, and for consistency, Word adjusts the font size of all text in the diagram to match.

Can I control the size and position of the diagram on the page?
Yes. You can size the diagram using its handles. Word sets the default position on the diagram in line with your text. You can position the diagram by dragging it.

continued ▶

No SmartArt diagram comes with all the shapes you need to create your diagram, but you can easily add shapes at any place in the diagram to accommodate your needs. And when circumstances change, you can easily revise a diagram by adding or deleting shapes as appropriate.

To keep your diagrams interesting, you can apply styles to diagrams. Styles enhance the appearance of a diagram, providing a professional look and adding dimension and depth to the diagram. These style enhancements draw a reader's attention to a diagram and help you get your point across.

Work with Diagrams (continued)

Add or Delete Shapes

1 Click the **SmartArt Tools Design** tab.

2 Click the shape above or beside which you want to add a shape.

A Handles (◯) surround the shape.

3 Click ▼ beside **Add Shape**.

4 Select the option that describes where the shape should appear.

This example adds a shape after the selected shape.

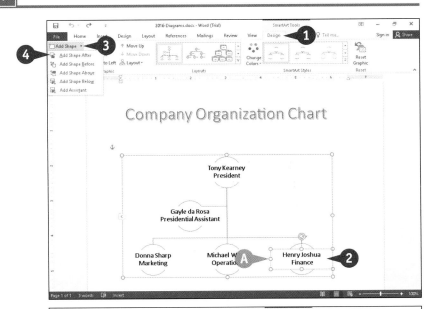

B The new shape appears.

You can add text to the new shape by following the steps in the previous subsection, "Add Text to the Diagram."

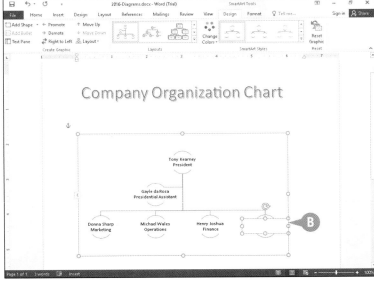

Apply a Diagram Style

1 Click the border surrounding the diagram.

2 Click the **SmartArt Tools Design** tab.

3 Click the **More** button (⊽) in the SmartArt Styles group to display the Quick Styles gallery.

Ⓒ The SmartArt Styles gallery appears.

You can slide the mouse (⬉) over an option in the gallery, and Live Preview displays the appearance of the diagram using that style.

4 Click a style.

Ⓓ Word applies the selected style to the diagram.

You can click anywhere outside the diagram to continue working.

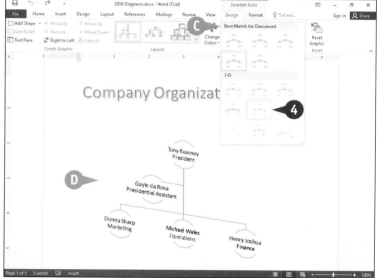

How can I delete a shape?

Click the outside border of the shape; handles (○) appear around the shape. Then, press Delete.

Can I change the layout of an organization chart diagram after I insert it?

Yes. Click the border of the organization chart to select it. Then click the **SmartArt Tools Design** tab and, in the Layouts group, click the **More** button (⊽) to display the Layouts gallery and select a different organization chart structure. To select a different type of diagram, you can click **More Layouts** at the bottom of the Layouts gallery to reopen the Choose a SmartArt Graphic dialog box.

CHAPTER 11

Customizing Word

Do you like the default Word settings? If not, you can easily customize portions of the Word program to make it perform more in line with the way you work. For example, you can easily create your own tab on the Ribbon and add to it the buttons you use most often.

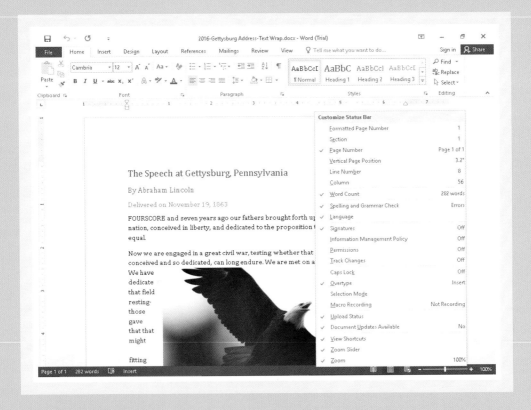

Control the Display of Formatting Marks

As described in Chapter 6, you can view the formatting marks that Word automatically inserts as you type. These formatting marks help you understand why your document looks the way that it looks — for example, why paragraphs seem farther apart than you expect. Formatting marks are always in documents, but they are hidden from you unless you display them.

Using the Show/Hide button (¶) displays all formatting marks. But you also can limit the formatting marks that Word displays to view just the ones that interest you.

Control the Display of Formatting Marks

1 Click the **Show/Hide** button (¶) on the Home tab to display formatting marks.

2 Click the **File** tab.

Backstage view appears.

3 Click **Options**.

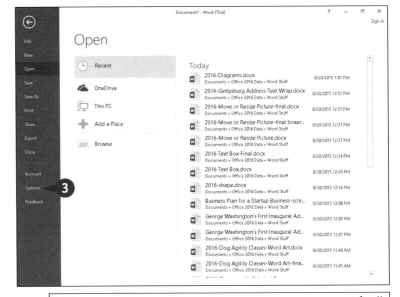

The Word Options dialog box appears.

4 Click **Display**.

Ⓐ You can select **Show all formatting marks** (☐ changes to ☑) to display all formatting marks.

5 Select the formatting marks you want to display (☐ changes to ☑).

6 Click **OK**.

Word displays only the selected formatting marks in your document.

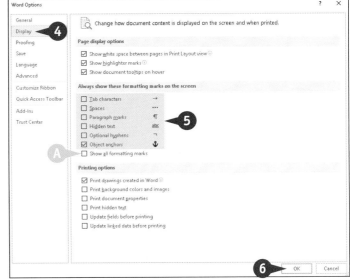

Customize the Status Bar

ou can customize the status bar to display information you want visible while you work. By default, Word displays some information on the status bar, such as the page number and number of pages and words in your document. You can add a wide variety of information, such as the position of the insertion point by line and column number or by vertical page position. You also can display indicators of spelling and grammar errors and typing mode — insert or overtype.

Customize the Status Bar

1 Right-click the status bar to display the Customize Status Bar menu.

2 Click the option you want to display on the status bar.

A check appears beside the option.

3 Repeat Step **2** for each option you want to display.

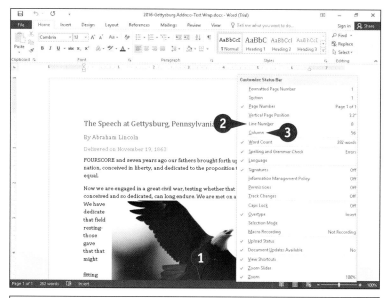

A Word displays the option(s) you selected on the status bar.

You can click anywhere outside the menu to close it.

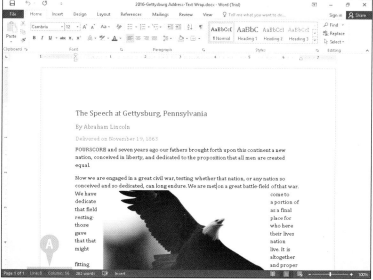

Hide or Display Ribbon Buttons

By default, Word pins the Ribbon on-screen, but you can unpin the Ribbon to hide it while you work and then redisplay it when you need it. Unpinning the Ribbon can make your screen appear less crowded and less distracting, enabling you to concentrate on your document as opposed to the controls you use as you prepare it.

When you unpin and hide the Ribbon, you hide the buttons on each tab, but the tab names continue to appear. When you click a tab name, the Ribbon reappears. Note that unpinning the Ribbon has no effect on the Quick Access Toolbar.

Hide or Display Ribbon Buttons

A By default, Word displays the Ribbon.

1 Click the **Unpin the Ribbon** button (⌃).

B Word unpins the Ribbon, hiding the buttons but continuing to display the tabs.

2 Work in your document as usual.

3 When you need a Ribbon button, click that Ribbon tab.

Note: You can click any Ribbon tab, but you will save time if you click the tab containing the button you need.

Word redisplays the Ribbon buttons.

④ Click the button you need.

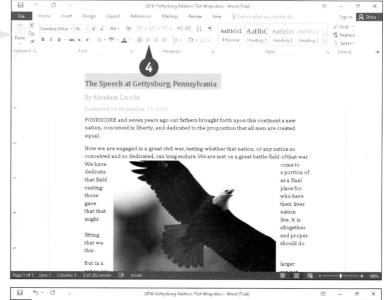

Word performs the button's action.

⑤ Click anywhere outside the Ribbon.

Word hides the Ribbon buttons again.

How can I redisplay the Ribbon buttons permanently?
Click any Ribbon tab to display the Ribbon. Then click the **Pin the Ribbon** button (➖) in the lower right corner of the Ribbon.

Is there another way to hide the Ribbon buttons?
Yes. You can click the **Ribbon Display Options** button (⬆) to display a menu. The Auto-hide Ribbon option hides Ribbon buttons, tabs, and the controls to minimize, maximize, and restore the window. The Show Tabs option hides Ribbon buttons but displays the other controls. The Show Tabs and Commands option displays everything: the Ribbon tabs and buttons and the window control buttons.

Add a Predefined Group to a Ribbon Tab

You can customize the Ribbon to suit your working style. You can work more efficiently if you customize the Ribbon to place the groups of buttons that you use most often on a single Ribbon tab.

For example, suppose that most of the buttons you need appear on the Home tab, but you often use the Page Setup group on the Page Layout tab to change document margins and set up columns. You can add the Page Setup group to the Home tab. That way, you do not need to switch tabs to get to the commands you use most often.

Add a Predefined Group to a Ribbon Tab

1 Click the **File** tab.

Backstage view appears.

2 Click **Options**.

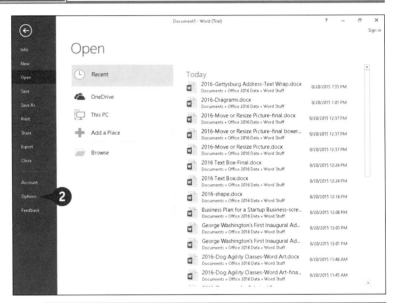

3 In the Word Options dialog box, click **Customize Ribbon**.

4 Click ⌄ and select **Main Tabs**.

5 Click ⊞ beside the tab containing the group you want to add (⊞ changes to ⊟).

6 Click the group you want to add.

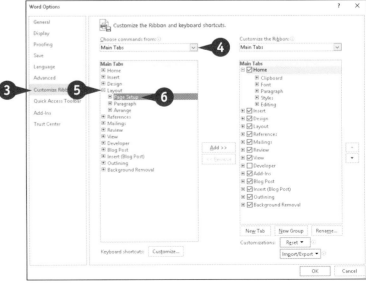

272

7 Click ⊞ beside the tab where you want to place the group you selected in Step **6** (⊞ changes to ⊟).

8 Click the group you want to appear on the Ribbon to the left of the new group.

9 Click **Add**.

Ⓐ Word adds the group you selected in Step **6** below the group you selected in Step **8**.

10 Repeat Steps **5** to **9** as needed.

11 Click **OK**.

Ⓑ Word adds the group you selected to the appropriate Ribbon tab.

Ⓒ Word might collapse other groups to fit the new group on the tab. In this example, Word collapsed the Editing group.

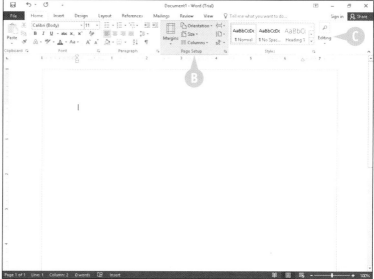

How do I add a single button — rather than a group — to one of the existing groups on the Ribbon?
Create your own group that contains only those buttons you want to use, and then hide the default group that Word displays. See the next section, "Create Your Own Ribbon Group."

If I change my mind, how can I eliminate the changes I made to the Ribbon?
Complete Steps **1** to **3**. In the column on the right, select the Ribbon tab and group you added. Just above the OK button, click **Reset**, and from the menu that appears, click **Reset only selected Ribbon tab**. Then click **OK**.

Create Your Own Ribbon Group

You cannot add or remove buttons from predefined groups on a Ribbon tab, but you can create your own group and place the buttons you want in the group. Creating your own groups of Ribbon buttons can help you work more efficiently, because you can place all the buttons you use regularly together and save yourself the time of switching groups and even Ribbon tabs.

To create your own Ribbon group, you first make a group, placing it on the tab and in the position where you want it to appear. Then you name it, and finally you add buttons to it.

Create Your Own Ribbon Group

Make a Group

1 Click the **File** tab.

Backstage view appears.

2 Click **Options**.

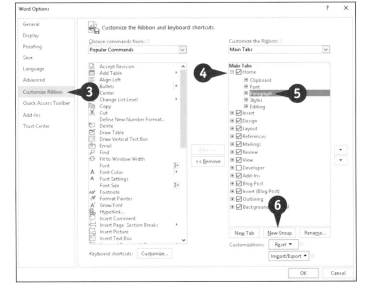

The Word Options dialog box appears.

3 Click **Customize Ribbon**.

4 Click ⊞ beside the tab to which you want to add a group (⊞ changes to ⊟).

5 Click the group you want to appear on the Ribbon to the left of the new group.

6 Click **New Group**.

Word adds a new group to the tab below the group you selected in Step **5** and selects the new group.

continued ▶

TIP

Can I move the location of my group to another tab?

Yes. Complete Steps **1** to **3**. Then follow these steps:

1 Click ⊞ beside the tab containing the group you want to move and the tab to which you want to move the group to display all groups on both tabs.

2 Click the group you want to move.

3 Click the arrows (▲ or ▼) repeatedly to position the group.

4 Click **OK** to save your changes.

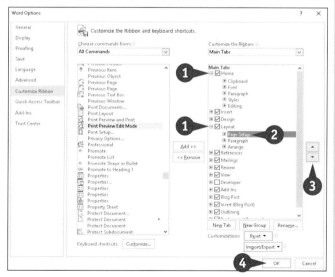

After you add a group to a tab, you can assign a name to it that you find meaningful — for example, something that describes the buttons you intend to include in the group or something that differentiates the group you created from the standard groups on the default Ribbon.

After you name your group, you can then add whatever buttons you need to the group. You are not limited to selecting buttons that appear together on one of the default Ribbon tabs; you can include buttons from any Ribbon tabs and buttons that do not ordinarily appear on the Ribbon.

Create Your Own Ribbon Group (continued)

Assign a Name to the Group

1 Click the group you created in the previous subsection, "Make a Group."

2 Click **Rename**.

The Rename dialog box appears.

3 Type a name for your group.

4 Click **OK**.

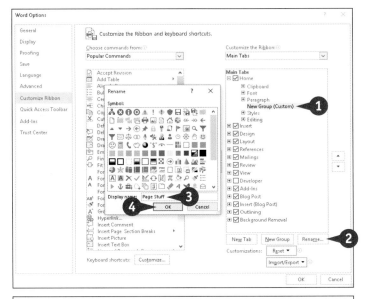

Ⓐ Word assigns the name to your group.

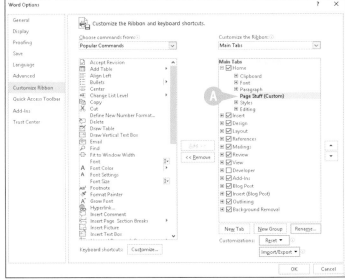

Add Buttons to Your Group

1 Click the group you created.

2 Click a command.

Ⓑ If the command you want does not appear in the list, click ⌄ and select **All Commands**.

3 Click **Add**.

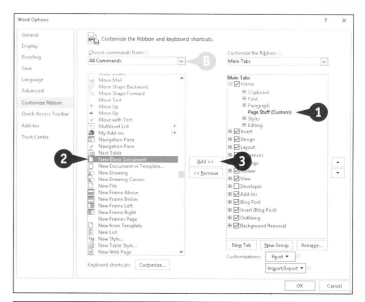

Ⓒ The command appears below the group you created.

4 Repeat Steps **2** and **3** for each button you want to add to your group.

5 Click **OK** to save your changes.

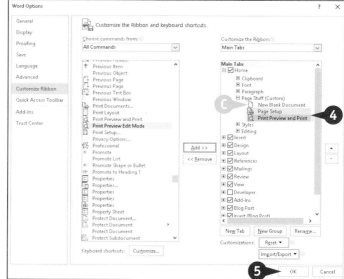

Are there any restrictions for the names I assign to groups I create?
No. In fact, you can even use a name that already appears on the Ribbon, such as Font, and you can place that custom group on the Home tab, where the predefined Font group already exists.

Can I assign keyboard shortcuts to the buttons I add to my group?
Word assigns keyboard shortcuts for you, based on the keys already assigned to commands appearing on the tab where you place your group. If you place the same button on two different tabs, Word assigns different keyboard shortcuts to that button on each tab.

Create Your Own Ribbon Tab

I n addition to creating groups on the Ribbon in which you can place buttons of your choosing, you also can create your own tab on the Ribbon.

Creating your own tab can help you work efficiently; you can store the buttons you use most frequently in groups on your tab. Then you can position your tab on the Ribbon so that it appears by default when you open Word. With all the buttons you use most frequently automatically visible, you save the time of locating the buttons you need on the various Ribbon tabs.

Create Your Own Ribbon Tab

Make a Tab

1 Click the **File** tab.

Backstage view appears.

2 Click **Options**.

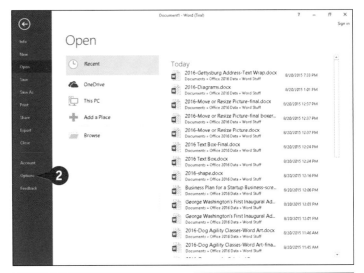

The Word Options dialog box appears.

3 Click **Customize Ribbon**.

4 Click the tab you want to appear to the left of the new tab.

5 Click **New Tab**.

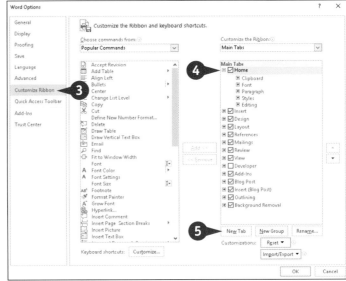

Ⓐ Word creates a new tab below the tab you selected in Step **4**, along with a new group on that tab.

Can I reposition my tab?

Yes. And if you place your tab above the Home tab, it appears as the first tab each time Word opens, giving you instant access to the commands you use most often. Follow these steps:

① Complete Steps **1** to **3**.

② Click your tab.

③ Click ▲ or ▼ until your tab appears where you want.

Note: On the Ribbon, Word displays your tab to the right of the tab above it in the Options dialog box.

Ⓐ To make your tab visible immediately every time you open Word, place it above the Home tab.

④ Click **OK** to save your changes.

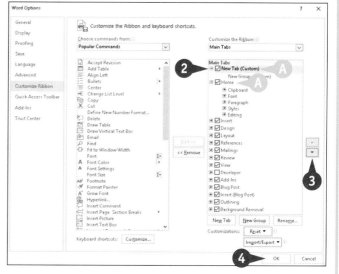

continued ▶

When you create a custom tab, Word automatically creates one group for you so that you can quickly and easily add buttons to the new tab. You can add other groups to the tab and place buttons in them; see the section "Create Your Own Ribbon Group," earlier in this chapter.

You should assign names to both the new tab and the new group that are meaningful to you. For example, you might name your tab to describe its content. Assign group names based on the buttons you intend to place in the group.

Create Your Own Ribbon Tab (continued)

Assign Names

1 Click the group you created, labeled as **New Group (Custom)**.

2 Click **Rename**.

The Rename dialog box appears.

3 Type a name for your group.

4 Click **OK**.

5 Click the new tab you created, labeled as **New Tab (Custom)**.

6 Repeat Steps **2** to **4** to rename your new tab, renamed in this example to **File Stuff**.

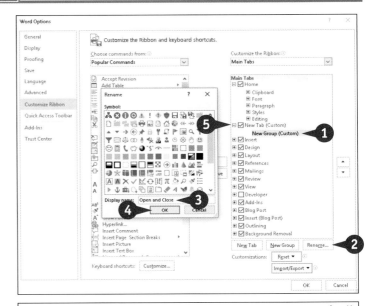

Ⓐ Word assigns names to your tab and your group.

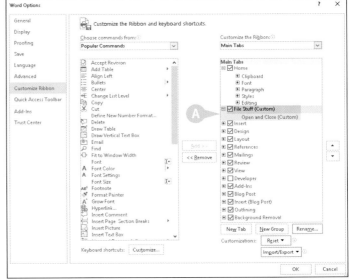

Add Buttons to Your Group

1 Click the group on the tab you created.

2 Click a command.

 If the command you want does not appear in the list, click ⌄ and select **All Commands**.

3 Click **Add**.

 The command appears below the group you created.

4 Repeat Steps **2** and **3** for each button you want to add to the group.

5 Click **OK**.

 The new tab appears on the Ribbon, along with the group containing the buttons you added.

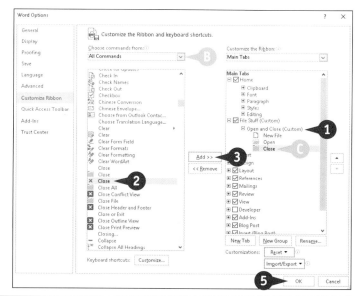

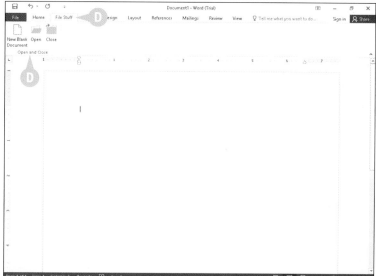

TIP

Is there a way to not display my tab without deleting it?
Yes, you can hide the tab. Complete Steps **1** to **3** in the subsection "Make a Tab." Deselect the tab you want to hide (☑ changes to ☐), and click **OK**. Word redisplays the Ribbon without your custom tab, but your custom tab remains available. In the Options dialog box, simply reselect it (☐ changes to ☑) to display it.

Work with the Quick Access Toolbar

You can customize the Quick Access Toolbar (QAT). The QAT is always visible as you work in Word, so, like a customized Ribbon, a customized QAT can help you work more efficiently if you place buttons on it that you use frequently.

By default, the QAT contains three buttons: the Save button, the Undo button, and the Redo button. You can remove any of these buttons as well as quickly and easily add other commonly used commands, and without much additional effort, you can add not-so-commonly used commands. You also can control the position of the QAT, displaying it above or below the Ribbon.

Work with the Quick Access Toolbar

Change Placement

1. Click the **Customize Quick Access Toolbar** ▾.

   Word displays a menu of choices.

2. Click **Show Below the Ribbon**.

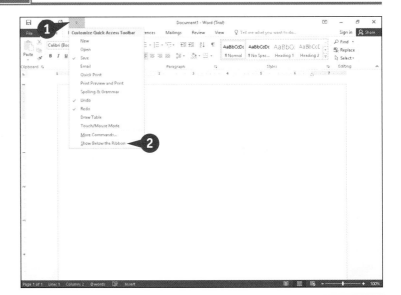

Ⓐ The Quick Access Toolbar (QAT) appears below the Ribbon instead of above it.

You can repeat these steps to move the QAT back above the Ribbon.

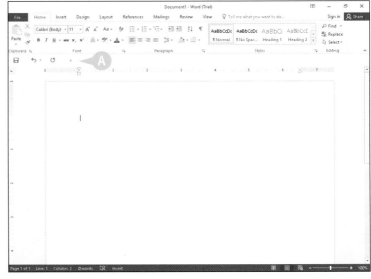

Add Buttons to the QAT

1 Click **Customize Quick Access Toolbar** ⊽.

B A check mark (✓) appears beside commands already on the QAT.

C You can click any command to add it to the QAT and skip the rest of these steps.

2 If you do not see the command you want to add, click **More Commands**.

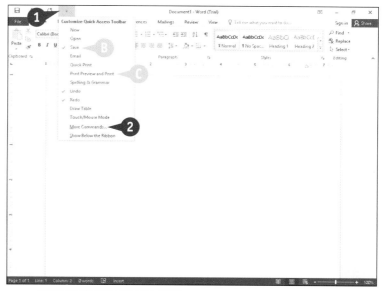

The Word Options dialog box appears, showing the Quick Access Toolbar customization options.

D You can add any of these commands to the QAT.

E If the command you want to add does not appear in the list, click ⌄ and select **All Commands**.

F Commands already on the QAT appear here.

G You can click ⌄ to customize the QAT for all documents or just the current document.

TIP

Is there an easy way to get rid of changes I made to the QAT?
Yes. You can remove an individual button by right-clicking it on the QAT and clicking **Remove from Quick Access Toolbar**. Or, you can reset it by following these steps: Complete Steps **1** and **2** in the subsection "Add Buttons to the QAT." In the Word Options dialog box that appears, click **Reset** and then click **Reset only Quick Access Toolbar**. The Reset Customizations dialog box appears, asking if you are sure of your action. Click **Yes**, and Word resets the QAT. Click **OK** to return to a document.

continued ▶

The buttons on the Quick Access Toolbar are smaller than their counterparts on the Ribbon, but their size should not discourage you from using the QAT. You can always position the mouse (⟍) over a button to see a ScreenTip describing its function.

In addition to repositioning the QAT either below or above the Ribbon and adding buttons to or removing buttons from the QAT, you can reorganize the order in which buttons appear on the QAT. You also can quickly add a button on the Ribbon to the QAT, as described in the tip at the end of this section.

Work with the Quick Access Toolbar (continued)

③ Click ⌄ to display the various categories of commands.

Ⓐ You can select **All Commands** to view all commands in alphabetical order regardless of category.

④ Click a category of commands.

This example uses the **Commands Not in the Ribbon** category.

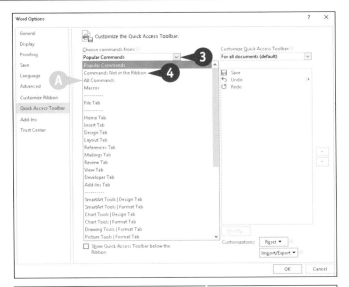

⑤ Click the command you want to add to the Toolbar.

⑥ Click **Add**.

Ⓑ Word moves the command from the list on the left to the list on the right.

⑦ Repeat Steps **3** to **6** for each command you want to add to the Quick Access Toolbar.

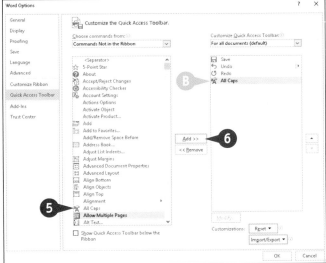

Reorder QAT Buttons

1 While viewing QAT customization options in the Word Options dialog box, click a command in the right column.

Note: Complete Steps **1** and **2** in the subsection "Add Buttons to the QAT" to view QAT customization options.

2 Click ▲ or ▼ to change a command's placement on the Quick Access Toolbar.

3 Repeat Steps **1** and **2** to reorder other commands.

4 Click **OK**.

C The updated Quick Access Toolbar appears.

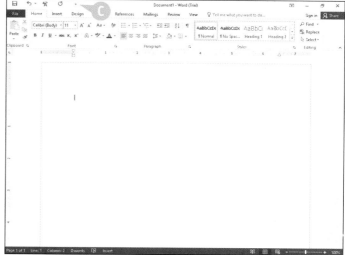

TIP

How do I add a button from the Ribbon to the Quick Access Toolbar?

To add a button from the Ribbon to the Quick Access Toolbar, right-click the button (**A**) and click **Add to Quick Access Toolbar**. Word adds the button to the QAT.

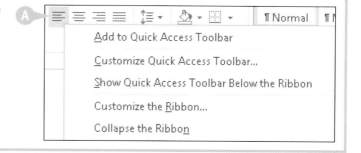

Add Keyboard Shortcuts

You can add keyboard shortcuts for commands you use frequently. Using a keyboard shortcut can be faster and more efficient than clicking a button on the Ribbon or the QAT because you can keep your hands on your keyboard, increasing typing speed and efficiency.

You might think that a command must appear on either the Ribbon or the Quick Access Toolbar in order to create a keyboard shortcut for it. But, in fact, whether a command appears as a button on the Ribbon does not affect whether you can create a keyboard shortcut. You can create keyboard shortcuts for any command.

Add Keyboard Shortcuts

1 Click the **File** tab.

Backstage view appears.

2 Click **Options**.

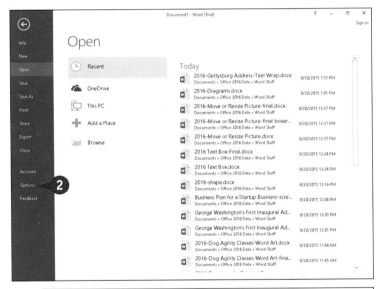

The Word Options dialog box appears.

3 Click **Customize Ribbon**.

4 Click **Customize**.

The Customize Keyboard dialog box appears.

Ⓐ Categories of commands appear here.

Ⓑ Commands within a category appear here.

5 Click the category containing the command to which you want to assign a keyboard shortcut.

6 Click the command.

Ⓒ Any existing shortcut keys for the selected command appear here.

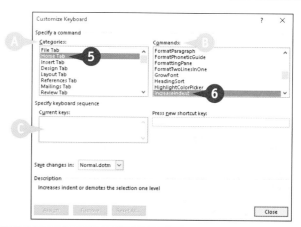

7 Click here, and press a keyboard combination.

Ⓓ The keys you press appear here.

Ⓔ The command to which the shortcut is currently assigned appears here.

Note: To try a different combination, press `Backspace` to delete the existing combination and repeat Step **7**.

8 Click **Assign**.

9 Click **Close**.

10 Click **OK**.

Word saves the shortcut.

How can I test my shortcut to make sure it works?
You can press the keys you assigned. You also can position the mouse (🖰) over the tool on the Ribbon; any assigned keyboard shortcut, whether user-assigned or Word-assigned, appears in the ScreenTip. If you do not see keyboard shortcuts in the ScreenTips, open the Word Options dialog box, click **Advanced** on the left, and in the Display section, select **Show shortcut keys in ScreenTips** (☐ changes to ☑).

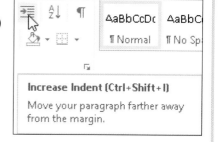

Increase Indent (Ctrl+Shift+I)
Move your paragraph farther away from the margin.

Create a Macro

You can create a macro to save time and repetitive keystrokes. A macro combines a series of actions into a single command. For example, suppose that you often type tables that must fit on the page in landscape orientation. Although you can use commands on the Ribbon to change the page orientation, you can save time and keystrokes if you create a macro that changes the page orientation from portrait to landscape.

Most people find it easiest to create a macro by recording the keystrokes that they use to take the action they want to store in the macro.

Create a Macro

Ⓐ Display the Macro Recording indicator (⊞) on the status bar by right-clicking the status bar and choosing **Macro Recording** from the Customize Status Bar menu.

① Click the **View** tab.

② Click the bottom half of the **Macros** button.

③ Click **Record Macro**.

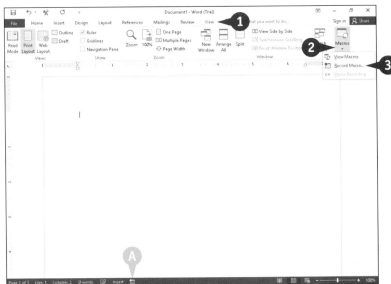

The Record Macro dialog box appears.

④ Type a name for the macro.

Note: Macro names must begin with a letter and contain no spaces.

⑤ Type a description for the macro here.

⑥ Click **OK**.

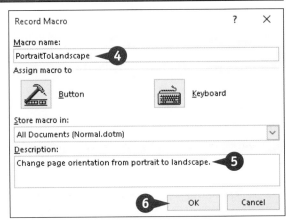

B The Macro Recording indicator (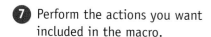) changes to a Stop Recording indicator (□).

C Stop Recording and Pause Recording buttons appear when you click the bottom half of the **Macros** button.

The mouse (⇧) changes to ⇧.

7 Perform the actions you want included in the macro.

Note: Macros can include typing, formatting, and commands. You cannot use the mouse (⇧) to position the insertion point.

8 When you have taken all the actions you want to include in the macro, click the **Stop Recording** indicator (□) on the status bar.

Word saves the macro, and the Macro Recording indicator returns to its original appearance.

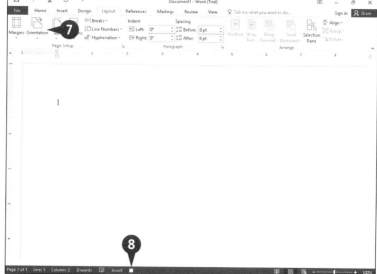

In the Record Macro dialog box, what do the Button and Keyboard buttons do?

They enable you to assign a macro to a button on the QAT or to a keyboard shortcut at the same time that you create the macro. You can always assign a macro to a QAT button or a keyboard shortcut after you create it. See the next section, "Run a Macro."

Do I need to re-create my macros from an earlier version of Word?

No. If you upgrade from an earlier version, Word 2016 converts the Normal template you used in that version, which typically contains all your macros.

Run a Macro

You can save time by running a macro you created because Word performs whatever actions you stored in the macro. The method you choose to run a macro depends primarily on how often you need to run it. If you use the macro only occasionally, you can run it from the Macros window. If you use it often, you can assign a macro to a keyboard shortcut or a Quick Access Toolbar button.

To record a macro, see the previous section, "Create a Macro."

Run a Macro

Using the Macros Dialog Box

If your macro is dependent upon the position of the insertion point, click in your document where you want the results of the macro to appear.

1 Click the **View** tab.

2 Click **Macros**.

The Macros dialog box appears.

Ⓐ Available macros appear here.

3 Click the macro you want to run.

Ⓑ The selected macro's description appears here.

4 Click **Run**.

Word performs the actions stored in the macro.

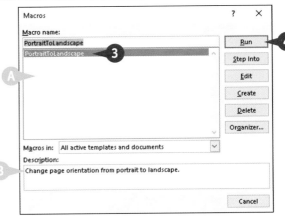

Assign and Use a QAT Button

1 Click the **File** tab.

Backstage view appears.

2 Click **Options**.

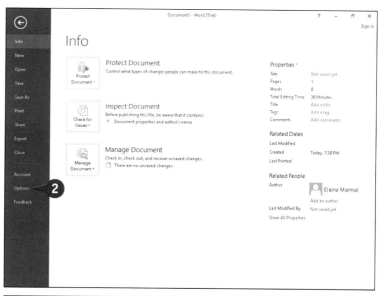

The Word Options dialog box appears.

3 Click **Quick Access Toolbar**.

4 Click ⌄ and select **Macros**.

5 Click the macro to add to the QAT.

6 Click **Add**.

Ⓒ Word adds the macro to the QAT.

7 Click **OK**.

8 Click the macro's button on the QAT to perform the actions stored in the macro.

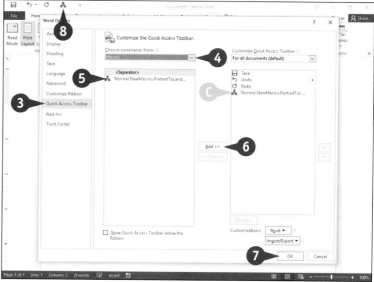

How do I assign a keyboard shortcut to a macro?

Follow the steps in the section "Add Keyboard Shortcuts, earlier in this chapter. In Step **5**, scroll to the bottom of the list and select **Macros**. In Step **6**, select the macro.

Can I create a ScreenTip for my QAT button that contains a name I recognize?

Yes. Complete Steps **1** to **6** in the subsection "Assign and Use a QAT Button." In the list on the right, click the macro, and below the list, click **Modify**. In the Modify Button dialog box, type a name for your macro in the **Display Name** text box below the button symbols.

CHAPTER 12

Working with Mass Mailing Tools

Form letters are particularly useful when you need to impart the same information to a large number of people. You can not only create form letters, but you also can create labels for your letters.

Create Letters to Mass Mail

Using a form letter and a mailing list, you can quickly and easily create a mass mailing that merges the addresses from the mailing list into the form letter. Typically, the only information that changes in the form letter is the addressee information. Wherever changing information appears, you insert a placeholder that Word replaces when you merge.

You can create the mailing list as you create the mass mailing, you can use a mailing list that exists in another Word document or an Excel file, or you can use your Outlook Contact List. This example uses an Excel file.

Create Letters to Mass Mail

Set Up for a Mail Merge

1 Open the Word document that you want to use as the form letter.

Note: The letter should not contain any information that will change from letter to letter, such as the inside address.

2 Click the **Mailings** tab.

3 Click **Start Mail Merge**.

4 Click **Letters**.

The screen flashes, indicating that Word has set up for a mail merge.

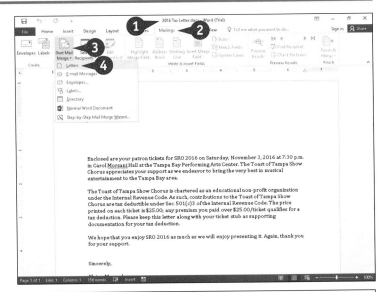

Identify Recipients

1 Click **Select Recipients**.

2 Click to identify the type of recipient list you plan to use.

This example uses an existing list in an Excel file.

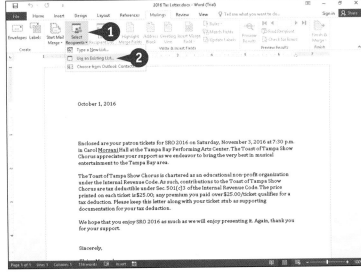

The Select Data Source dialog box appears.

3 Navigate to the folder containing the mailing list file.

4 Click the file containing the mailing list.

5 Click **Open**.

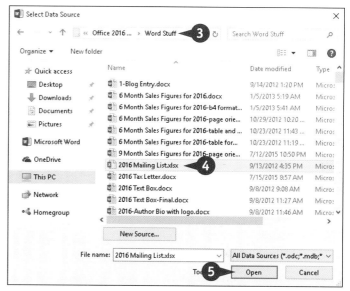

Word links with Excel, and the Select Table dialog box appears.

Note: If the Excel notebook contains multiple sheets, you can select a specific sheet in the Select Table dialog box.

6 If necessary, select a sheet.

7 Click **OK**.

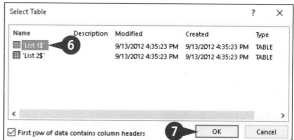

TIP

How do I create a mailing list?
To create a mailing list, perform the steps that follow: In Step **2** in the subsection "Identify Recipients," click **Type New List**. In the New Address List dialog box, type recipient information for each addressee (**Ⓐ**), and click **OK**. Save the file in the Save Address List dialog box that appears. Skip to the subsection "Create the Address Block" to finish the steps.

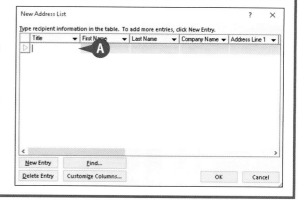

continued ▶

Create Letters to Mass Mail (continued)

Y ou are not limited to sending letters to all recipients in a list; you can select specific recipients from the mailing list to receive the form letter.

You use merge fields, which are placeholders, to identify the location in your document where the recipient's address and greeting should appear. You can modify the appearance of both the recipient's address and the greeting line. For example, in the address block, you can include or exclude titles such as "Mr." in the recipient's name; and in the greeting line, you can address the recipient formally, using a title and last name, or informally, using a first name.

Create Letters to Mass Mail (continued)

8 Click **Edit Recipient List**.

The Mail Merge Recipients window appears.

A A check box (☑) appears beside each person's name, identifying the recipients of the form letter.

9 Deselect any addressee for whom you do not want to prepare a form letter (☑ changes to ☐).

10 Click **OK**.

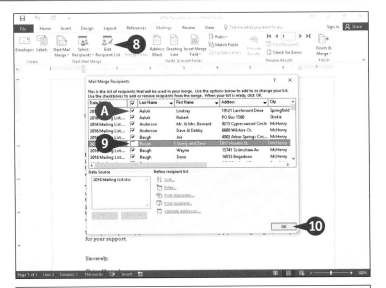

Create the Address Block

1 Click the location where you want the inside address to appear in the form letter.

2 Click **Address Block**.

The Insert Address Block dialog box appears.

3 Click a format for each recipient's name.

B You can preview the format here.

4 Click **OK**.

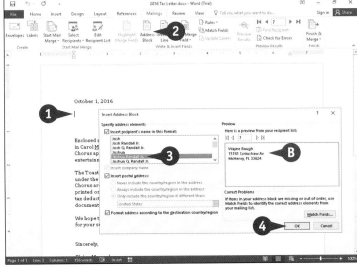

ⓒ The <<Address Block>> merge field appears in the letter.

Create a Greeting

① Click at the location where you want the greeting to appear.

② Click **Greeting Line**.

The Insert Greeting Line dialog box appears.

③ Click these (∨) to select the greeting format.

ⓓ A preview of the greeting appears here.

④ Click **OK**.

ⓔ The <<Greeting Line>> merge field appears in the letter.

Preview and Merge

① Click **Preview Results** to preview your merge results.

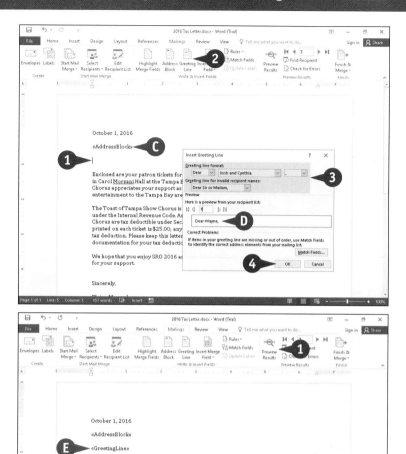

TIP

What should I do if the preview in the Insert Address Block dialog box is blank or incorrect?
Perform the steps that follow: After you complete Step **3** in the subsection "Create the Address Block," click **Match Fields**. The Match Fields dialog box appears. Beside each field you use in your merge, click ∨ and select the corresponding field name in your mailing list file. Click **OK** and continue with Step **4** in the subsection "Create the Address Block." Word matches your fields.

continued ▶

You can preview the letters; information from your mailing list replaces the merge fields that were acting as placeholders. Word gives you another opportunity to select specific recipients before creating individual letters.

After you review the letters, you can print them. Or, if your mailing list contains email addresses, you can send the letters as email messages; Word prompts you for a subject line and a format — HTML, plain text, or an attachment — and then places the message in the Outlook outbox. You must finish by opening Outlook and sending the messages.

Create Letters to Mass Mail (continued)

Ⓐ Word displays a preview of the merged letter, using the unchanging content of the letter and the changing information from the address file.

Ⓑ You can click the **Next Record** button (▶) to preview the next letter and the **Previous Record** button (◀) to move back and preview the previous letter.

Ⓒ You can click **Preview Results** to redisplay merge fields.

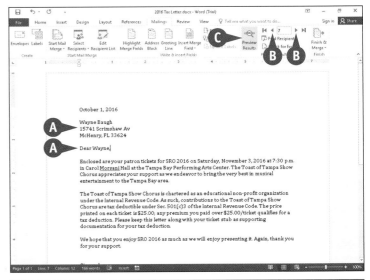

② Click **Finish & Merge**.

③ Click **Edit Individual Documents**.

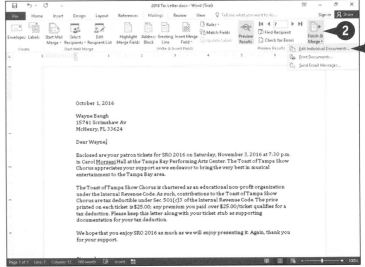

The Merge to New Document dialog box appears.

④ Select an option to identify the recipients of the letter (○ changes to ⦿).

The **All** option creates a letter for all entries on the mailing list; the **Current record** option creates only one letter for the recipient whose letter you are previewing; and the **From** and **To** option creates letters for recipients you identify by their numeric position in the address list, not by their names.

⑤ Click **OK**.

Ⓓ Word merges the form letter information with the mailing list information, placing the results in a new document named Letters1.

Ⓔ The new document contains individual letters for each mailing list recipient.

⑥ Click the **Customize Quick Access Toolbar** ⤓.

⑦ Click **Quick Print**.

Ⓕ You can click the **Save** button (💾) on the Quick Access Toolbar (QAT) and assign a new name to save the merged letters.

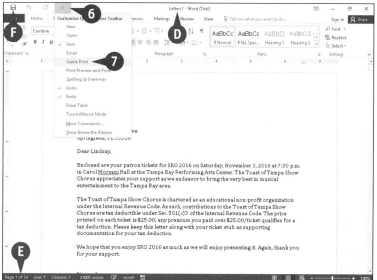

TIP

Can I create envelopes to go with my form letter?
Yes. Display the form letter containing merge fields. Click **Envelopes** to display the Envelopes and Labels dialog box. Click **Add to Document** to place an envelope in your document. You can type a return address in the upper left corner of the envelope. Click in the lower center of the envelope to locate the address box; dotted lines surround it. Complete the steps in the subsections "Create the Address Block" and "Preview and Merge."

Create Labels for a Mass Mailing

In addition to creating personalized form letters for a mass mailing, you can use the Merge feature to create mailing labels for mass mailing recipients. Mailing labels can be useful when you do not want to use your printer to print separate envelopes for your letters. For example, your mailing might include more than a letter so that you must use larger envelopes than your printer can print. By creating mailing labels, you can automate the process of addressing your larger envelopes.

Word's Mass Mailing feature enables you to select from a wide variety of commonly used labels from various manufacturers.

Create Labels for a Mass Mailing

Select a Label Format

1 Start a new blank document.

Note: See Chapter 2 for details on starting a new document.

2 Click the **Mailings** tab.

3 Click **Start Mail Merge**.

4 Click **Labels**.

The Label Options dialog box appears.

5 Select a printer option (○ changes to ◉).

6 Click ∨ to select a label vendor.

7 Use the scroll arrows (∧ and ∨) to find and click the label's product number.

A Information about the label dimensions appears here.

8 Click **OK**.

Word sets up the document for the labels you selected.

Note: If gridlines identifying individual labels do not appear, click the **Table Tools Layout** tab and then click **View Gridlines**.

Identify Recipients

1 Click **Select Recipients**.

2 Click to identify the type of recipient list you plan to use.

In this example, an existing list in an Excel file is used.

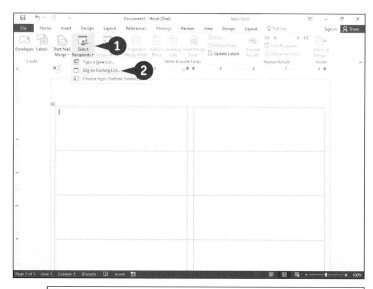

The Select Data Source dialog box appears.

3 Navigate to the folder containing the mailing list file.

4 Click the file containing the mailing list.

5 Click **Open**.

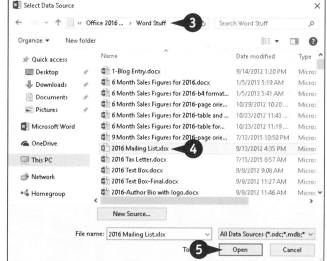

TIPS

What happens if I click Details in the Label Options dialog box?

A dialog box appears, displaying the margins and dimensions of each label, the number of labels per row, and the number of rows of labels, along with the page size. Although you can change these dimensions, you run the risk of having label information print incorrectly if you do.

What happens if I click New Label in the Label Options dialog box?

A dialog box appears that you can use to create your own custom label. Word bases the appearance of this dialog box on the settings selected in the Label Options dialog box. Type a name for the label, and then adjust the margins, height and width, number across or down, vertical or horizontal pitch, and page size as needed.

continued ▶

Using your label options, Word sets up a document of labels to which you attach a file containing recipient information. You can use an existing file or your Outlook contacts, or you can create a new recipient list. You also can select specific recipients from the mailing list for whom to create labels.

You use a merge field, which serves as a placeholder, to identify the location in the label document where the recipient's address should appear. You can modify the appearance of the recipient's address to, for example, include or exclude titles such as "Mr."

This example uses addresses stored in an Excel file.

Create Labels for a Mass Mailing (continued)

Word links with Excel, and the Select Table dialog box appears.

Note: If the Excel notebook contains multiple sheets, you can select a specific sheet in the Select Table dialog box.

⑥ If necessary, select a sheet.

⑦ Click **OK**.

Ⓐ Word inserts a <<Next Record>> field in each label except the first one.

Add a Merge Field

① Click the first label to place the insertion point in it.

② Click **Address Block**.

The Insert Address Block dialog box appears.

③ Click a format for each recipient's name.

Ⓑ You can preview the format here.

④ Click **OK**.

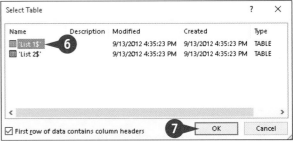

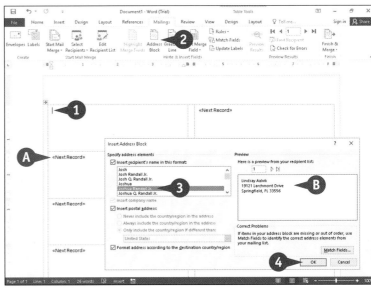

C Word adds the <<Address Block>> merge field to the first label.

Note: When you merge the information, Word replaces the merge field with information from the mailing address file.

5 Click **Update Labels**.

D Word adds the <<Address Block>> merge field to every label.

Preview and Print

1 You can click **Preview Results** to preview your merged results.

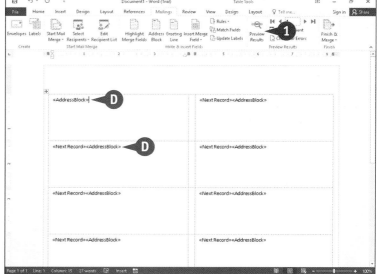

TIP

Can I selectively create labels using an existing file?
Yes. Perform the steps that follow: Click **Edit Recipient List**. The Mail Merge Recipients dialog box appears. Deselect any addressee for whom you do not want to create a mailing label (☑ changes to ☐), and click **OK**.

continued ▶

Create Labels for a Mass Mailing (continued)

You can preview the labels before you print them. Information from your mailing list replaces the placeholder merge field. Word gives you another opportunity to select specific recipients before creating sheets of labels.

After you review the labels, you can print the label document, or you can remerge the label sheets directly to your printer. Although you can send a label as an email message, it probably will not mean much to the recipient because the email body contains the recipient address only. You might consider this option if you need to confirm physical addresses.

Create Labels for a Mass Mailing (continued)

Word displays a preview of your labels, replacing the merge field with information from the mailing list file.

Ⓐ You can click the **Next Record** button (▶) to preview the next label and the **Previous Record** button (◀) to move back and preview the previous label.

② Click **Preview Results** to redisplay merge fields.

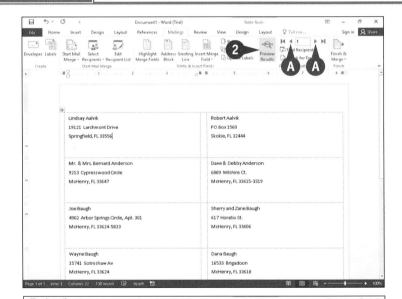

③ Click **Finish & Merge**.

④ Click **Edit Individual Documents**.

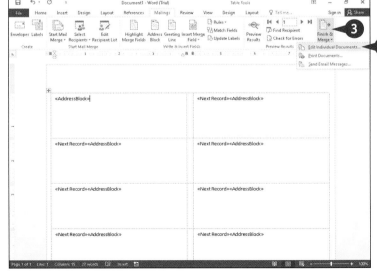

The Merge to New Document dialog box appears.

5 Select an option to identify the recipients of the letter (○ changes to ●).

The **All** option creates a label for all entries on the mailing list, the **Current record** option creates only one label for the recipient you are previewing, and the **From** option creates labels for recipients you specify.

6 Click **OK**.

Ⓑ Word creates the labels in a new Word document named Labels1.

The new document contains individual labels for each mailing list recipient.

7 Click the **Customize Quick Access Toolbar** ▾.

8 Click **Quick Print**.

The labels print.

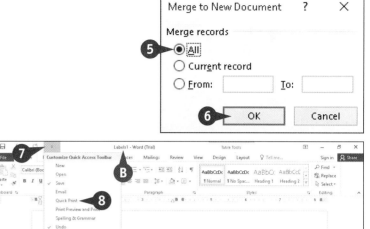

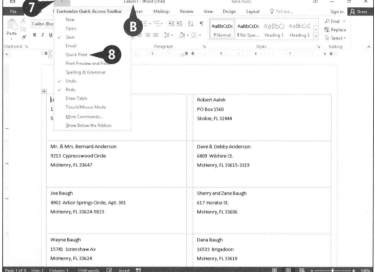

TIP

What does the Check for Errors button on the Ribbon do?
When you click this button, Word gives you the opportunity to determine whether you have correctly set up the merge. In the Checking and Reporting Errors dialog box that appears, select an option (○ changes to ●) and click **OK**. Depending on the option you choose, Word reports errors as they occur or in a new document.

Checking and Reporting Errors   ?   ✕

○ Simulate the merge and report errors in a new document.

● Complete the merge, pausing to report each error as it occurs.

○ Complete the merge without pausing. Report errors in a new document.

OK   Cancel

CHAPTER 13

Word and the World Beyond Your Desktop

You can use Word to reach beyond your desktop. You can email a document, post to your blog, or work with documents stored in your OneDrive cloud storage. You also can use the Word online app.

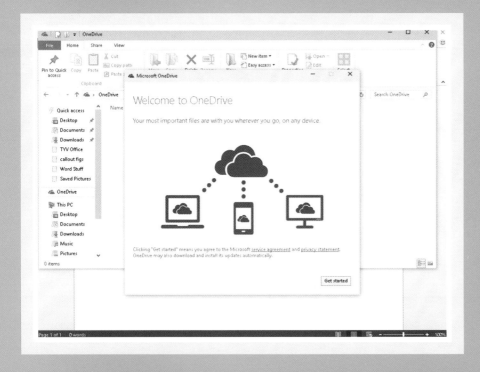

Email a Document

You can share a Word document with others via email. Although you could create a new email message in your email program and add the file as an attachment, you really do not need to go to the extra trouble. Instead, you can email a Word document from Word. Word sends the document as an attachment in a variety of formats.

Although you do not need to send the document from your email program, your email program must be set up on your computer. Note that, to open the file, recipients must have the appropriate software on their computer.

Email a Document

1 With the document you want to share via email open, click the **File** tab.

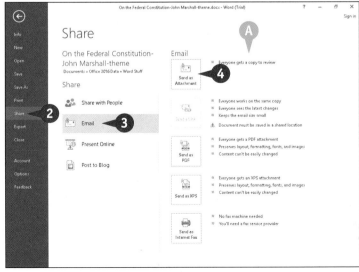

Backstage view appears.

2 Click **Share**.

3 Click **Email**.

A Options for emailing the file appear here.

4 Click a method to send the document.

Note: This example sends the document as an attachment.

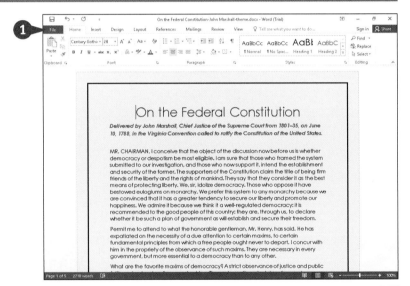

A new message window in Outlook appears.

Ⓑ The name of your file appears in the window's Subject line.

Note: Subjects are not required, but including one is considerate. Word automatically supplies the document name for the subject; you can replace the document name with anything you want.

Ⓒ The file is attached to the message.

⑤ Type the message recipient's email address in the **To** field.

Note: To send to multiple recipients, separate the email addresses with a semicolon (;) and a space.

⑥ Type your text in the body of the message.

⑦ Click **Send**.

Outlook places the message in the Outbox and closes the email message window.

Note: You must open Outlook and, if Outlook does not automatically send and receive periodically, send the message.

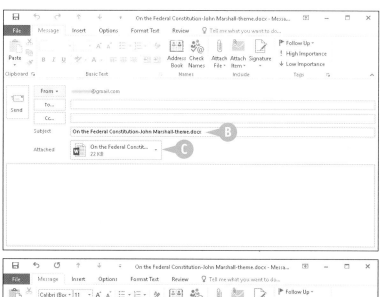

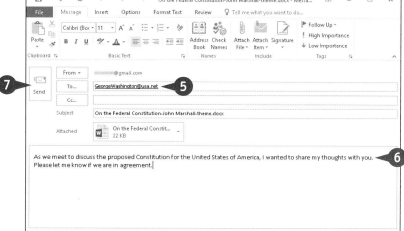

TIPS

What should I do if I change my mind about sending the email message while viewing the email message window?
Click the **Close** button (✖) in the email message window. A message might appear, asking if you want to save the email message. Click **No**.

What happens if I choose Send as PDF in Step 4?
Word creates a PDF version of the document and attaches the PDF version to the email message instead of attaching the Word file. The recipient cannot edit the PDF file with Word; to edit the document, the recipient would need special software, such as Adobe Acrobat.

Create a Hyperlink

You can create a hyperlink in your Word document. You use hyperlinks to connect a word, phrase, or graphic image in a Word document to another document on your computer or in your company's network or to a web page on the Internet. Hyperlinks are useful when you want to refer, in your Word document, to other information that you want the reader to be able to view quickly and easily.

The hyperlink you create in a Word document works just like the ones you use on web pages you browse. Clicking a hyperlink takes you to a new location.

Create a Hyperlink

1. Select the text or graphic you want to use to create a hyperlink.

2. Click the **Insert** tab.

3. Click **Links**.

4. Click **Hyperlink**.

   You can right-click the selection and click **Hyperlink** instead of performing Steps **2** and **3**.

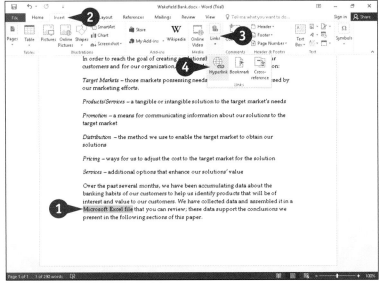

   The Insert Hyperlink dialog box appears.

5. Click **Existing File or Web Page**.

Ⓐ Files in the current folder appear here.

6. Click ⌄ and navigate to the folder containing the document to which you want to link.

7. Click the file to select it.

8. Click **ScreenTip**.

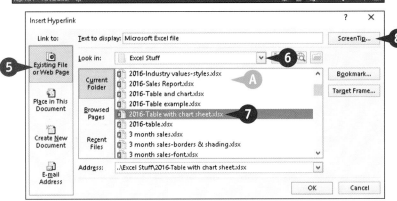

The Set Hyperlink ScreenTip dialog box appears.

9 Type text that should appear when a user positions the mouse (⌖) over the hyperlink.

10 Click **OK**.

11 Click **OK** in the Insert Hyperlink dialog box.

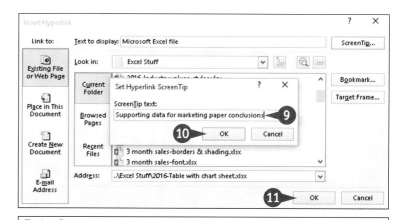

B Word creates a hyperlink shown as blue, underlined text in your document.

12 Slide the mouse (⌖) over the hyperlink.

C The ScreenTip text you provided in Step **9** appears, along with instructions to the reader on how to use the hyperlink.

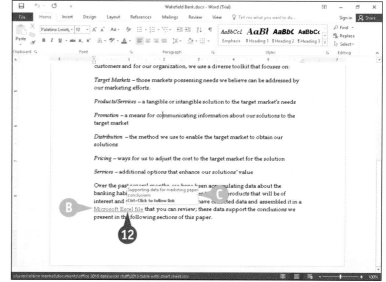

TIPS

How do I use a hyperlink that appears in a Word document?
Press and hold Ctrl as you click the hyperlink. The linked document or web page will appear.

My hyperlink to a file does not work anymore. Why not?
In all likelihood, the file no longer exists at the location you selected in Step **6**. If you moved the file to a new folder, edit the hyperlink to update the file location. To edit the hyperlink, slide the mouse (⌖) over it and right-click. From the menu that appears, click **Edit Hyperlink**. Then follow Steps **5** to **7**.

Post to Your Blog

If you keep an online blog, you can use Word to create a document to post on it. This enables you to take advantage of Word's many proofing and formatting tools. You can then post the blog entry directly from Word.

To post your blog entry, you must first set up Word to communicate with the Internet server that hosts your online blog; the first time you post a blog entry from Word, the program prompts you to register your blog account. Click **Register Now**, choose your blog provider in the dialog box that appears, and follow the on-screen prompts.

Post to Your Blog

Note: You must be connected to the Internet to complete this section.

1 Click the **File** tab.

2 Click **New**.

3 Click **Blog post**.

Word displays details about the Blog Post template.

4 Click **Create**.

Word opens the blog post document.

Note: The first time you use the blog feature, Word prompts you to register your blog account. Click **Register Now**, choose your blog provider in the dialog box that appears, and follow the on-screen prompts.

Ⓐ You can use the buttons in the Blog group to manage blog entries. For example, you can click Manage Accounts to set up blog accounts.

Ⓑ You can use the tools in the other Ribbon groups to format text as you type.

Ⓒ You can use the buttons on the **Insert** tab to incorporate tables, pictures, clip art, shapes, graphics, screenshots, WordArt, symbols, and hyperlinks in a blog entry.

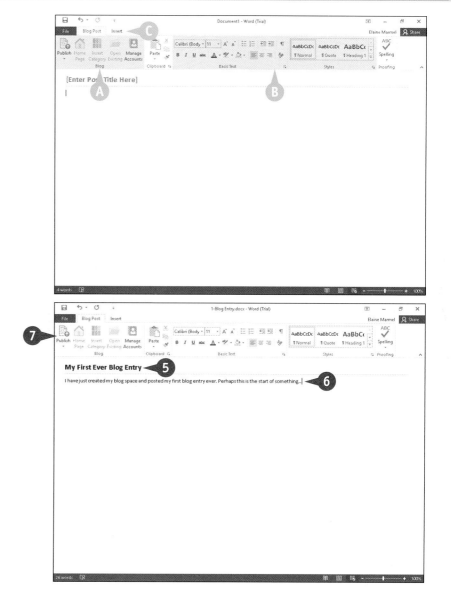

❺ Click here and type a title for your blog entry.

❻ Click here and type your entry.

Note: You can save your blog entry on your hard drive the same way you save any document.

❼ Click **Publish**.

Word connects to the Internet, prompts you for your blog username and password, and posts your entry.

A message appears above the blog entry title, identifying when the entry was posted.

Can I edit my blog accounts from within Word?
Yes. Click the **Manage Accounts** button on the Blog Post tab when viewing a blog page in Word to open the Blog Accounts dialog box. Here, you can edit an existing account, add a new account, or delete an account that you no longer use.

Can I post entries as drafts to review them before making them visible to the public?
Yes. Click ▼ on the bottom half of the **Publish** button, and click **Publish as Draft**. When you are ready to let the public review your entry, open it in Word and click **Publish**.

Office and the Cloud

Today, people are on the go but often want to take work with them to do while sitting in the doctor's office waiting room, the airport, or a hotel room. Using Word 2016, you can work from anywhere using almost any device available because, among other reasons, it works with SharePoint and OneDrive, Microsoft's cloud space. From OneDrive, you can log in to cloud space and, using the Word online app — essentially, a tool with which you are already familiar — get to work.

You also can download the Word universal app for Windows Phone, Android, or iPad. You can share documents across platforms.

Sign In to the Cloud

Signing in to Office Online or to your Office 365 subscription connects your Office programs to the world beyond your computer. Office Online offers free access to the online, limited-edition versions of the Word and other Office programs that you can use on any computer. Purchasing an Office 365 subscription gives you access to full versions of the Office desktop programs and the online versions of the products. Signing in gives you access to online pictures and clip art stored at Office.com and enables Word to synchronize files between your computer, OneDrive, and SharePoint.

OneDrive and Office 2016

The OneDrive app, Microsoft's cloud storage service, comes with Word 2016; 15GB are free, and you can rent additional space. Word 2016 saves all documents by default to your OneDrive space so that your documents are always available to you.

Using Office Online Apps

You can open and edit Word, Excel, OneNote, and PowerPoint documents from your OneDrive using Office online apps, which are scaled-down editions of Office programs that you can use to easily review documents and make minor changes.

Take Your Personal Settings with You Everywhere

Word 2016 keeps track of personal settings like your recently used files and favorite templates and makes them available from any computer. Word and PowerPoint also remember the paragraph and slide you were viewing when you close a document, and they display that location when you open the document on another machine, making it easy for you to get back to work when you move from one work location to another.

Your Documents Are Always Up to Date

Word 2016 saves your documents by default in the OneDrive folder you find in File Explorer. As you work, Word synchronizes files with changes to your OneDrive in the background. And the technology does not bog down your work environment because Word uploads only changes, not entire documents, saving bandwidth and battery life as you work from wireless devices.

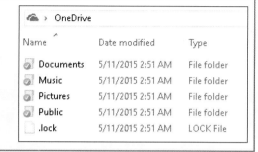

Share Your Documents from Anywhere

You can share your documents both from within Word and from your OneDrive. And from either location, you can email the document to recipients you choose, post a document to a social media site, or create a link to the document that you can provide to users so that they can view the document in a browser. You also can use Microsoft's free online presentation service to present Word and PowerPoint documents online.

Take Advantage of the Office Store

The Office Store contains add-in applications that work with Microsoft Word 2016. For example, the dictionary you use to look up words in Word does not automatically install when you install the program. But when you need an add-on for Word, you can download it from the Office Store.

Office 2016 On Demand

Office 2016 comes in "traditional" editions, where you buy the program; you can install any traditional edition on one machine. Office 2016 also comes in "subscription" editions; essentially, you pay an annual rental fee to use the software on five PCs or Macs.

Subscription editions include the Office On Demand feature; subscribers can run temporary instances of Word on computers where they normally would not be able to install software. To keep the process fast, only parts of the application actually download as needed, and it runs locally. When you close Word, it uninstalls itself.

Subscribers must be online and logged in to validate their right to use Office On Demand.

Sign In to Office 365

You can use Office Online or your Office 365 subscription to work from anywhere. While signed in from any device, you can use one of the free Office online apps, including the one for Word. Word remembers some of your personal settings such as your Recent Documents list so that you always have access to them. Desktop product users typically sign in using an Office 365 subscription, as described in this section and, for the most part, throughout the book.

When you work offline, Word creates, saves, and opens your files from the local OneDrive folder. Whenever you reconnect, Word uploads your changes to the cloud automatically.

Sign In to Office 365

1 Open Word.

The Word Start screen appears.

2 Click the **Sign in** link.

Note: If you are viewing a document, you can click the **Sign in** link in the upper right corner of the screen.

The Sign In window appears.

3 Type the Microsoft account email address associated with your Office 365 subscription.

4 Click **Next**.

5 Type your password.

Ⓐ If you have trouble signing in, you can click this link to reset your password.

6 Click **Sign in**.

B Your name in this area indicates that you have signed in to Office 365.

Note: Office Online offers free access to the online, limited-edition versions of the Office programs that you can use on any computer. Office 365 is a subscription you purchase to use full versions of the Office programs; Office 365 includes both the desktop and the online versions of the products.

TIP

How do I sign out of Office 365?
In any Office program, follow these steps:

1 Click the **File** tab.

2 Click **Account**.

Note: In Outlook, click **Office Account**.

3 Click **Sign out**.

A The Remove Account dialog box appears, warning you that continuing removes all customizations and synchronization might stop.

Note: In most cases, it is perfectly safe to click **Yes**. If you are unsure, check with your system administrator.

4 Click **Yes**.

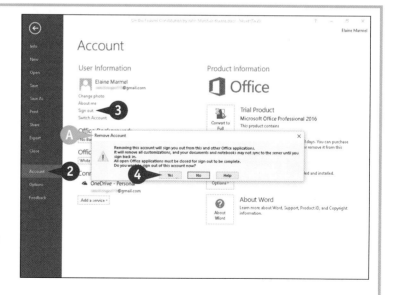

Open a Cloud Document

You can open and edit a document stored in the cloud. The process is quite similar to opening any document as described in Chapter 2. To open a document stored in the cloud, you use your local OneDrive folder.

Documents stored in the local OneDrive folder are automatically synchronized with your cloud storage so that all versions are up to date. Further, the synchronization technology ensures that synchronization occurs quickly because only changes are synchronized, which is particularly useful if your Internet connection bandwidth is not particularly good or if you are working on a wireless device with low battery life.

Open a Cloud Document

1 Make sure you are signed in to your Office 365 subscription by looking for your name here.

Note: See the section "Sign In to Office 365" if your name does not appear.

2 Click the **File** tab.

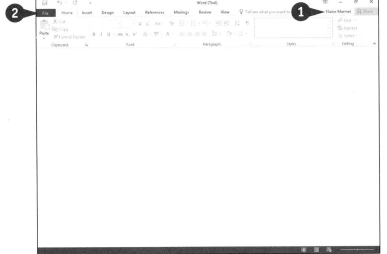

Backstage view appears.

3 Click **Open**.

Note: If you are viewing the Word Start screen, click **Open Other Documents**.

4 Click your OneDrive space.

Ⓐ What you see here when you select your OneDrive space depends on how you have organized the OneDrive space.

5 Navigate to the location where you stored the file you want to open.

B In this example, the file is stored in the Documents\Word Documents folder.

6 Click the file you want to open.

The document stored in the cloud appears on-screen.

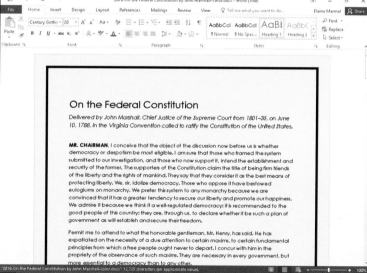

What happens if I am not signed in to Office 365?

Instead of signing in to Office 365, you can edit the local version of the cloud document by browsing to the OneDrive folder found in File Manager and opening the document, as described in Chapter 2. As you work, notifications let you know that you are working offline. If you save the local version of the cloud document to your OneDrive folder, Word alerts you that changes to your file are pending upload to the cloud.

Save a Document to the Cloud

By default, Word 2016 saves all your documents to the local OneDrive folder. Installing Word 2016 automatically gives you 15GB of cloud storage space for free, and you can rent additional space.

The first time you save a document to your OneDrive, Word sets up automatic synchronization for you. So each time you subsequently save changes to the document, synchronization between the local file and the file stored in your cloud storage space at OneDrive happens automatically. If you do not want your files automatically saved to your OneDrive, you can change that option.

Save a Document to the Cloud

1 With the document that you want to save to your OneDrive open, click the **File** tab.

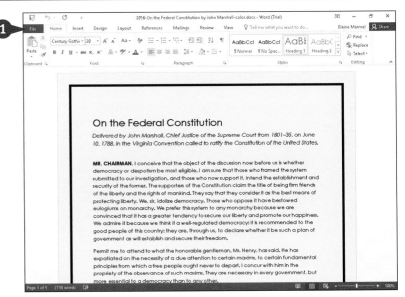

Backstage view appears.

2 Click **Save As**.

3 Click your OneDrive.

4 If the folder where you want to save the document appears in these lists, click that folder; otherwise, click **Browse**.

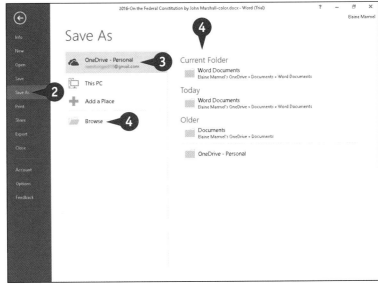

The Save As dialog box appears.

5 Click your OneDrive in the folder list.

6 Open the OneDrive folder where you want to place the document.

7 Provide a filename.

Note: If you opened the document from your OneDrive space, you will be prompted to replace it; click **Yes**.

8 Click **Save**.

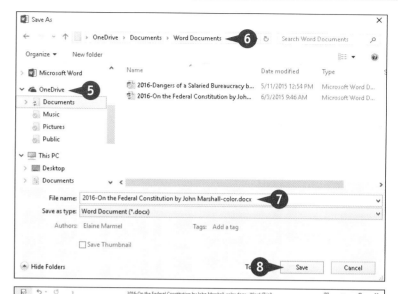

A Your document uploads to your OneDrive.

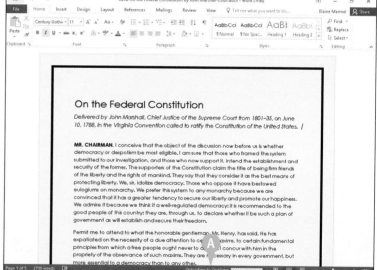

TIP

What should I do if I do not want Word automatically synchronizing with my OneDrive?
Perform the steps that follow: Click the **File** tab, and then click **Options** to display the Word Options dialog box. Click **Save** in the left pane. Select **Save to Computer by default** (☐ changes to ☑), and then click **OK**.

Share a Document from Word

You can easily share documents using Office 365. You can share an Office document by posting it using a social network or to a blog or sending a document as an email attachment. You also can take advantage of a free online presentation service Microsoft offers and share your document by presenting it online. Or, as shown in this section, you can send a link to your OneDrive — as part of Office 2016, you receive free cloud space at OneDrive — where the recipient can view and even work on a shared document. When you finish, you can stop sharing the document.

Share a Document from Word

Share a Document

Note: You must be signed in to Office 365 and the document you want to share must be stored in the cloud. See the tip at the end of this section for details.

1 With the document you want to share on-screen, click **Share**.

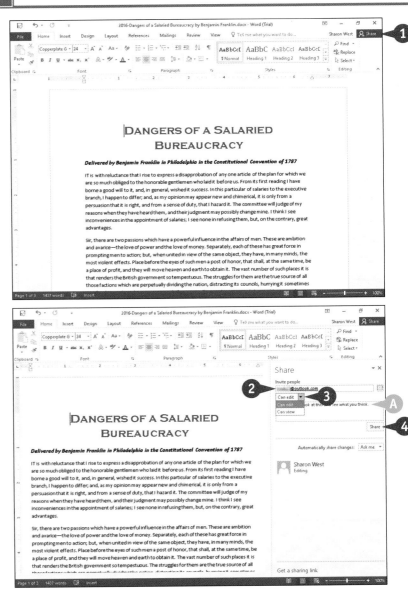

The Share pane appears.

2 In the **Invite People** box, type email addresses of people with whom you want to share.

Note: If you enter multiple addresses, Word separates them with a semicolon (;).

3 Click ▼ and specify whether these people can edit or simply view the document.

A You can type a personal message to include with the invitation.

4 Click **Share**.

Office sends email messages to the people you listed.

Ⓑ Recipients with whom you shared the document appear here.

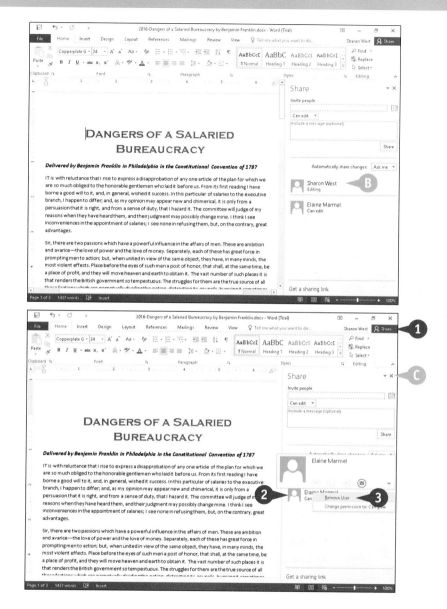

Stop Sharing

① Open the document you want to stop sharing, and click the **Share** button.

② In the Share pane, right-click the recipient with whom you no longer want to share.

③ Click **Remove User**.

The program updates document permissions and removes the user from the screen.

Ⓒ You can click ✖ to close the Share pane.

Why do I see a screen indicating I must save my document before sharing it?

If you have not previously saved your document to your OneDrive, Word will prompt you to do so before starting the Share process. By default, Word saves all your documents to your OneDrive, but if you changed that option, click the **Save to Cloud** button that appears. The program displays the Save As pane of Backstage view; click your OneDrive and then click a folder in the Recent Folders list, or click **Browse** to navigate to the OneDrive folder where you want to place the document.

Download Apps from the Office Store

You can use the Office Store to download add-on applications, or *apps*, for Word. For example, you can add the Merriam-Webster Dictionary to look up words in Microsoft Word 2016; this dictionary does not automatically install when you install Word.

In addition to add-on apps you have used in the past, the Office Store also contains add-on apps created by developers outside Microsoft — apps that work with Word. The developer can choose to charge for an app or make it available for free.

Download Apps from the Office Store

1 Click the **Insert** tab.

2 Click **My Add-ins**.

Ⓐ The Office Add-ins dialog box appears, displaying the My Add-ins tab.

3 Click the **Store** tab to search for new apps.

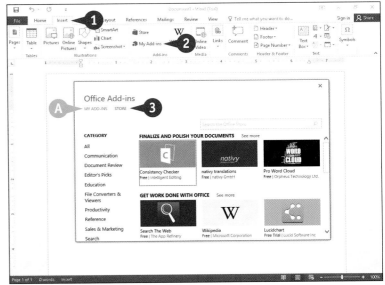

4 Click in the search box and type criteria to search for apps.

Ⓑ You also can narrow your search by clicking a category.

5 Click the app you want to add.

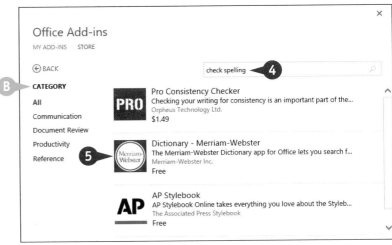

The details for the app appear.

Note: This section adds the Merriam-Webster Dictionary to Word as an example.

6 Click **Trust It**.

The app loads.

C For the Merriam-Webster Dictionary app, a pane opens on the right side of the Word screen, enabling you to type a word to look up.

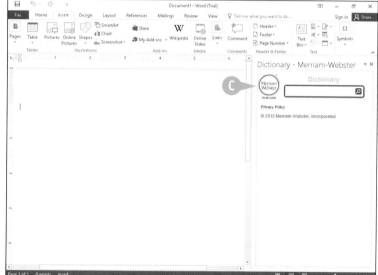

Do I need to keep the Merriam-Webster Dictionary pane open all the time to use the dictionary?
No. Click ✖ in the pane to close it.

Do I need the Merriam-Webster Dictionary to check spelling in Word?
No. Word comes with its own spell-checking dictionary. The Merriam-Webster Dictionary is simply an add-on to provide additional information for you.

Using the Word Online App in OneDrive

From OneDrive, you can use the Word online app to open and edit Word documents with the same basic editing tools you use in Microsoft Word.

Do not let the limitation of "basic editing tools" stop you; although you cannot perform advanced functions like creating or using macros, you still can perform key functions. For example, in the Word online app, you can apply character and paragraph formatting, such as bold or italics, align text, change margins, insert a table or a picture stored on the local drive, and add clip art available from Microsoft's clipart collection.

Using the Word Online App in OneDrive

Open the Document

1 Sign in to OneDrive at https://OneDrive.live.com.

2 Open the folder containing the document you want to open.

3 Click the document.

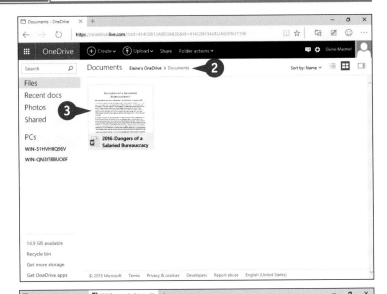

The document appears in the online app for viewing only.

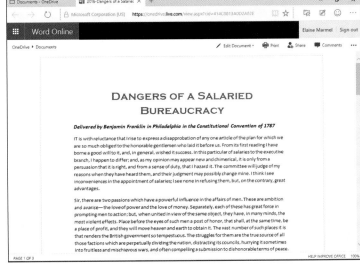

Edit Online

1 Perform Steps **1** to **3** in the previous subsection, "Open the Document."

2 Click **Edit Document**.

3 Click **Edit in Word Online**.

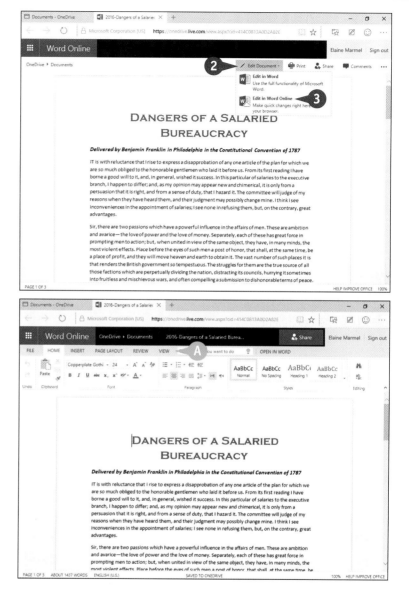

The document appears in the Word online app.

A The Ribbon contains fewer tabs.

How do I save my work in the Word online app?

As you work, the Word Online app automatically saves your document. But, you have options: Click the **File** tab and then click **Save As**. Word gives you the option to save the document to OneDrive, rename it, and download a copy to your computer as a Word document, a PDF, or an ODT document.

How do I close a document I opened in the cloud?

Each online app opens in its own browser tab. Close the browser tab.

Index

Index

Index

Index